LOUIS SICILIANO

QUANTUM MUSIC THERAPY

MUMEx Generative Sound Fields

FOREWORD

GENNARO RISPOLI

MAGIC&UNIQUE BOOKS

MAGIC&UNIQUE BOOKS ©

First Edition: 2026
Published by MAGIC&UNIQUE BOOKS
London, Los Angeles, Rome
ISBN: 9789697660001

https://www.magicandunique.com/magicuniquebooks

Foreword

I have known Louis Siciliano for many years; I delight in his compositions and regularly receive the gift of his research in advance. All this from a physician who esteems and does not underestimate the therapeutic contribution of music. Louis Siciliano drew me in because he is an extraordinary creative phenomenon, capable of moving from the music of the spheres of Pythagoras to electronic musical rhythms, from the sounds of the body to the vibrations existing in nature. He is an undisputed master who moves like a tireless bee and recognizes no limit on the frontier of research. He is a free spirit but he knows the synthetic method of the "Summa," which requires, for a method to be taken seriously, that it contain all the knowledge and possibilities of a discipline, without however remaining a passive experience closed within static rules.

For more than twenty years, Louis Siciliano has had in mind this work, MUMEx, the fruit of a "mad and desperate" study, precious for those who will come after us to change our marvelous planet and its people for the better.

Sound in his work loses its identity as a static recording and is considered a dynamic field capable of interfacing with the patient's body, itself a changing structure. Human biology varies from embryonic cells to the fetus, to the child. Then it becomes an adult body, mature, with different structures and sensitivities, until maturity and senescence. Cerebral, hormonal, and sexual functions influence the mind, body perception, and sensitivity to the environment. Even the embryo and the fetus, suspended in the mother's amnion, which contains them, listen to sounds from the external environment that surrounds them. Every cell, every organ, every system has different vibrational fields over time. Breath, intestinal borborygmi, and heart rhythm possess sonorities that are a model of investigation and a testimony of influences. Sometimes cells and tissues move in harmony and in unison; at other times harmony dissolves and dispersion creates chaos in human biology, and thus pathology.

The construction of a human being is slow and dynamic; one need only observe the dynamics of embryonic development, swift and obedient to the chronology of temporal events that themselves act as a stimulus to a dynamic cascade. Even death cannot be contained in the instant of the declaration of death, but is rather a complex biological event that endures in the dynamic phases of autolysis, always in becoming.

The central point of Louis's thinking is to succeed in producing sound vibrations that create an environmental field where a changing body and a sound that modifies itself according to perception enter into dialogue. The therapist can use electronic instruments and artificial intelligence but must be capable of perceiving how to improve human perception. MUMEx is a complex method explained in a work of 35 chapters, with a synthetic introduction and as many as five therapeutic appendices.

Louis's thought goes from theoretical formation to the patient's perceptual frontier, creating a sound field useful for stimulating well-being—never euphoria—and improving the perception of those who are near him. In short, MUMEx is not the administration of music but a composition of perceptual fields. Indeed, the result is "parsimonious" breathing, a tolerance for silences, a different vocal emission, and, above all, an expanded perceptual ability.

In his opera omnia, Siciliano describes the human mind as a field laboratory influenced by context, interference, the measure of things, and state transitions. Nonlinear cognitive processes use judgment, decision, and memory in an intellectual composition validated by the logic of quantum probability. The music therapist must intervene before the symptom appears, organizing and balancing the human state, which represents an authentic clinical subject. The body, in attention, in memory, in the image of time, of relationship, and of choices, benefits from the generative sound field chosen by the therapist.

The therapist observes somatic indicators such as breath, jaw tone, eyelid tone, and voice. Thus, the method is, in fact, the architecture of generative sound fields: the body becomes a vibrating field and the mind a possibility to resonate in unison. The generative sound is a transformative and responsible environment that uses the gentleness of a perceptual reintegration to avoid dissociation. The therapist's skill lies in finding an optimal sound gateway to assess the state of the body. The usual techniques proposed therefore range from the traditional performance of a piece to the realization of a field that perceives becoming, following the method of resonance, suspension, gentle perturbation, perceptual collapse, and reintegration. All these sound methods, thoroughly explained in the text, do not follow a fixed sequence but are administered according to the patient's state during the session.

Louis Siciliano's work deserves every success, also for the goal he sets himself: to improve human perception and feeling, with man within a changing nature. Following nature, in fact, according to its etymology (future participle of *nascor*), means expecting from it a slow and constant change, for "natura" means the things that will be born... Thus, Louis Siciliano is well aware of continuous change in man, in the therapist, in the environment.

Finally, although I am not an expert in music therapy, I know the sonic importance of rhythm and tone that influence the patient, and therefore I gladly accepted to read and introduce this accomplished creation of Louis Siciliano: the generative sound field. As a scholar of the history of medicine, I know hundreds of nursery rhymes and chants used for healing. As a surgeon, I tell you that even in our craft as body artisans we use rhythmic words to differentiate the various phases of a technical gesture: it serves to relax but also to contain the time of a specific phase of the intervention (for example, the clamping of a vessel that leads to temporary ischemia of an organ). Rhythm helps to rebalance within the team the passing of an instrument, or the placing of a stitch, or the tightening of a thread with a knot.

One evening fifty years ago, I was a young resident in Paris, following a master of colorectal surgery, Jean Duhamel. That evening I was part of the team, together with others, in an emergency surgery performed by Jean Duhamel alongside Lucien Léger, a master of vascular surgery and semiotics. At the end, we all complimented one another on the good result, delighted by the spectacle of four hands at work on a truly difficult case. Jean Duhamel deflected the praise, and as we were returning home, night having fallen, he stopped in front of the Sainte-Chapelle and knocked on the sacristy door. He woke the abbot to gain access to the organ in the church: he played Bach divinely for us young people, who were astounded by his skill; he smiled and said simply, "We, as surgeons, at most resemble a cobbler, a carpenter, a tailor... while music is capable of carrying you to the stars and to God." I learned that lesson, and in Louis I have found the same modest confidence to guide us toward the infinite, without frontiers.

Gennaro Rispoli
Surgeon
Director of the Museum of Medical Arts of Naples, Italy

From the Musical Piece to the Sound Field

For a long time, we have thought of music as language. A language older than speech, more plastic than grammar, closer to the body than any concept. Music therapy has built much of its greatness on this evidence: music communicates where words break, organizes where discourse fails, opens relationship where verbal contact is not enough.

This truth remains intact. The path that begins here does not intend to deny it. It intends to move beyond it.

Music is not only language. It is environment. It is temporal pressure. It is the geometry of perceived space. It is the vibration of tissues. It is an invitation to movement. It is the architecture of breath. It is memory that needs no sentence. It is a field of perceptual forces in which the subject can change internal position before even knowing what is happening.

When a person listens, sound does not remain in front of them like an object. It reaches them, surrounds them, penetrates them, orients them. A rhythm can modify gait; a drone can slow the breath; a voice can loosen the throat; a bell can open an inner distance; silence can make perceptible what mental noise had covered. Sound does not merely describe the state. It touches it.

From here the central thesis arises: sound can be treated as a state operator.

By state, we mean a complex configuration of body-mind: physiological activation, attentional quality, emotional tone, perception of time, implicit memory, sense of safety, relational availability, posture, breath, imagination. A state does not coincide with an isolated emotion. It is the way the whole organism organizes itself at a given moment.

Music therapy has always worked with states. It does so in anxiety regulation, rehabilitation, trauma work, dementia, depression, the autism spectrum, disability, palliative care, childhood, the mother-child relationship, voice, movement, and group work. Systematic reviews show promising effects in several areas, although with differences in methodological quality, heterogeneity of interventions, and a need for further studies. Cochrane, for example, has reported that music therapy added to treatment as usual appears more effective than treatment as usual alone in depression; other reviews of music interventions in oncology indicate possible benefits for anxiety, pain, fatigue, depression, and quality of life. A 2025 meta-analysis on anxiety included 51 studies and 93 effect sizes, confirming growing interest in the effect of music therapy interventions on psychological and physiological outcomes (de Witte et al., 2025).

These data do not close the discussion. They open it. They indicate that music can affect clinically relevant dimensions, while leaving a finer question open: which sonic configurations act on which states, in which subjects, in which contexts, along which trajectories, with which risks, and with what possibility of measurement?

The answer cannot come from a playlist. A playlist is a sequence of already closed musical objects. It can be useful, emotionally powerful, and culturally meaningful. Yet it remains bound to a fixed form. The patient changes; the piece remains identical. The therapist can choose, interrupt, replace, or comment. The sonic material does not possess an operational memory of the session.

MUMEx is born from another hypothesis: to build generative sound fields. A MUMEx field is not a piece to be played back. It is an evolving configuration. It has parameters, density, timbre, rhythm, space, microvariation, formal memory, and the possibility of adaptation. It can be designed to accompany an entry phase, a phase of Suspension, Gentle Perturbation, a point of emergence, and Reintegration. It can avoid abrupt events, maintain a breath, reduce density when the voice emerges, and generate support without occupying the entire room.

The passage is decisive: from music as thing to music as environment; from the piece as closed form to the field as sonic organism; from listening as reception to the session as perceptual ecology.

This transformation is not only technological. It concerns the way we conceive the patient. If the person is understood as an organism in state, the therapeutic task changes. It is not only a matter of interpreting contents, evoking emotions, or facilitating expression. It is a matter of building conditions in which the state can reorganize. The anxious patient can recover a boundary. The depressed patient can perceive the world again. The traumatized subject can encounter a sound environment that does not assault. A person living fragmentation can experience continuity. A person imprisoned in the mental can return to the body.

The path will proceed along this line. First it will establish the conceptual field: music therapy, mind, state, quantum cognition, nonverbal hypnosis, perceptual reconstruction. Then it will descend into the body: vibration, internal organs, instruments, Resonance, radionics and radiesthetic frontiers. It will open to trance, to empty infinity, to Eastern and Western meditative practices. It will enter nature as a vibrating matrix: garden, woods, birds, animals, soundscapes. It will arrive at MUMEx as generative architecture, at immersive electronic sound, at the five operators, at the experiential laboratory. Finally, it will enter into dialogue with neuroscience, depth psychology, cosmos, alterity, experimental protocols, and the final manifesto.

This breadth does not arise from accumulation. It arises from a conviction: sound does not belong to one domain. Sound is biological, cultural, spiritual, clinical, technological, animal, cosmic. The music therapy to come must know how to speak with all these dimensions without losing the center of human relationship.

For this reason, the book maintains one rule: distinguish the planes. When data belong to clinical research, they will be treated as such. When a practice belongs to a spiritual tradition, it will be respected within its genealogy. When a territory is frontier, it will be approached as frontier. When a technology produces data, those data must be readable, recordable, and criticizable. Freedom does not need confusion. It needs precision.

The word quantum enters the title because it indicates the deep structure of the project: not a music that acts mechanically on a passive body, but a sound field that enters into relationship with a living system of possibilities. In this sense, the patient is not a receiver. The patient is part of the field. The therapist is not an applicator. The therapist is guardian of the field. MUMEx is not a substitute. It is a generator of conditions.

The operational model will revolve around five operators: Resonance, Suspension, Gentle Perturbation, Perceptual Collapse, and Reintegration. They make it possible to translate the music therapist's intuition into sonic parameters: density, register, dynamics, rhythm, silence, spatialization, microvariation, controlled unpredictability. They will not be formulas to apply. They will be maps for designing and observing.

Resonance builds compatibility between body and sound. Suspension opens a space of possibility. Gentle Perturbation moves without invading. Perceptual Collapse accompanies the emergence of an internal form. Reintegration restores orientation, body, speech, and return. In every session, these operators may combine, recede, repeat, or interrupt one another. The life of the human state does not follow a schedule. The model exists so we do not lose ourselves while exploring.

The relationship with nonverbal hypnosis will be crucial. Marco Paret's work, with its attention to fascination, gaze, presence, and the perceptual frontier, allows us to understand a zone that music therapy knows but often does not name with sufficient radicality: the preverbal transformation of state. Sound can function as the acoustic counterpart of the hypnotic gaze. Where the gaze fixes and leads, sound envelops and suspends. Where fascination brings consciousness to a threshold, the sound field builds the environment of that threshold.

This research will not turn music therapy into hypnosis. It will keep open the dialogue between two powers: the power of the gaze and the power of the sound field. Both act before explanation. Both require responsibility. Both can transform when held by a capable presence.

The body will have a central role. In many contemporary practices, sound is still thought of as something that reaches the ear and then the mind. This is a poor reduction. Sound enters the chest, the sternum, the diaphragm, the abdomen, the bones, the skull. The therapist's voice is not only melodic information: it is a body touching another body by vibratory means. A bell, a drum, a gong, an electronic drone, a controlled sub-bass can make forgotten internal zones perceptible. Vibratory stimulation must be studied seriously, especially when speaking of internal organs, electromedical systems, vibroacoustic beds, biofeedback, and advanced devices. No naivete: here the boundary among somatic experience, well-being, clinical intervention, and medical claim must remain legible.

Nature will enter as a teacher of generativity. The garden is not scenery. It is a sonic organism. The forest is not relaxation. It is a living architecture of breath. Birdsong offers models of repetition and variation that a generative system can study with extreme refinement. The animal world returns to the human body a voice less domesticated, more instinctive, less imprisoned by the mental. MUMEx will be able to enter into dialogue with these landscapes without copying them, transforming them into field matrices.

Neuroscience will provide part of the necessary language: autonomic nervous system, entrainment, rhythm, memory, emotion, plasticity, heart rate variability (HRV), electroencephalography (EEG), neuroaesthetics. Here too, measure will be necessary. Neuroscience must not become a decoration of authority. It must help us formulate better questions: what happens to breath? to heart-rate variability? to the perception of time? to absorption? to the return after the session?

The Q-MUMEx State Modulation Protocol (SMP-001) will arise from this need: to observe, in healthy adult subjects, whether a generative sound field produces variations different from fixed music or a neutral condition. Not to declare a cure. To build a first ground for verification. Authentic research does not extinguish vision. It gives vision legs.

There will be frontier chapters: radionics, radiesthesia, previous lives, Michael Wolf, aliens, cosmic music therapy. These territories must be approached without submission to preventive ridicule and without naivete. The human being has always used sound to speak with what exceeds human measure: gods, the dead, ancestors, animals, stars, spirits, invisible worlds. Even when science cannot validate such experiences as objective facts, they remain psychic, symbolic, bodily, and cultural events. Music therapy, if it wants to become fully adult, must also know how to listen to what does not fit comfortably into the standard forms of institutional rationality.

This does not mean giving up scrutiny. It means not abandoning to ignorance what could become research. It means not allowing fear of judgment to prevent exploration. Sound has always crossed boundaries. Research will follow its nature.

In the end, the entire path can be summarized in one sentence: MUMEx produces sound environments capable of entering into relationship with the human state. Everything else begins here. The generative sound field is not spectacle. It is not automatic therapy. It is not technological decoration. It is a new possibility for music therapy: to build environments of perception, vibration, memory, and Reintegration with a level of continuity, adaptability, and traceability that constitutes a novelty for the discipline.

The path therefore begins with a decisive passage. With a simple and immense question: what sound world can help a human being return to inhabiting themselves?

It is not a matter of bringing the machine into the therapist's room. It is a matter of generating a larger room, a subtler field, a listening able to include body, memory, nature, and consciousness within the same sonic architecture.

Reader's Guide

The book can be read linearly, from the Foreword to the final Manifesto, or by following three consultation trajectories. The structure by parts allows the reader to enter through the theoretical foundation, the clinical practice, or the visionary frontier, while always maintaining reference to the five operators: Resonance, Suspension, Gentle Perturbation, Perceptual Collapse, and Reintegration.

THEORETICAL PATH—Chapters 1–5, 19, 21, 26–28, and 33–34. For readers who wish to understand the conceptual, epistemological, neuroscientific, and methodological foundation of MUMEx Quantum Music Therapy.

CLINICAL-PRACTICAL PATH—Chapters 6–9 and 20–25, and Appendices B–D. For music therapists, therapists, applied researchers, and professionals interested in operational tools, design sheets, safety, composite cases, and session practice.

VISIONARY PATH—Chapters 10–18 and 29–32. For readers who wish to explore the relationship among sound, empty infinity, nature, meditation, symbol, cosmos, alterity, and frontier territories of consciousness.

Each chapter maintains its own epistemological level. Reading can therefore proceed by interest, discipline, or degree of evidence, without confusing clinical research, theoretical model, wisdom tradition, and frontier territory.

PART	CHAPTERS	THEME	DOMINANT OPERATOR
I	1-5	Founding the field: music therapy, mind, state, hypnosis, perceptual reconstruction	Foundation of the model
II	6-9	Vibrating body, internal organs, instruments, resonance	Resonance
III	10-13	Trance, empty infinity, Nada Yoga, sacred chant	Suspension

PART	CHAPTERS	THEME	DOMINANT OPERATOR
IV	14-18	Garden, forest, birds, animals, soundscape	Gentle Perturbation
V	19-25	MUMEx, generative fields, immersive electronics, operators, laboratory	All operators
VI	26-29	Neuroscience, depth psychology, interoception, archetype	Perceptual Collapse
VII	30-34	Cosmos, alterity, SMP-001 protocol, final manifesto	Reintegration

List of Plates

Plate 1—The Five Operators. The five operators are presented as dynamic functions of the field. The sequence indicates a possible trajectory, not a mandatory procedure.

Plate 2—The Human State. The human state includes body, breath, attention, memory, emotional tone, posture, relationship, safety, and possibility of choice.

Plate 3—The MUMEx Sound Field. The field is represented as a variable generative environment with density, register, timbre, movement, formal memory, and clinical orientation.

Plate 4—Session Trajectory. The trajectory visualizes entry, Resonance, Suspension, Gentle Perturbation, Perceptual Collapse, and Reintegration. It is a flexible map, not a rigid sequence.

Plate 5—The MUMEx Room. The room is conceived as a shared space among patient, therapist, instruments, loudspeakers, and generative sound field.

Plate 6—Body–Vibration Map. The body map indicates resonance zones and safety boundaries. Every application requires consent, gradualness, observation, and respect for contraindications.

Plate 7—SMP-001 Protocol. The Q-MUMEx State Modulation Protocol (SMP-001) unfolds across multiple phases and sessions, from participant selection to debriefing, follow-up, and data reading.

Plate 8—Epistemological Spectrum. The spectrum distinguishes established evidence, theoretical model, wisdom tradition, frontier narrative, and authorial speculation.

Iconographic Orientation Plates

The following plates offer the professional reader a visual compass. They do not replace the text; they condense the grammar of the model, making operators, human state, MUMEx field, session trajectory, setting, vibrating body, experimental protocol, and epistemological levels immediately legible.

THE FIVE OPERATORS

Dynamic functions of the MUMEx field

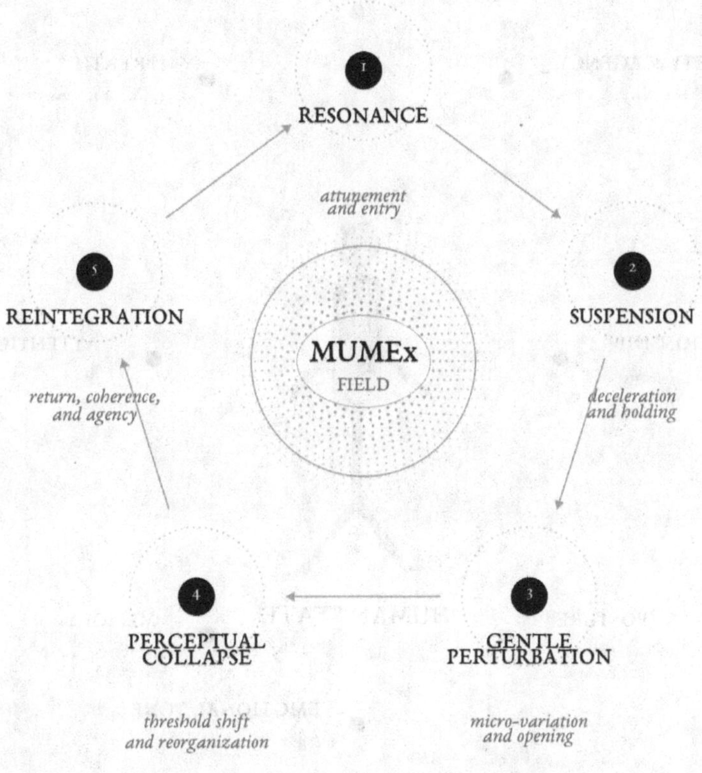

The operators form a responsive cycle. A session may linger, repeat, overlap, or reverse according to the human state and the therapeutic relationship.

THE HUMAN STATE

A multidimensional clinical model

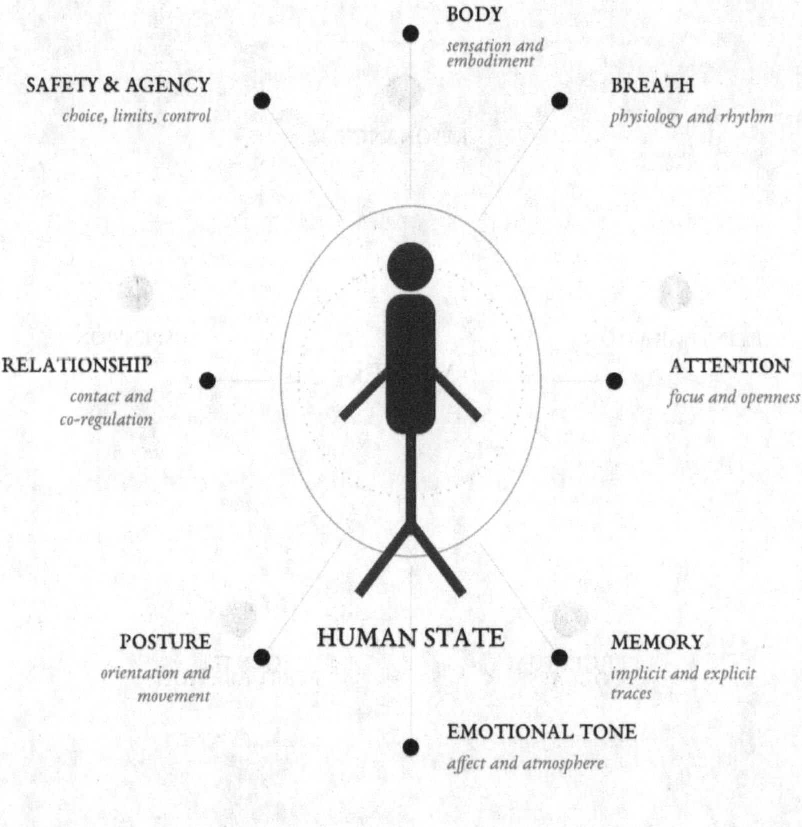

The human state is a living configuration of body, breath, attention, memory, emotion, posture, relationship, safety, and possibility of choice.

THE MUMEX SOUND FIELD

A variable generative environment

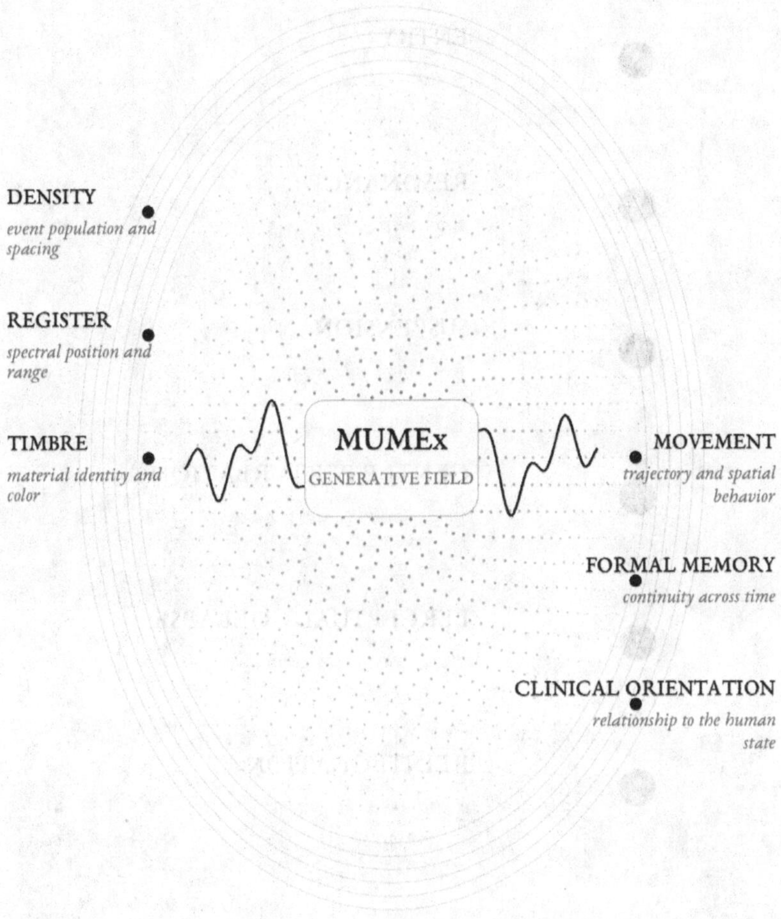

A MUMEx field remains coherent without becoming fixed: it can evolve, remember, respond, change density, and be oriented to the person and the session.

SESSION TRAJECTORY

A flexible arc of state transformation

ENTRY

arrival, orientation, consent

RESONANCE

attunement and compatibility

SUSPENSION

deceleration and opening

GENTLE PERTURBATION

micro-variation and movement

PERCEPTUAL COLLAPSE

emergence and reorganization

REINTEGRATION

return, coherence, agency

The trajectory is a map rather than a rigid sequence. It may repeat, suspend, or return according to the person, the field, and the therapist's judgment.

THE MUMEX ROOM

Shared therapeutic space

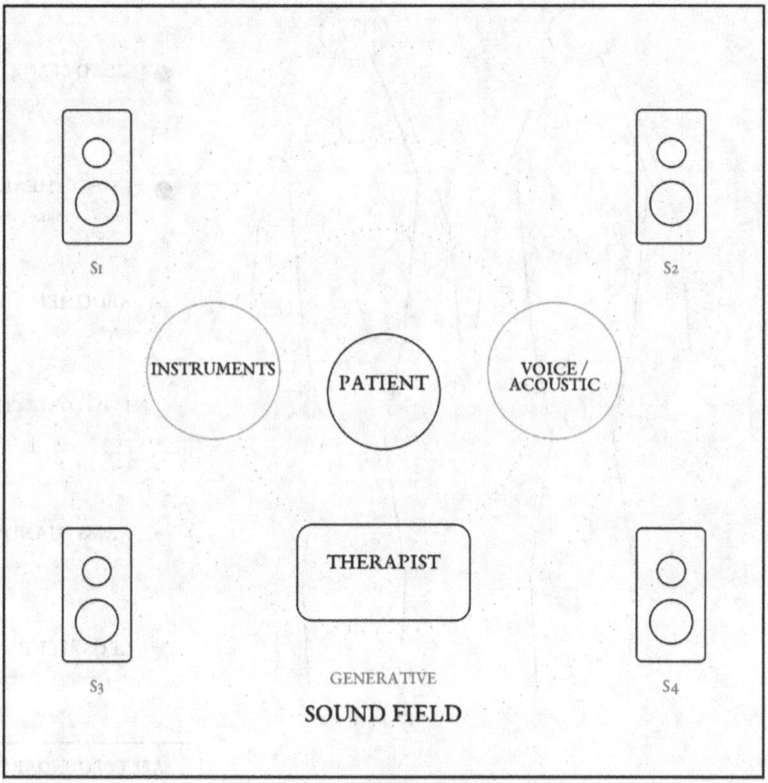

PATIENT	*center of experience and meaning*
THERAPIST	*presence, guidance, restraint*
INSTRUMENTS	*acoustic, electronic, hybrid*
LOUDSPEAKERS	*spatialization without domination*

The room is a relational architecture. Technology serves the encounter; it does not become the center of the session.

BODY–VIBRATION MAP

Resonance zones and safety boundaries

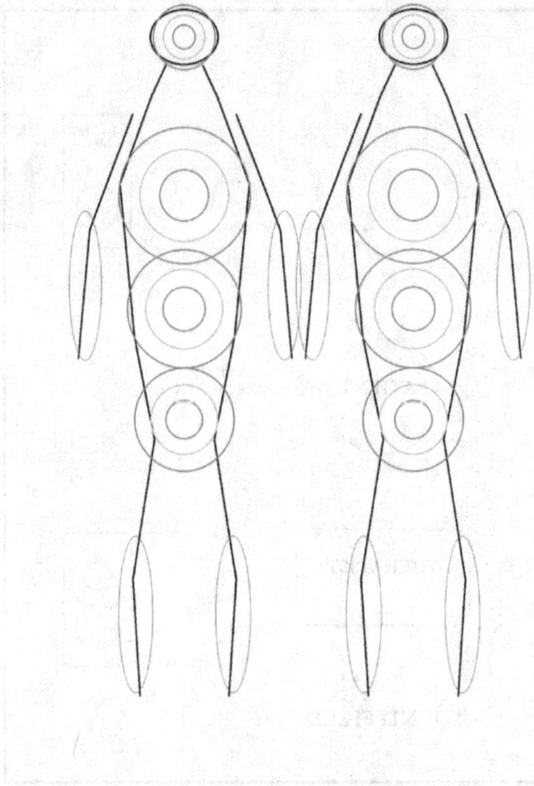

● **HEAD / FACE**
perception and cranial resonance

● **CHEST / HEART**
breath, emotion, vocal support

● **ABDOMEN**
interoception and grounding

● **PELVIS / LOWER CENTER**
weight, stability, locomotion

● **ARMS / HANDS**
expression and contact

● **LEGS / FEET**
support and orientation

SAFETY BOUNDARY
consent · gradualness
observation · contraindications
right to stop

The map is descriptive, not diagnostic. Every application requires consent, gradualness, careful observation, respect for contraindications, and a clear path of return.

SMP-001 PROTOCOL

Q-MUMEx State Modulation Protocol

1. **SCREENING**
   Eligibility, exclusion criteria, informed consent
2. **BASELINE**
   Clinical, psychological, physiological reference
3. **CONDITION A**
   MUMEx generative field sequence
4. **CONDITION B**
   Comparison condition or alternative field
5. **DEBRIEFING**
   Immediate report, well-being, qualitative feedback
6. **FOLLOW-UP**
   Delayed observations and any change
7. **DATA INTERPRETATION**
   Quantitative, qualitative, phenomenological reading

The protocol turns exploratory field practice into a structure that can be described, repeated, compared, criticized, and progressively improved.

EPISTEMOLOGICAL SPECTRUM

Different planes of validity

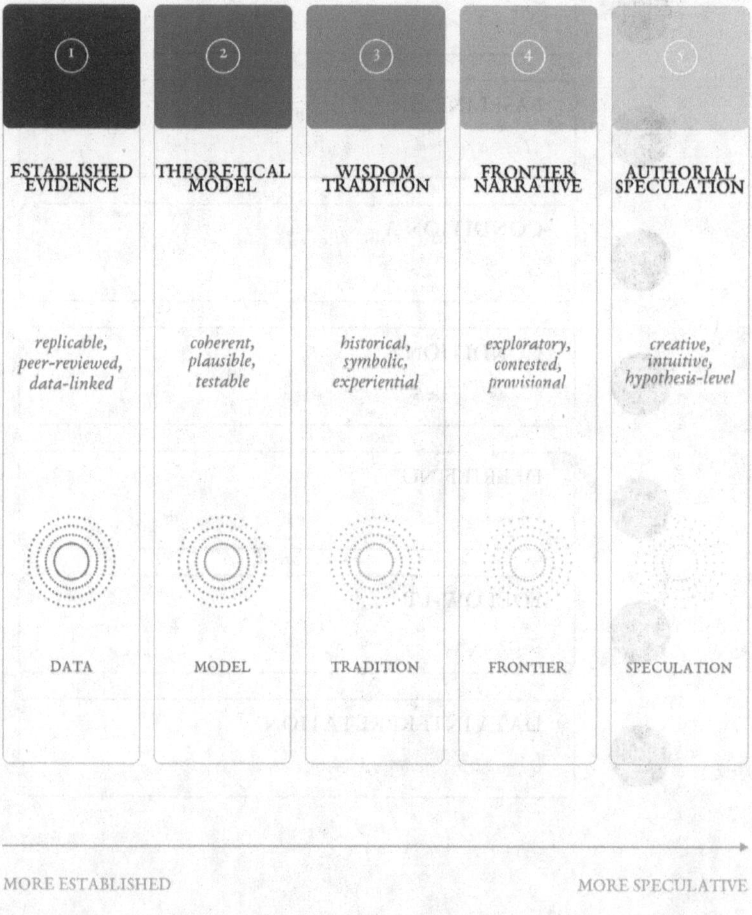

The categories are not interchangeable. The task is to preserve freedom of exploration while keeping evidence, model, tradition, frontier narrative, and speculation clearly distinguished.

PART ONE

FOUNDING THE FIELD

CHAPTER 1

Music Therapy Before Its New Frontier

EPISTEMOLOGICAL LEVEL: *Established evidence / theoretical model. Professional foundation of music therapy, MUMEx generative extension, and the distinction between clinical relationship and sonic technology.*

Music therapy enters our time with a responsibility larger than its own history. It has already shown itself to be a clinical relationship, an artistic practice, an educational resource, a rehabilitative presence, and a method for reopening channels of communication where speech has grown thin or rigid. Now it is being asked to recognize something further: that sound can become a dynamic environment, an adaptive field, a perceptual architecture capable of affecting the configuration of the human state.

This passage must be understood with precision. Music therapy already possesses a recognized professional identity. The American Music Therapy Association defines it as the clinical and evidence-based use of music interventions to accomplish individualized goals within a therapeutic relationship, conducted by a qualified professional. In Europe, the European Music Therapy Confederation describes music therapy as an independent profession grounded in specific musical interventions, evidence-based knowledge, clinical research, and therapeutic alliance. These definitions are not institutional ornaments. They are boundaries, structure, and responsibility (American Music Therapy Association & Certification Board for Music Therapists, 2015; Certification Board for Music Therapists, 2025).

MUMEx Quantum Music Therapy is born within this responsibility, not outside it. Its founding gesture is to move music therapy toward a new class of sonic phenomena: generative, nonlinear sound fields, endowed with memory, sensitive to context, capable of evolving in time without repeating the closed form of the musical piece. This shift moves the center of the question. The issue is no longer only which music to offer, which song to choose, or which improvisation to support. The question becomes: what sound field can enter into relationship with this human state, at this moment, within this relationship?

MUMEx does not inaugurate the replacement of the music therapist by a machine. That would be a poor reduction, born of the same technical mentality that confuses innovation with automation. MUMEx opens the possibility of a sound environment that the therapist can design, inhabit, modulate, interrupt, and allow to breathe. The center remains human. The field becomes larger.

Every young discipline knows a phase in which it must defend itself. It must explain that it exists, distinguish itself from adjacent practices, build a vocabulary, produce studies, and seek recognition. Music therapy has known this labor. It has had to show that it is not entertainment for fragile patients, not generically comforting music, not simple sonic animation. It has had to affirm the specificity of the setting, the competence of the professional, and the need for goals, assessment, documentation, and supervision.

Today music therapy can speak from a different position. The clinical literature is broad, though heterogeneous. Cochrane reviews on depression indicate that music therapy added to treatment as usual may reduce depressive symptoms and anxiety compared with treatment as usual alone. The World Health Organization report on the arts and health synthesized more than three thousand studies, recognizing a role for artistic practices in prevention, health promotion, and the management of several conditions across the life span. More recent meta-analyses on anxiety signal relevant effects, along with methodological heterogeneity and the need for stronger designs (Aalbers et al., 2017; Bradt et al., 2021; de Witte et al., 2022, 2025; Fancourt & Finn, 2019).

These data must be read without triumphalism and without subservience. Scientific evidence is not a request for permission. It is a way of building verifiable power. Music therapy does not need to disguise itself as pharmacology in order to deserve legitimacy. Its strength lies in the singular nature of music: a temporal, bodily, relational, symbolic event able to act on planes that no purely discursive language reaches with the same immediacy.

A discipline is adult when it can open a new question without betraying its origin. The present passage arises here: to integrate generative technologies and models of state without losing the relational nucleus that makes music therapy what would otherwise be mere sonic administration.

Before speaking about MUMEx, we must name what no generative system will ever be allowed to confiscate: the relationship. A music therapy session is not a stream of musical stimuli applied to an organism. It is an encounter. It is a room in which one human being listens to another human being with instruments that include sound, silence, breath, gesture, waiting, rhythm, error, and response.

The music therapist brings more than musical competence. The therapist brings the capacity to read state. The therapist sees a shoulder drop, a hand seeking the edge of the chair, a voice breaking, a pause that lasts too long, a silence that is full or a silence that is closed. The therapist knows when to support and when to remove; when repetition is containing and when it is becoming a prison; when variation opens a passage and when it invades.

The voice remains the original instrument. Even when the session uses acoustic instruments, electronic instruments, or generative environments, the voices of the therapist and the patient retain ontological priority. Voice contains breath, identity, vulnerability, and body. Before communicating a meaning, it emits presence. A murmur, a chant almost without pitch, a suspended vowel, a note held in the chest can modify the state more than a precise explanation.

Improvisation is the second nucleus. In music therapy, improvising does not mean playing freely in order to display creativity. It means building a shared event in real time, with rules born from listening. Improvisation is a form of embodied thought. The patient produces a sonic gesture and that gesture is recognized, mirrored, transformed. Here the person is not the object of an intervention; the person becomes coauthor of the field.

Any technology entering music therapy must kneel before this fact: therapeutic sound is born from relationship. MUMEx will have value only if it knows how to serve that relationship, expanding its space without occupying it.

Recorded music has had, and still has, an important role. A piece can carry memory, identity, belonging, consolation, activation, and ritual. It can hold a precise biographical story. It can be the song of a father, the melody of childhood, a cultural fragment that reopens a sense of continuity. Music therapy must not renounce this inheritance.

Yet the fixed piece has a structural limit: it returns identical to itself. Its form is closed. Every detail is already decided. The patient may change, the body may shift, the breath may accelerate or settle, but the piece continues along its own trajectory. This stability can be precious. It can also become rigidity.

In clinical practice, fixed music can impose an already written dramaturgy on a state that needs to be followed. A harmonic progression may arrive too soon. A crescendo may exceed the limit of tolerance. A melody may saturate the symbolic space. A rhythm may become excessively prescriptive. In all its beauty, the piece can ignore the body present before the therapist.

So-called therapeutic playlists reveal the problem even more sharply. They often simplify the relationship between music and human state by imagining linear correspondences: calm music to relax, cheerful music to lift mood, natural sounds to soothe, low frequencies to ground. The reality of the session is more complex. Music that is theoretically calm can irritate. A bright piece can wound. A natural sound can activate an unpleasant memory. The patient is not a category of sonic consumption.

The limit of fixed music does not erase its value. It indicates the point at which a new class of environments becomes necessary: sound fields capable of maintaining coherence without fixity, form without closure, direction without imposition.

The entrance of technology into music therapy requires severe lucidity. Every device carries a temptation: to make us believe that the power of the instrument authorizes a diminishment of human listening. The recent history of care is full of objects presented as revolutionary and then used to standardize, accelerate, and simplify what in fact required presence.

Sonic technology can become intrusive. It can turn the patient into a user, the therapist into an operator, the session into a procedure, and physiological data into a fetish. It can generate spectacular environments that impress without helping. It can seduce the professional with the beauty of control and draw that professional away from the living opacity of the clinical process.

For this reason, a clear position is required: technology enters MUMEx Quantum Music Therapy as an extension of sensitivity, never as a replacement for responsibility. A sensor can inform; it cannot decide. An algorithm can generate; it cannot interpret. A sound field can support; it cannot know the patient by itself. Judgment remains with the therapist, and with judgment remain responsibility for opening, duration, intensity, and return.

Recent literature on musical technologies for health, rehabilitation, and well-being shows an expanding field: digital systems, accessible interfaces, monitoring tools, personalization, biofeedback, and interactive environments. This expansion contains real opportunities and radical questions. The question is not how sophisticated the machine can become. The question is what human form its use can assume (Edwards et al., 2023; Seo, 2026; Wei & He, 2026).

MUMEx must be born with this internal discipline. Its strength will not be the quantity of sound it can generate. Its strength will be its capacity to generate fields that know how to withdraw, fall silent, simplify themselves, make room for the voice, and respect the living limit of the body. A therapeutic technology is also measured by its capacity not to act.

The decisive word in this research is field. It allows us to leave both the logic of the piece and the logic of the device. A field is not an isolated sonic object. It is an environment of forces, relationships, tensions, and possibilities. It has duration, form, density, edge, depth, and a field of action. It is inhabited, not merely listened to.

To think in terms of field is to recognize that sound acts together with space, body, time, and relationship. A drone is not merely a sustained frequency. It changes according to volume, room, posture, breath, the presence of the therapist, the memory it evokes, and the length of time for which it is held. A drum stroke is never only an acoustic event. It is distance, intention, gesture, vibration, expectation, and response.

Music therapy has always worked in fields, even when it did not use the word. The setting itself is a field. The relationship is a field. Improvisation is a field in which each gesture modifies the next one. The novelty of MUMEx consists in making part of this sonic dynamic programmable and traceable without reducing it to mechanism.

A generative sound field has specific characteristics: it can evolve over time; it can vary without losing identity; it can preserve memory of what has occurred; it can respond to external parameters; it can differentiate phases; it can create a trajectory of entry, Suspension, Gentle Perturbation, and Reintegration. Its value arises from the possibility of tuning form and state.

The passage from device to field also implies a change in the therapist's posture. The task is not to start a system and observe the effect. The task is to inhabit an environment with the patient, knowing that every sonic choice modifies the perceptual landscape of the session.

MUMEx is introduced in this research as an engine for generative sound fields. Its function is not to produce new music in the aesthetic sense, although musical quality remains decisive. Its function is to generate sound environments that can be conceived in relation to the human state.

Three elements distinguish it from a playlist or an ambient track. The first is generativity. A MUMEx field does not proceed like a closed recording: it can produce variations, branches, micro-events, and adaptations. The second is memory. The system can maintain a relationship with what has happened before, avoiding blind repetition and building continuity. The third is potential adaptivity. If connected to physiological signals or to the therapist's choices, the field can modulate density, register, timbre, rhythm, space, and silence.

From this perspective, music therapy does not receive a gadget. It receives a new kind of matter. As electricity transformed the guitar without abolishing the musician's hand, the generative sound field can transform the landscape of the session without abolishing the therapist's body. The question is aesthetic, clinical, and epistemological.

MUMEx allows us to think of the session as a trajectory. Not as continuous background, but as an arc: entry, Resonance, Suspension, Gentle Perturbation, possible emergence, and Reintegration. Each phase can be designed through specific parameters. Each parameter can be observed. Each session can leave a trace in a logbook. This allows vision to become research.

The real novelty is not the machine that generates sounds. It is the possibility of building sound fields with a grammar of state.

The frontier before music therapy does not concern technology alone. It concerns the very idea of what a sonic intervention is. Until now, the discipline has worked primarily through three great modalities: performance, improvisation, and listening. A fourth is now added: the construction of generative environments.

Performance brings form. Improvisation brings relationship in real time. Listening brings reception, memory, and containment. The generative sound field brings a fourth quality: an evolving sound environment able to support a trajectory without coinciding with a closed piece and without requiring the therapist to maintain continuous manual sound production.

This fourth modality can liberate new practices. A session can open with a Resonance field while the therapist observes the patient's body without having to play immediately. A spontaneous vocalization can emerge over an environment that thins out to make space for it. An anxious patient can be supported by a field that is almost ritual, predictable and alive. Work on memory can be prepared by a timbral Suspension that does not push toward already codified images. A return phase can be accompanied by a field that reduces complexity and brings the body back to the room.

The music therapist does not lose a role. The responsibility changes. The therapist becomes more clearly architect, guardian, and interpreter of the field. Not only the one who plays, chooses, or listens, but also the one who designs sonic conditions so that a state can change without being violated.

This frontier is also political in the highest sense of the word. Every dominant paradigm tends to defend its own instruments, languages, and hierarchies. A living thought must have the courage to press against the border. Generative music therapy does not ask to be authorized by those who confuse rigor with immobility. It builds method, produces experiences, gathers data, and calls the most courageous professionals to verify in the field what theory glimpses.

An essay that proposes a new frontier must hold together three words that are often separated: evidence, experience, and method. Evidence without experience becomes disembodied statistics. Experience without method becomes fragile testimony. Method without vision becomes administration of the already known (Edwards et al., 2023; Robb et al., 2025).

Music therapy lives at the exact point where these three dimensions touch. Each session contains observable data and subtle material. It contains changes in breath and images reported by the patient; variations in muscle tone and memories; assessment scales and silences; physiological parameters and symbolic gestures. The error would be to choose one level and declare it sovereign.

MUMEx can contribute to this integration because each field can be recorded in its parameters: density, dynamics, timbre, rhythm, silence, variation, spatialization, duration, transitions. The logbook makes it possible to connect the quality of experience to the qualities of the field. In this way the music therapist does not lose clinical subtlety; the therapist acquires technical memory of the process (Hanson-Abromeit, 2025; Robb et al., 2025).

The initial method must be modest and strong. Modest because it will begin with nonclinical protocols, healthy subjects, exploratory observations, and comparison among a MUMEx field, fixed music, and a neutral control. Strong because it will formulate precise questions: does a generative sound field modify state differently from a fixed track? Does it produce greater absorption? Does it favor a richer perception of the body? Does it affect breath, HRV, attention, the perception of time? Does it generate denser experiential narratives?

A frontier discipline becomes credible when it faces difficult questions. The future of MUMEx Quantum Music Therapy must pass through that point: the patient construction of evidence suited to the nature of the phenomenon, with promise replaced by protocols, observations, comparison, and responsibility.

The music therapist who enters this territory does not become a sound technician. The therapist becomes a professional able to govern a broader complexity. Musical competence remains, yet it expands toward field design, psychophysiological reading, comprehension of generative parameters, and management of the perceptual edge.

This new figure does not abandon the acoustic instrument. The therapist brings it into an ecosystem. A drum can enter into dialogue with a generative drone. A voice can emerge within an electronic field that withdraws. A gong can be integrated into immersive spatialization. A silence can be treated as a structural event, not as an empty space between two interventions.

The therapist must learn to distinguish intensity from depth. An immersive field can be intense and useless. A barely perceptible sound can be extremely deep. Spectacle is a constant threat. The therapeutic field must not impress. It must create conditions for transformation.

This figure must also safeguard the return. Every practice that works with states, trance, vibration, memory, body, and openness can open delicate material. Reintegration is not an accessory phase. It is the ethical seal of the work. The patient must leave the session more present, not more dispersed; more inhabitable to themselves, not more dependent on the field. MUMEx must be designed with this inner law: every opening requires a way back.

The music therapist of the generative sound field will therefore be artist, clinician, listener, designer, and guardian. No machine can take this place because no machine is morally answerable for the human state it helps to modify.

The new frontier of music therapy can be stated in an essential formula: from the musical piece to the field; from the field to the state; from the state to transformation. This formula does not erase previous history. It carries it forward.

The piece remains. Improvisation remains. Voice remains. The instrument remains. The setting remains. To these elements the generative sound field is added: a temporal organism capable of modulating presence, density, Suspension, Gentle Perturbation, and return.

MUMEx is not the final answer. It is an opening. Its legitimacy will depend on the quality of the fields produced, the sensitivity of the therapists who use it, the precision of the protocols, the willingness to correct, and the capacity to gather data without sterilizing experience. Every new discipline is born fragile. It becomes strong when it can build a language capable of speaking to body, practice, and research.

Music therapy before its new frontier must choose whether to remain inside already recognized boundaries or expand its gesture. This research chooses expansion: it gives clinical work a larger horizon, offers the relationship a field in which to breathe more widely, removes care from technocracy, and obliges technology to become more human.

The next step is to understand what model of mind can sustain this vision. If sound becomes field, the mind can no longer be conceived as a linear mechanism. It must be understood as a system of possibilities, a mobile place in which memory, desire, fear, imagination, and choice coexist before taking form. From here the second chapter begins.

CHAPTER 2

The Mind as a Field of Possibility

EPISTEMOLOGICAL LEVEL: *Theoretical model. The mind as a field of possibility, and a quantum-like use of state, measurement, context, and interference without improper physical claims.*

To understand fully what MUMEx Quantum Music Therapy may become, we must abandon a figure of the mind that is too poor. The mind does not resemble a straight corridor in which one cause produces one effect, a symptom derives from a trauma, a word corrects a thought, and a musical piece induces a predetermined emotion. The human mind is wider, more unstable, more contradictory. It resembles a field in which different states coexist, attract one another, repel one another, disguise themselves, weaken, strengthen, and eventually allow an event to produce an experienceable form.

The patient who enters a music therapy room is a complex configuration. They bring the desire to be helped and the fear of changing. Thcy bring memories and silences, images and defenses. They bring the body. Sometimes they arrive with an apparently clear sentence—I feel bad, I am anxious, I am blocked—while beneath that sentence many possibilities are moving without yet having names.

This chapter establishes the book's second pillar: the mind as a field of possibility. This is not an ornamental metaphor. It is a way of thinking about music therapy with greater fidelity to clinical and experiential reality. Before speech, before choice, before a coherent narrative, the human being often lives in a plurality of partial states. Sound can enter that plurality with a force that discursive language possesses only in part because sound works in time, in the body, in waiting, in implicit memory, and in the transformation of presence.

Quantum cognition offers a valuable formal reference here. Its value for this research does not lie in importing quantum physics into therapy. Its value lies in showing that certain mental processes can be modeled through states, contexts, interferences, and measurements. The mind changes when it is questioned. One judgment modifies the next. One possibility can interfere with another. The order of questions changes the answers. A decision often arises from the reduction of an inner plurality into a chosen form. All of this speaks directly to the music therapist, even when no mathematical formula is being used: every session is a field of moving states (Busemeyer & Bruza, 2012; Huang et al., 2025; Pothos & Busemeyer, 2013).

Western therapeutic traditions have often inherited a mechanical image of the psyche. One seeks a cause, isolates a symptom, identifies a link, intervenes upon a function. This schema has produced important tools. It has made it possible to classify, observe, measure, and treat. Its limit appears when psychic life is reduced to a linear chain.

Those who work with sound know the insufficiency of this reduction well. The same music can calm one person and irritate another. Silence can be rest, threat, emptiness, listening, waiting, abandonment. A rhythm can ground or oppress. A voice can open or close. The meaning of the sonic event is born from the field in which it occurs: body, history, relationship, setting, memory, physiological state, the patient's expectation, and the therapist's presence.

The mechanical mind presupposes already given properties: anxiety, sadness, fear, calm, openness. The mind as field invites us to think of these properties as configurations that emerge. An anxious person is not simply the carrier of anxiety; that person is a system in which anxiety coexists with desire for trust, shame, hypervigilance, remaining resources, memory of safety, capacity for bond, and fantasy of control. Therapeutic work does not add a new state from outside. It supports the reorganization of forces already present, often separated or made inaccessible.

Precisely because of its temporal nature, sound can move inside this field without forcing it immediately into an explanation. A stable drone allows a possibility to last. A minimal perturbation makes a difference perceptible. A pause lets an image emerge. A repetition makes time inhabitable. Music does not explain the state. It traverses it, holds it, shifts it, modifies it.

In the scientific field, the expression quantum cognition refers to a research program that applies quantum probability theory to cognition. The most cautious formulation is also the most useful for our work: the probabilistic and geometric rules of quantum theory are used as modeling tools without committing us to the hypothesis of physical quantum processes in the brain.

Reviews by Pothos, Busemeyer, and their collaborators show how these models have been applied to judgment, decision-making, memory, perception, conceptual combination, order effects, disjunction, conjunction, similarity, and causality. A 2025 synthesis explicitly describes quantum cognition as the application of quantum probability to cognitive modeling, that is, the use of probability rules for assigning likelihoods to events drawn from quantum mechanics, without subatomic physics. This clarification is decisive: the model matters because of the structure of thought, not because of a metaphysical promise (Huang et al., 2025; Pothos & Busemeyer, 2013).

The strength of quantum probability is its ability to describe situations in which context changes the state of a system. In classical probability, one often imagines that an event has an already determined property that measurement merely reveals. In quantum-like models, measurement participates in the constitution of the result. Transposed with caution into psychology, this idea helps us understand why a question, a listening, a gesture, a silence, or a sound can modify the mental state it claims to observe.

The music therapist sees this continually. If the therapist immediately asks the patient what they feel, the answer may be different from the one that would emerge after five minutes of listening. If the therapist proposes a drum rather than a vocal drone, the field is oriented differently. If the therapist allows a silence, the state may organize itself through a dynamic that an immediate word would have interrupted. The session does not merely observe the patient; it participates in the formation of the state the patient may later recognize.

To make the dialogue between quantum cognition and music therapy fertile, three words must be translated: state, observable, measurement. In the vocabulary of physics these words have technical definitions. In our model they are used as conceptual instruments, able to organize experience without pretending that a session is an experiment in quantum mechanics.

The state is the subject's overall configuration at a given moment. It includes attention, posture, breath, muscle tone, active memory, imagination, affectivity, perception of time, sense of safety, degree of absorption, and relational availability. None of these elements is sufficient by itself. The state is the way they hold together.

An observable is a quality of the state that can become perceptible or measurable. In the session we can observe breath, pulse, voice, movement, gaze orientation, the capacity to remain within sound, the emergence of images, the post-experience account, and possible physiological measures such as HRV or skin conductance. An observable does not exhaust the subject. It makes one cut of the field accessible.

Measurement is the act that brings a quality into manifestation. It can be a question, a numeric scale, a physiological recording, an invitation to vocalize, a debriefing, or a choice between two sounds. Every measurement modifies something. Asking a person to name an emotion produces a different effect from asking where they feel a vibration. Inviting a person to choose a sound produces a different effect from allowing the sound to act without a task.

This awareness avoids two errors. The first is believing that measurement is neutral. The second is giving up measurement because one fears impoverishing experience. The mature path is another one: to measure while knowing that every measurement is an intervention. In music therapy, this means building instruments of observation that respect the life of the field.

One of the most fertile concepts, when handled precisely, is superposition. In quantum physics it indicates a combination of possible states before measurement. In psychology it must be used as a formalizable image, not as a physical identity. Psychological superposition describes the coexistence of incompatible tendencies, emotions, images, and directions that have not yet assumed a stable form.

A patient may want to speak and desire silence. They may ask for help and defend themselves against help. They may seek calm and fear calm because calm allows what agitation kept away to emerge. They may desire contact and experience contact as threat. Psychic life is often composed of such impossible cohabitations. Ordinary language tends to resolve them too soon, forcing the subject to choose one version of the self. Sound can keep the coexistence open for a longer time.

Here music therapy possesses a rare strength. A sound field can hold two states without obliging them to become narrative immediately. A low timbre can contain weight; a high figure can let the possibility of opening filter through. A slow rhythm can hold the body; a microvariation can let the patient feel that something is moving. The patient does not have to declare which part is true. The patient can remain within a wider configuration.

MUMEx allows this coexistence to be programmed with greater precision. A field can have a stable nucleus and mobile peripheries; low density with distant micro-events; a repetition that does not become a loop; a harmonic tension that remains inhabitable. In this way the system does not offer the patient a prepackaged emotion. It offers an acoustic space in which several inner possibilities can breathe together.

Quantum cognition assigns great importance to interference. In a classical model, the probabilities of different alternatives can be added according to linear rules. In quantum-like models, possibilities can interfere: the presence of one modifies the weight of another. This idea describes many clinical and experiential situations with surprising efficacy.

Fear of change interferes with the desire to heal. The memory of abandonment interferes with the possibility of trusting the therapist. A sentence heard in childhood interferes with the present perception of one's own voice. Music loved in the past can interfere with grief, transforming itself from a source of joy into the sonic body of sorrow. The mind does not simply add elements. It makes them act upon one another.

Sound makes this logic audible. Two nearby frequencies produce beats. Two rhythms create friction or interlock. A timbre can color another. Silence changes the meaning of the sound that precedes it. Music, before theory, teaches that the relationship among elements produces new qualities. This is decisive for Quantum Music Therapy: the sonic intervention does not merely add stimuli; it modifies the relationships among internal possibilities.

A MUMEx field can be designed as a space of controlled interference. Not an accumulation of events, but a composition of subtle tensions: continuity and difference, support and movement, predictability and openness, body and image. Therapeutic quality does not arise from the isolated sound. It arises from the way the field modifies the probability that certain internal configurations will emerge.

Among the phenomena most studied by quantum cognition are order effects. The answer to a question can change if the question is asked before or after another one. A judgment changes the context of the following judgment. The order of events participates in the formation of the result. In therapy this is evident: the same question, asked at a different moment, meets a different human being (Trueblood & Busemeyer, 2011).

In music therapy, order is everything. A percussion intervention proposed too early can activate defense. The same percussion, after a long work of Resonance, can give body and grounding. Silence at the beginning can be an anguished emptiness. The same silence after a containing sonic phase can become integration. A sung voice can feel invasive at the entrance of the session and salvific after a period of shared listening.

This logic prevents us from thinking of music as a repertoire of effects. No sound has a universal therapeutic value separated from context. Context includes the patient's history, the moment in the session, the setting, the therapist's presence, the sequence of events, the intensity of the field, the possibility of control, and the way the sound is introduced and withdrawn.

MUMEx must therefore be designed as a temporal architecture, not as a collection of materials. The entry field prepares the next field. Suspension prepares perturbation. Perturbation requires the possibility of return. Each phase modifies the meaning of the following phase. Generativity becomes useful when it respects the deep order of experience.

In the language of this research, Perceptual Collapse indicates the moment in which a plurality of internal possibilities assumes a lived form. The term must be understood psychologically and phenomenologically. It does not describe a physical event in the brain. It indicates an experiential passage: what was diffuse becomes image, word, gesture, tear, decision, memory, quiet, orientation.

Clinical practice knows these passages. A patient listens for ten minutes without saying anything and then says they have seen a house, a face, a road. Another person suddenly feels their chest after months of bodily estrangement. An adolescent who refused any verbalization strikes three notes on a drum and that gesture becomes the first declaration of presence. An older person with cognitive decline recognizes a melodic fragment and, for a few seconds, biography has a center again.

Perceptual Collapse is not spectacle. It is a delicate event, often minimal. Its importance arises from the fact that the internal field reorganizes. The person can say: now I feel. Now I see. Now I remember. Now I breathe. Now this part of me has a form. Transformation of state does not always coincide with strong emotional change; often it coincides with the emergence of a form stable enough to be integrated.

The music therapist must recognize these moments without appropriating them. Interpreting too soon is a way of colonizing the patient's experience. The more respectful question concerns body and presence: what is happening? Where do you feel it? Do you need to remain in silence? Would you like to say something? In MUMEx, Perceptual Collapse requires a field that can converge and then withdraw. Sound prepares emergence, then makes space for the human.

If the mind is a field of possibility, the patient cannot be reduced to a diagnosis. Diagnosis can orient, protect, indicate risks, and guide clinical choices. It remains a partial map. The real person is a living configuration of possible states. This statement changes the way the session is designed.

A depressed patient is not only a subject with low mood, anhedonia, or slowing. That patient is also a system in which micro-possibilities of contact, sonic memories, traces of pleasure, annihilated desires, frozen anger, bodily needs, and hunger for the world survive. Music therapy searches for these subtle possibilities without disguising them as optimism.

An anxious patient is not only hyperactivation. They carry a demand for control and a demand for surrender, fear of the world and need for support, often an extremely acute acoustic sensitivity and a capacity for orientation that can be reeducated through rhythms, repetitions, and sonic boundaries. The therapeutic field does not fight anxiety frontally; it builds conditions in which other states may become more probable.

A traumatized patient is not only the bearer of painful memory. They carry living parts that remained outside the story, anesthetized parts, hypervigilant parts, parts capable of play, parts that already know the way back to the body. In this context sound must be handled with extreme precision because it can reopen powerful sensory material. The model of possible states helps us not confuse intensity with progress.

To think of the patient as a configuration of states produces a different ethics. The therapist stops searching for the immediate result and begins working on the probabilities of the field: more safety, more presence, more breath, more tolerance for silence, more possibility of choice, more contact with the body. This is a subtle science made of minute transitions.

In this architecture, sound becomes an operator. An operator is not a simple cause. It is a transformation applied to a state. In our language, a sound field operates upon the subject's psychophysical state in relation to context, therapist, history, the moment of the session, and the person's perceptual availability.

We can express the idea synthetically: rho_H(t + Delta t) = E_{S,C} (rho_H(t)). The formula does not claim to measure the full complexity of the human being. It fixes the principle. The human state rho_H evolves over time through the joint action of the sound field S and the context C. Context includes setting, relationship, voice, silence, safety, intention, debriefing, and the possibility of interrupting the experience.

This formula prevents a frequency reductionism. Sound alone is not enough. The same frequency, drone, or rhythm can have different effects in different contexts. MUMEx Quantum Music Therapy does not worship the isolated frequency. It studies the relationship among sound field, human state, and therapeutic context.

Sound operates on many dimensions: rhythm, timbre, density, register, dynamics, spatialization, microvariation, silence, recognizability, unpredictability, duration. MUMEx makes these dimensions programmable and traceable. The music therapist can therefore think not only about what is sounding, but about what transformation of state the field makes possible.

The power of MUMEx emerges when sonic generation is conceived as a geometry of states. A sound field does not merely proceed through time; it draws a perceptual space. It brings nearer or farther. It densifies or rarefies. It stabilizes or troubles. It moves the subject toward the body or toward image. It makes time more linear, more circular, more suspended, more breathing.

In a quantum-like model, we can imagine that the subject's state is represented by a distribution of possibilities. Some concern calm, others activation, bodily attention, memory, voice, or defense. The sound field does not impose a result; it modifies the landscape of possibilities. It makes some configurations more accessible and others less dominant.

A field of Resonance increases the probability of bodily safety. A field of Suspension increases the probability of images and tolerable ambivalences. A Gentle Perturbation increases the probability of micro-transitions. A field of Reintegration increases the probability of stable return. This language does not replace clinical intuition; it makes it discussable, designable, and shareable.

The geometry of states also helps avoid fascination with complexity. A MUMEx field that is too rich can generate confusion, spectacle, saturation. A poor field can be very deep if it precisely orients the required transformation. The criterion is not the autonomous beauty of the sound. The criterion is coherence among sound, state, and relationship.

In the classical model of decision, to choose means to select an option among alternatives already available. In real psychic life, choice is often born while it is being searched for. The person does not know in advance what they want; they discover it in contact with situations, words, images, bodies, sounds. Choice is an event of formation, not only of selection.

Sound has a deep relationship with this dimension. A patient may not know whether they wish to speak. Then they listen to a low voice and feel they can emit a note. Another does not know whether they want to move. Then a rhythm invites them to shift weight from one foot to the other. A person unable to name anger may recognize it in a percussion. An inexpressible memory may choose a bell, a tremolo, a descending interval.

Music therapy often works with tiny choices: choosing an instrument, a volume, a distance, a duration, a gesture, a point in the room. In a wounded mind, such choices have enormous value because they rebuild agency. The patient experiences that they can affect the field and therefore their own state. This experience precedes many verbal elaborations.

MUMEx can make choice part of generation. The patient can modify a simple parameter: nearer, farther, denser, rarer, lower, brighter, more still. The machine records, the therapist observes, the field changes. Choice becomes audible. The subject hears in the sound the effect of their own gesture. Here technology does not replace the relationship; it makes the patient's capacity to transform the environment perceptible.

Every powerful concept carries a danger. The mind as field can become a vague formula. Perceptual Collapse can be mistaken for magic. The word quantum can be used as decoration. For this reason the language of the book must remain demanding. A metaphor has value only when it produces method, observation, and responsibility.

Quantum cognition authorizes us to use formal structures of state, context, interference, order, and measurement. It does not authorize claims of quantum healing, unproven universal vibrations, absolute causalities between frequencies and organs, or arbitrary equivalences between physics and psyche. Pioneering freedom does not consist in saying anything at all. It consists in carrying intuition farther than dominant language permits while building instruments capable of withstanding verification.

In the present chapter, caution does not function as a brake. It functions as a blade. It cuts away what is rhetorical and leaves passage for what can become research. The mind as a field of possibility is a strong thesis because it can be translated into operational questions: which states are present? Which observables make them legible? Which sound modifies the field? Which sequence favors transition? Which measurement respects the process? Which return integrates the experience?

This discipline of language protects the work from two opposite enemies: academicism that sterilizes experience and enthusiasm that makes it indemonstrable. MUMEx Quantum Music Therapy must stand at the most difficult point: broad vision, concrete method, writing able to name the new without selling it cheaply.

Thinking of the mind as a field of possibility changes practice in at least five ways. First, the session is designed as a trajectory of state, not as a sequence of activities. The initial question concerns the possible passage: from hypervigilance to orientation, from closure to contact, from dispersion to body, from mutism to voice, from fragmented memory to sustainable image.

Second, sound is chosen for its function within the field. A drum, a voice, a drone, an interval, a natural sample, an electronic spatialization are not neutral elements. Each modifies the internal distribution of possibilities. The therapist must know what function they intend to assign to each sonic event.

Third, time becomes part of care. Order, duration, moment of entry, moment of subtraction, and final silence have structural value. The same sonic matter can open or close depending on when it appears. A music therapy of fields cannot be hurried.

Fourth, observation becomes more refined. The therapist observes micro-transitions: a change in breath, a shift of the jaw, an eyelid lowering, a hand releasing contraction, a voice becoming barely more sonorous. These are small and decisive events because they indicate that the field is changing.

Fifth, return becomes part of the model. Every opened state must be integrable. The session must not leave the patient in a vastness without orientation. Quantum Music Therapy seeks transitions, not irresponsible dissolutions. For this reason Reintegration, one of the five central operators, is an ethical principle before being a technical one.

This chapter prepares the theoretical heart of the next. If the mind is a field of possibility, Quantum Music Therapy must clarify what it means to transform a human state. Transformation is not a superficial change of mood. It means modifying the overall organization of body, attention, memory, image, time, relationship, and choice.

A person can leave a session without euphoria and yet be profoundly different: breathing with less effort, feeling the chest, tolerating silence, remembering without being overwhelmed, managing to emit a sound, recognizing a part of themselves, perceiving the world with one more degree of inhabitability. These are events of state. Clinical work should learn to respect them as much as it respects dramatic declarations of change.

MUMEx enters here as an instrument of amplification and precision. Not to produce guaranteed effects, but to build fields capable of entering into dialogue with the complexity of the human state. The machine generates the field; the therapist safeguards the relationship; the patient moves within their own configuration; the method records what happens; research slowly learns to distinguish intuition, effect, transformation, and evidence.

The mind as a field of possibility is not an accessory image in this book. It is its deep grammar. Without this model, MUMEx would risk appearing to be an advanced sonic technology. With this model, MUMEx becomes a laboratory for studying how sound intervenes in the mobile form of consciousness.

CHAPTER 3

Quantum Psychology and the Transformation of the Human State

EPISTEMOLOGICAL LEVEL: *Theoretical-clinical model. Transformation of the human state, quantum psychology in an operational sense, and caution around diagnosis, causality, and therapeutic promise.*

Quantum Music Therapy is born from a radical decision: to take the human state seriously. Before the symptom, before the story, before the diagnosis, before interpretation, there exists a living configuration made of body, attention, memory, breath, images, fear, desire, orientation, energy, and waiting. This configuration changes continuously. At times it hardens until it seems like destiny. At times it opens for an instant and lets a new form appear. At times it remains suspended in an obscure point where the person knows they must change and at the same time fears the change. Music therapy has always worked in this territory, even when it has not named it this way. Sound does not meet an abstract subject. It meets a state.

To call this territory Quantum Psychology is to propose a grammar of transformation. The term must be assumed in its force, without reducing it to ornament, spiritual fashion, or an automatic guarantee of efficacy. In this research, quantum indicates above all field, possibility, context, interference, measurement, transition of state, and reorganization of experience. It indicates a conception of the mind broader than linear psychology: a mind that does not always proceed through simple causes and predictable reactions because it simultaneously contains divergent impulses, layered memories, opposing fears, images not yet verbalized, and bodily tensions that anticipate speech.

The most fertile scientific reference is quantum cognition, a research program that uses the formalism of quantum probability to model cognitive processes in which classical probability proves insufficient or too rigid. Research by Busemeyer, Pothos, Trueblood, Yearsley, Khrennikov, and others has shown that judgment, decision-making, memory, perception, conceptual combination, and order effects can be described through models in which mental state changes according to context and to the very act of questioning. This point touches therapeutic practice directly: every intervention modifies the field it intends to observe. A question changes the possible answer. A silence changes the quality of memory. A timbre changes the way the body is disposed. A rhythm modifies the internal time in which an emotion can form.

The Quantum Psychology proposed in this essay does not claim to prove that the brain is a quantum device. The physical question of quantum consciousness belongs to a specific and complex debate, marked by fascinating hypotheses and open problems. Our task is different. We must build an operational model for understanding how sound can intervene in the transformation of the human state. From this perspective, the word quantum describes a structure of mental behavior: uncertainty, coexistence of possibilities, dependence on context, variation produced by observation, and emergence of a form from a larger field.

A patient arrives in session saying: I am anxious. The sentence seems simple. In reality it contains an entire field. There is the declared anxiety, yes. There is the body that has learned to anticipate threat. There may be a remote memory in which thc environment was not reliable. There is the desire to be seen. There is the shame of being unable to calm down. There is one part asking for control and another part wanting to surrender. There is fear of silence because in silence the inner noise becomes louder. There is a respiratory rhythm that says much more than the sentence. Linear psychology risks taking anxiety as an object. A psychology of state sees the living constellation that sustains it.

The same is true of depression. Depression is not only sadness, low mood, or loss of interest. It is often a radical transformation of the perceptual field. The world loses relief. Sounds become distant or useless. The body is heavy. Time flattens. Future possibility darkens. In the music therapy room, this state cannot be addressed through the naive idea of a sound that should cheer it up. One must enter its architecture. A sound field that is low, slow, bodily, and undemanding may not produce immediate emotion and yet may reopen a minimal possibility of presence. Transformation of state often begins with a tiny change: a less contracted breath, attention that does not flee, a vibration felt in the sternum, a pause that does not fall into emptiness.

In trauma, the field assumes another form. The person may live in a double temporality: the present of the room and the frozen time of the event. The body reacts before thought. A sudden noise crosses defenses, breath breaks, gaze loses orientation. In terms of state, trauma does not only preserve painful content; it preserves a perceptual mode. Music therapy can then become a work of reconstructing the present. Sound must restore continuity, predictability, control, the possibility of interruption, and bodily return. Here the power of the sound field must be governed with extreme precision. Transformation does not arise from the force of the stimulus; it arises from the possibility of living a sonic experience without being seized again by alarm.

Quantum Psychology assumes that the person never coincides with the dominant state of the moment. This is decisive. The human being is not their anxiety, depression, defense, dissociation, or creative block. Every dominant state tends to present itself as totality, to occupy the whole psychic sky. Yet beneath or alongside it, other possibilities remain active in weak, silent, marginal form. The function of sound may consist precisely in increasing the probability of access to these nondominant possibilities. A blocked person may encounter a micro-movement. A closed person may tolerate a shared vibration. A fragmented person may feel temporal continuity. A person invaded by thought may experience one minute of bodily presence.

This way of thinking changes the role of the music therapist. The therapist is not a technician applying a sound to a disorder. The therapist is a reader of states, a builder of conditions, an interpreter of the relational and perceptual field. The therapist must understand when sound must contain, when it must rarefy, when it can intensify, when it must withdraw. The therapist must recognize the moment in which the person can sustain variation and the moment in which variation would be violence. The therapist must feel the clinical value of repetition, slowing, a timbre that stays near the body, a silence that does not collapse into abandonment.

The transformation of the human state does not always occur through meaning. In many situations, meaning arrives later. First the breath changes. First a tension in the jaw loosens. First the patient feels the feet. First a hand begins to move. First a voice manages to come out. First an internal image appears without explanation. Only afterward does the person find words. Therapeutic culture has often attributed absolute primacy to speech. Music therapy reminds us that speech is one form of integration, not the first layer of experience. Sound works where concept has not yet taken possession of lived experience.

The word state must therefore be distinguished from the word emotion. Emotion is part of the state, not its totality. State includes posture, vegetative tone, orientation, internal rhythm, spatial perception, muscular tension, implicit memory, imagination, relational availability, level of energy, and quality of attention. A person can declare calm while the body remains in alarm. A person can cry and feel finally stable. A person can be silent and undergo a deep transformation. A person can smile as defense. The music therapist must read the whole field, without trusting a single signal.

Quantum probability offers a rigorous image for thinking this complexity: a state is not simply a list of already given properties. It is a configuration that can manifest different aspects according to the measurement. In therapy, a measurement can be a question, a gesture, a sound, an instruction, an instrumental choice, a pause. Asking the patient to speak about pain produces one manifestation. Inviting them to listen to a drone produces another. Asking them to choose a sonic object produces another. None of these manifestations exhausts the person. Each reveals and modifies part of the field.

From this vision follows a precise responsibility: the session cannot be conceived as the simple collection of data about the patient. The session participates in the creation of the conditions in which those data emerge. If the patient appears closed, one must ask what field has made that closure possible: the room, the first sound, the initial question, the therapist's posture, the memory activated, the expectation of performance. Quantum Psychology removes the therapist from the comfortable idea of being an external observer. Every therapeutic relationship is a co-construction of state.

This principle does not weaken research. It makes it more adult. The old dream of absolute neutrality has produced many illusions. In complex systems, observing means intervening. The issue is not to eliminate intervention, but to make it legible, traceable, and discussable. Here MUMEx offers a decisive advantage. A generative sound field can be documented through its parameters: density, register, dynamics, timbre, rhythm, microvariation, duration, degree of unpredictability, and formal evolution. If clinical observations, light physiological measures, and careful debriefings are added to these parameters, work on state gradually becomes studyable.

Transforming the human state through sound requires a theory of time. The ordinary time of the suffering mind is often deformed. In anxiety, the future invades the present. In depression, the future disappears. In trauma, the past does not pass. In grief, time splits between what continues and what can no longer return. Sound intervenes directly in this matter because it is organized time. A rhythm does not describe time; it builds it. A drone does not stop time; it dilates it. A pause does not interrupt time; it makes it perceptible. A generative sequence does not repeat time; it makes it evolve.

MUMEx can become a technology of internal time. Its generativity allows us to avoid two extremes: the fixed piece that imposes a closed form, and sonic chaos that disperses. A MUMEx field can vary without losing identity, change without tearing, and maintain a memory of what has happened. This formal memory is essential. The patient is not thrown into a series of disconnected events; the patient moves within an environment that preserves traces, returns, transformations. The continuity of the field can help the continuity of the state.

Quantum Psychology also asks us to rethink choice. Many human decisions are not born from explicit calculation among already defined alternatives. They are born from a transformation of state in which certain possibilities become accessible. A person does not choose to trust because someone has logically explained trust. They arrive at being able to trust when their internal field makes that configuration practicable. A person does not decide to breathe better; they enter a rhythm that makes another breath possible. Music therapy works precisely on these predecisional conditions.

In this light, Perceptual Collapse is not a spectacular act. It is the moment in which a configuration becomes experience. The patient says: now I feel it. Or: I saw an image. Or: a memory returned. Or: my body expanded. Or the patient remains silent, yet their presence has changed. Before that moment, many possibilities were distributed in the field. After it, a form has become available. The therapist's task is to guard this passage, avoiding both interpretive emphasis and abandonment of the experience to itself.

Quantum Psychology has operational consequences. If the mind is field, treatment must concern the field. If context modifies state, setting becomes part of the intervention. If measurement modifies what it measures, debriefing must be designed with care. If possibilities interfere, the therapist must listen not only to what appears, but also to what prevents something else from appearing. If the order of events counts, the session must be composed as a temporal form. If sound acts before speech, music therapy has primary responsibility in the transformation of the human state.

This perspective opens a new idea of sonic diagnosis. Not medical diagnosis, not labeling, not a replacement for clinical work. Diagnosis in the etymological sense of discernment: listening deeply. How does this subject breathe before a low sound? What happens when rhythm enters? Does silence calm or threaten? Does voice bring the patient closer or expose them? Does unpredictability intrigue or frighten? Does a melodic figure organize or carry the person away? Each answer helps map the state, not to imprison it, but to find the sonic passage best suited to transformation.

MUMEx Quantum Music Therapy can therefore develop a practice of dynamic mapping. Not a fixed map of the person, but a cartography of the relationships between states and sound fields. One patient may respond well to low densities and poorly to sudden spatial openings. Another may need rhythmic movement in order not to sink into stasis. Another may tolerate the drone only if the therapist's voice remains present. These pieces of information are not secondary details. They are the concrete grammar of sonic care.

The risk of every large model is that it becomes ideology. The word quantum can also become ideology if used to cover what is not known. To avoid this, Quantum Psychology of sound must remain demanding. It must accept verification, critique, replicability when possible, and an accurate description of limits. It must distinguish powerful experience from proof. It must leave to the clinic what belongs to the clinic, to philosophy what belongs to philosophy, to art what belongs to art. The force of revolutionary thought does not consist in ignoring differences, but in connecting them without flattening them.

Intellectual freedom is not arbitrariness. A pioneer does not repeat the academy but knows its language well enough to go beyond it. In this research, Quantum Psychology does not ask permission from a reductionist vision of the human being. It affirms that the mind is wider than the measurement that claims to close it, that the body contains subtle intelligences, that sound acts on planes still insufficiently understood. At the same time, every affirmation must become work, method, protocol, describable experience. Audacity without form consumes itself. Audacity with form builds territory.

From here arises the function of MUMEx. The system is not a simple musical generator. It is a field device. It can create sound environments that do not merely decorate the session but participate in the reorganization of state. It can generate continuity, variation, memory, perturbation, and return. It can work with parameters fine enough to make sound a living environment. Its value does not lie in replacing the therapist or automating care. It lies in giving the music therapist a new kind of matter: a sound field that evolves and can be studied.

Transformation of the human state occurs at the point where body and meaning cease to appear separate. A vibration in the sternum can become safety. A rhythm in the feet can become the desire to move. A distant timbre can become memory. A shared silence can become trust. The mind does not simply receive sound; it incorporates it, interprets it, resists it, transforms it, responds to it. Every music therapy session is a microphysics of experience.

Quantum language allows us to name this microphysics without impoverishing it. State, field, interference, measurement, collapse, observable, context: these words must not remain distant concepts. They must become tools for seeing more clearly what happens in the room. When the therapist changes the register of the sound, the field changes. When the therapist waits before speaking, measurement changes. When the therapist allows two opposing emotions to coexist, a psychological superposition is supported. When the therapist accompanies the emergence of an image without capturing it, Perceptual Collapse is guarded. When the therapist returns the person to the body, Reintegration occurs.

Quantum Psychology, in this sense, does not add mystery to music therapy. It makes visible the mystery that was already contained there. Every experienced music therapist knows that a session can change because of a minimal detail: a note held one second longer, a pause left open, a bell played farther away, a voice lowered, a drum that stops. The quantum-like model does not trivialize these details. It recognizes them as acts capable of reorganizing the field of possibilities.

The previous chapter showed music therapy before a new frontier. This chapter has established its theoretical necessity: if the mind is a field of possibility, then sound can be an operator of transformation. MUMEx Quantum Music Therapy is born from this convergence. On one side, the clinical and artistic wisdom of the music therapist. On the other, a model of the human state capable of thinking context, ambivalence, interference, and passage of form. At the center stands sound: not as simple language, not as emotional ornament, but as a temporal environment in which the human being can become something other than what the dominant state had made them believe they were.

The next step will be to specify more precisely what we mean by transformation of the human state. It is not enough to say that music moves us emotionally. We must understand how sound shifts attention, modifies breath, reorders time, makes the body perceptible, opens images, and changes the relationship between fear and possibility. Quantum Psychology gives the conceptual map. MUMEx prepares the sound laboratory. The music therapist remains the living presence that decides when to open the field, when to hold it, when to transform it, and when to close it.

CHAPTER 4

Nonverbal Hypnosis, Fascination, and the Perceptual Field

EPISTEMOLOGICAL LEVEL: *Established evidence / theoretical model. Hypnosis, altered attention, fascination, suggestive risk, and the sonic translation of the perceptual field.*

Nonverbal hypnosis compels music therapy to look at its most ancient center: the transformation of state before explanation. Before a sentence orders experience, before the patient finds an acceptable narrative, before consciousness builds a coherent version of itself, there is a primary zone in which the body decides whether to open, defend, contract, trust, remain still, flee, or listen. In that zone, language arrives late. Gaze, posture, distance, the rhythm of breath, the quality of presence, and the pressure of silence arrive first. Music therapy has always known this precedence because sound operates in the same territory. A held note, a drone, a low voice, a distant drum, a bell slowly disappearing can modify the state without asking the patient to understand immediately what is happening.

Modern hypnosis has often been imprisoned by two opposite caricatures: on one side, the spectacle of dominated will; on the other, its reduction to a verbal technique of relaxation and suggestion. Both caricatures impoverish the phenomenon. In contemporary clinical research, hypnosis is generally described through focused attention, reduced peripheral awareness, and increased responsiveness to suggestion. This definition is useful provided we do not forget that suggestion is not only a verbal command. A room suggests. A light suggests. A still body suggests. A pause suggests. A sound held motionless for several minutes suggests a different relationship to time. Suggestion, in the deepest sense, is the art of configuring a field in which an internal possibility becomes more accessible (Elkins et al., 2015).

Nonverbal hypnosis carries this evidence to its most naked point. The subject is not guided primarily by sentences, explanations, or discursive inductions, but by bodily signs: gaze, hands, orientation, proximity, microgestures, rhythm, presence. Fascination belongs to this territory. The term must be handled carefully because it carries an ancient, magnetic, sometimes theatrical aura. Yet it contains a precise phenomenological nucleus: consciousness can be captured, gathered, concentrated, shifted, when a perceptual element assumes an organizing force greater than the others. The gaze that fixes is not merely an organ that sees. It becomes a gravitational center of attention. The gesture of the hand is not only movement. It becomes a trajectory that the nervous system follows. The facilitator's silence is not emptiness. It becomes perceptual pressure.

Marco Paret has brought this line back into contemporary discourse: mesmerism, magnetism, fascination, nonverbal hypnosis, bodily communication, the power of gaze and presence. His work belongs to a frontier where magnetic tradition, hypnotic practice, and training of presence touch. For this research, the essential point is not to turn Paret into a normative clinical authority, nor to superimpose his school upon professional music therapy without a filter. The point is to recognize that his work insists on a decisive truth: the human state can be modified before speech. This truth directly concerns MUMEx. If the gaze can function as a magnetic center of attention, sound can function as its acoustic counterpart.

EDITORIAL NOTE FOR THE NORTH AMERICAN EDITION: Marco Paret's work, situated at the frontier of nonverbal hypnosis and fascination studies, is treated here as an exploratory and experimental reference point. It is cited for its phenomenological and methodological interest, not as established clinical evidence or as a mainstream clinical authority.

Sound as the acoustic counterpart of the hypnotic gaze is one of the governing images of this research. Gaze concentrates; sound surrounds. Gaze fixes; sound orients in time. Gaze creates an axis; sound creates an environment. Gaze can gather consciousness into a point; sound can gather it into duration. Both act before concept, both intervene in the distribution of attention, both modify the relationship between body and world. The difference is decisive: gaze tends to produce a frontal axis; sound produces a multidirectional field. In MUMEx Quantum Music Therapy, this difference becomes method.

A music therapy session does not need to imitate nonverbal hypnosis in order to learn from it. It must understand that every sonic event has an inductive quality. A regular rhythm induces a way of inhabiting time. A drone induces permanence. A low pulsation induces a relationship to weight. A sharp intermittent figure induces vigilance or call. A spatialized sound induces orientation, distance, depth. Silence also induces because it obliges perception to search for support. The correct question is not whether sound induces a state, but which state it makes more probable and under what safety conditions.

Here music therapy must defend its ethical maturity. To work on preverbal states is to enter a powerful zone. Powerful does not mean automatically therapeutic. A sound field can calm, contain, organize; it can also invade, disorient, seduce, generate dependency, or produce openings the patient is not ready to integrate. Fascination, when separated from responsibility, can become manipulation. The therapist's presence must not become charisma that crushes. Sound must not become a command disguised as aesthetic experience. MUMEx Quantum Music Therapy must be born with a precise law: every modification of state requires consent, gradualness, possibility of interruption, observation of the body, and return to ordinary presence.

Fascination is an archaic technology of attention. It does not belong only to hypnotists. Every mother who calms an infant with the voice knows a primary form of sonic fascination. Every ritual that uses a constant drum knows the force of repetition that takes the nervous system and carries it into another arrangement. Every sacred chant understands that the human being can be gathered by a sound long before being convinced by an argument. Music therapy, when it works deeply, enters this same lineage but must translate it into clinical responsibility.

In nonverbal hypnosis, the body of the facilitator is not neutral. Posture, breath, gaze, hands, and rhythm become instruments. In music therapy the therapist's body is also always active, even when it does not play. The way a hand moves toward an instrument, the slowness with which a gong is approached, the distance from the patient, the therapist's breathing before singing, the quality of listening before responding: these elements configure the perceptual field. MUMEx does not abolish this bodily theater. It makes the need for it even greater because the therapist must prevent the generative field from becoming disembodied.

The perceptual field is the total arrangement in which the patient's attention is distributed. It includes visible space, acoustic space, bodily sensations, relational signals, memories activated by the setting, the patient's expectations, and the therapist's presence. Nonverbal hypnosis acts on this field by reorganizing attention. Music therapy acts on it through sound, gesture, silence, and relationship. MUMEx adds an evolving sonic layer that can be designed as part of the perceptual architecture.

The field can be narrow or wide, unstable or secure, saturated or sparse, frontal or enveloping, predictable or uncertain. An anxious patient may live in a field narrowed by threat. A depressed patient may live in a field emptied of attraction. A traumatized patient may live in a field where the present is constantly invaded by sensory traces of the past. Sound can intervene because it changes distance, depth, pulse, density, and temporal expectation.

Nonverbal hypnosis teaches the importance of the threshold. The decisive changes often occur at the border between ordinary attention and altered attention, between control and surrender, between verbal identity and bodily perception. Music therapy knows this threshold when a patient begins to listen differently, when the room seems to slow down, when the body becomes more present, when an image appears without being sought, when the voice emerges without being forced. MUMEx can help sustain this threshold by creating fields that neither push nor abandon.

A MUMEx field designed for threshold work must avoid spectacle. It must be coherent, slow enough to be followed, alive enough not to become mechanical, and respectful enough to leave the patient a margin of choice. A drone that never changes can anesthetize. A field that changes too much can scatter. The point is a living stability: a sonic environment that supports a modification of attention while preserving safety.

The concept of fascination must therefore be purified. In this book it does not mean domination, enchantment, theatrical power, or the surrender of will to an external authority. It means the gathering of attention around a perceptual center capable of modifying the organization of state. In music therapy, this center may be a voice, a pulse, a resonance, a spatialized sound, a silence, or a relationship between sound and gesture. The therapist's task is to ensure that the gathering of attention remains in the service of freedom, not dependency.

This distinction is crucial for the American and Canadian clinical context, where ethical clarity is not optional. Any work with hypnosis-related language, altered states, trance, suggestion, or fascination must avoid ambiguous promises. The patient must know that they can stop. The therapist must track signs of dissociation, overwhelm, or compliance. The protocol must include grounding, orientation, and debriefing. MUMEx fields intended for altered attention must be designed with explicit entrance and exit curves (American Music Therapy Association, n.d., 2019).

There is also a technical implication. A generative system can produce gradual transitions with a precision that human performance may not always sustain. It can reduce density imperceptibly, lengthen pauses, move sonic events farther away, maintain a low pulse, or thicken a harmonic body without a sudden break. This makes it a powerful instrument for work on attention. Yet the same precision can become dangerous if used to bypass the patient's agency. The system must be placed under the authority of the therapeutic relationship.

Nonverbal hypnosis also clarifies the role of silence. Silence is not the absence of intervention. Silence is a field event. A silence following a sound can intensify attention; a silence before a sound can create expectation; a silence shared by therapist and patient can become trust; a silence imposed too early can become abandonment. In MUMEx, silence must be designed, not left to chance. It can be an operator of Suspension, a place where perception reorganizes before a new form emerges.

The hypnotic gaze and the sonic field differ in their spatial ethics. The gaze can be too direct, too invasive, too frontal. Sound can be enveloping, yet enveloping sound can also become inescapable. For this reason spatialization requires caution. A sound behind the patient, a sudden lateral movement, a sub-bass under the body, or a source that seems too close can alter the perceptual field with great force. What is immersive in an artistic installation may be intrusive in a therapeutic session. The therapist must translate immersion into clinical tact.

Fascination, understood as attentional gathering, has a deep relation to rhythm. Rhythm can hold attention because it creates expectation. The body anticipates. The nervous system begins to predict. When the prediction is confirmed, a sense of continuity arises. When it is gently varied, a micro-change occurs. Too much predictability can become mechanical capture; too much unpredictability can become alarm. MUMEx can work in the narrow interval between these two extremes, producing rhythms that are stable enough to orient and alive enough to transform.

Voice is the most delicate hypnotic instrument in music therapy. It can carry lullaby, command, prayer, seduction, care, authority, and memory. A vocal sound can be more powerful than any electronic field because it announces another human body. The therapist's voice must therefore be used with sobriety. It should not overwhelm the patient's voice, and it should never occupy the place where the patient's sound might emerge. MUMEx can prepare a background, but the human voice remains the threshold at which sonic field becomes relationship.

The relationship between nonverbal hypnosis and music therapy must remain dialogic, not absorptive. Music therapy does not become hypnosis. It learns from hypnosis that state can be transformed before explanation. Hypnosis does not become music therapy. It reminds us that attention, suggestion, presence, and threshold are real forces. MUMEx enters as a third element: an architecture capable of supporting the perceptual field with continuity, memory, and controlled variation.

This triadic relationship—therapist, patient, field—must never obscure the asymmetry of responsibility. The patient may surrender attention for a while; the therapist must not surrender judgment. The patient may enter altered presence; the therapist must remain capable of reading signs, reducing intensity, grounding, naming, closing. The field can grow complex; the therapist must stay simple enough to notice the body.

A practical MUMEx protocol inspired by nonverbal hypnosis would begin with orientation: the patient knows where they are, what will happen, and how to stop. It would proceed through a field of Resonance, establishing safety. It would introduce a focal element—a tone, pulse, voice, or spatial point—only after the body shows tolerance. It would allow Suspension without rushing toward interpretation. It would include a Gentle Perturbation only if the patient remains present. It would close with Reintegration: breath, body, room, words, ordinary time.

This sequence is not a rigid script. It is a clinical grammar. Each patient will require another timing. Some will need more voice; others less. Some will tolerate stillness; others need a small rhythm to remain oriented. Some will find the sonic field containing; others may feel absorbed by it too quickly. The therapist's art consists in sensing when fascination is becoming concentration and when it is becoming capture.

The ethical risk of suggestion is particularly important. Suggestion can help when it opens a possibility already present in the patient. It becomes problematic when it implants a narrative, produces compliance, or confuses the therapist's imagination with the patient's experience. In sound work, suggestion may be less explicit yet equally powerful. A dark timbre can suggest threat; a rising figure can suggest transcendence; a soft voice can suggest safety. The therapist must know that no sonic sign is innocent.

For this reason debriefing is not administrative. It is part of the measurement and part of the return. After an altered attention experience, the patient should be invited to describe what occurred without being led. The therapist should privilege open questions, bodily orientation, and concrete perception. What did you notice? Where did you feel the sound? Did any moment feel too close, too intense, too distant? What helped you return? These questions protect the experience from premature interpretation and allow the field to become knowledge.

MUMEx can record what occurred while the patient describes the experience. The logbook can note where density changed, where silence entered, where a spatial movement occurred, where a pulse slowed, where the therapist intervened vocally. Over time, this creates a bridge between subtle experience and technical trace. The frontier becomes research not by flattening experience, but by remembering its conditions.

Nonverbal hypnosis also reminds music therapy that presence cannot be outsourced. A field may be generated, but presence cannot. The therapist's body, ethical stance, listening, and capacity for restraint are the actual container. A powerful field without a capable presence can become destabilizing. A simple field held by a refined presence can become transformative.

The chapter therefore does not propose a hypnotic turn of music therapy. It proposes a deeper recognition of the preverbal territory in which music therapy has always worked. The language of nonverbal hypnosis allows us to name attention, fascination, threshold, and suggestion with greater radicality. MUMEx allows us to translate these forces into generative sonic environments. The music therapist remains the guardian who ensures that every opening serves the patient's freedom.

At the end of this passage, the perceptual field becomes the central concept. The patient is not only a mind that thinks or a body that reacts. The patient is an organism immersed in a field of signals. To heal, or more carefully to transform, means also to reorganize that field so the person can inhabit the world with less fear, more breath, more choice, and more presence. The next chapter will enter exactly here: the reconstruction of the patient's perceptual-sensory world through sound.

CHAPTER 5

Reconstructing the Patient's Perceptual-Sensory World Through Sound

EPISTEMOLOGICAL LEVEL: *Clinical-operational model. Perceptual-sensory reconstruction, body, setting, gradualness, and return.*

The patient never enters a session carrying only a symptom. The patient carries a world. This world has odors, temperatures, voices, noises, tactile memories, distances, illuminated zones and mute zones. It has internal rooms, the noises of home, footsteps on stairs, closing doors, kitchens, hospitals, streets, family silences, sounds that protect and sounds that wound. No one suffers in the abstract. A person suffers inside a perceptual organization that has taken shape over time and that, at a certain point, may have become too narrow, too noisy, too empty, too threatening, or too flat to let life breathe.

Music therapy has a privileged path into this world because sound does not ask the patient to deliver a complete narrative immediately. Before the person knows how to explain, the body recognizes. A voice reaches a remote zone; a drone allows the chest to be felt; a rhythm returns the floor; a pause lets an image emerge; a low frequency makes a contraction visible; a metallic timbre reveals an alarm. Sound does not work only on emotions. It works on the sensory form through which the subject inhabits the self and the world.

To reconstruct the patient's perceptual-sensory world means assuming that every psychic state has a geography. Anxiety is not only fear. It is a way of listening to the world. Depression is not only sadness. It is a modification of brightness, weight, time, and distance from things. Trauma is not only painful memory. It is a reorganization of the body before stimuli, a brutal selection of what is perceived as danger, a difficulty in distinguishing the present from the sensory return of what happened. When music therapy works in depth, it does not merely produce emotional containment. It helps the person rebuild an inhabitable world.

This claim has a severe methodological consequence. Before proposing a sound field, one must understand what sound world the patient already inhabits. Diagnosis, clinical history, age, and declared musical preferences are not enough. A perceptual cartography is needed. Which sounds calm the patient without anesthetizing them? Which activate without invading? Which irritate immediately? Which generate memory, withdrawal, shame, pleasure, tears, movement? What distance from sound allows the patient to remain present? What density confuses them? Which silence heals and which silence throws them into emptiness? The therapist is not collecting musical tastes. The therapist is collecting data about the relationship among sound, body, and state.

The notion of perceptual world allows us to move beyond one of the poorest misunderstandings in sound practice: the idea that a state corresponds simply to a sound. Calm music for anxiety, cheerful music for depression, natural sounds for relaxation, low frequencies for grounding. These associations may work in some cases, but they become dangerous when treated as law. An anxious person may feel threatened by music that is too calm because calm entails loss of control. A depressed person may experience cheerful music as violence, an insult to their emptiness. A natural sound may evoke abandonment, grief, illness, isolation. A low frequency may offer support or oppression. The real session refutes every naive algorithm of well-being.

For this reason MUMEx Quantum Music Therapy must begin from a more precise question: what perceptual transformation is possible for this subject, at this moment, with this body, within this relationship? The work does not consist in changing mood as one changes the color of a room. It consists in gradually modifying the sensory conditions that make one state more probable than another. If the internal world is saturated, the sound field must create space. If it is empty, it must introduce presence without forced filling. If it is fragmented, it must produce continuity. If it is rigid, it must authorize microvariation. If it is invaded by mental noise, it must restore a bodily axis.

Depression, viewed from a perceptual point of view, often appears as a narrowing of the world. Not always as acute pain, more often as loss of relief. Things remain where they are, but they no longer call. Morning does not open, food does not sing, the body does not accompany, voices seem distant or excessive, time loses articulation. The depressed patient may have difficulty perceiving the future as a livable space; what will happen tomorrow appears without magnetism. In such a condition, sound must not pretend enthusiasm. It must reignite the minimal possibility of a sensory relationship with the world.

A sound field for depression, in this perspective, does not try to cheer. It tries to restore gradation. A warm drone, poor in events but not immobile, can offer the body a point of support. A timbral microvariation can let the patient feel that time is not completely dead. A slow pulsation can give form again to the passing of minutes. A nearby voice, used with restraint, can remind the patient that another human being exists in the room. The decisive quality is noninvasiveness: the field must call without demanding an answer, support without demanding performance, move without forcing vitality.

MUMEx allows this delicacy to be designed with precision. It can generate very low-density fields, avoiding the hypnotic-mechanical loop while producing microdifferences sufficient to prevent stasis. It can maintain formal memory so the patient is not exposed to disconnected events. It can slowly open register, modify the relationship between center and periphery, leave zones of silence, reduce predictability only when the body shows it can tolerate this reduction. In depression, generativity must be almost vegetal: growing without noise, making space without spectacle, returning the world one millimeter at a time.

Anxiety presents another architecture. Here the perceptual world is not narrowed by lack of relief; it is hyperlit. Certain signals dominate all others. The body lives ahead of itself, as though the future had already entered the room. Minimal noises become warnings, silences become expectations, sudden variations become threats. Attention narrows around what could happen. The anxious subject does not need simply to be calmed. They need to recover a hierarchical relationship with stimuli: figure and ground, near and far, alarm and information, noise and presence.

The sound field, in this case, must offer boundary. Boundary does not mean rigidity. It means a legible environment. A rhythm that is too insistent can impose control from outside; a texture that is too vague can increase uncertainty. What is needed is perceptible continuity, a sonic margin, a living predictability. The anxious patient must be able to anticipate enough to feel safe and receive variations discreet enough not to close down. Perturbation, when it arrives, must have the character of a gentle question, not of an attack.

MUMEx can modulate anxiety by working on density, distance, dynamics, and the frequency of events. A field can place a few elements in a stable spatial position, avoid sudden jumps in volume, maintain a nonoppressive low-middle register, and introduce variations through slow curves. It can support breath through a nonmilitary periodicity, allowing the body to regain internal time without feeling commanded. In a second phase, it can slightly move the position of certain events, opening the possibility of tolerating change. The sonic care of anxiety does not aim at sedation. It aims at restoring orientation.

In trauma, the question becomes even more precise. Trauma does not reside only in a memory. It remains in a sensory grammar. A slammed door, a tone of voice, an odor, a siren, a sudden silence, a certain kind of resonance can reactivate alarm long before the patient understands what is happening. The body recognizes patterns even when consciousness does not name them. For this reason, sonic work with traumatized people requires extreme sobriety. Intensity is not depth. A powerful session can be clinically wrong if it carries the patient beyond their capacity for regulation.

Reconstructing the perceptual world after trauma means giving the present a sensory consistency different from the past. The patient must be able to feel: this sound is here, in this room, with this therapist, in a time from which I can exit. The possibility of interrupting the field is part of the care. Physical distance from the sound sources is part of the care. The predictability of certain transitions is part of the care. Even minimal volume has ethical value. The field must not capture the patient. It must accompany the patient in recognizing that they can remain in the present while feeling something.

Applied to trauma, MUMEx must be designed through a logic of shared control. The therapist can establish safety parameters: no sudden attacks, no saturation, no spatialization behind the patient without consent, no bodily sub-bass before the somatic response has been checked, no increasing density without the possibility of return. The patient can intervene through simple signals: farther, lower, stop, continue, change. Technology becomes reliable here only if it accepts a superior clinical principle: the person's body decides the limit.

The body is the center of this cartography. There is no perceptual world without a body. Every sound is received by a nervous system, by bones, muscles, skin, diaphragm, viscera, posture. The ear is only one of the doors. A low sound can be felt in the sternum, a song can soften the throat, a percussion can reach the feet, a high texture can modify the forehead, a silence can let the heartbeat emerge. Music therapy must recognize the patient as an embodied acoustic landscape.

An important part of the session should consist in asking the body to testify. Not by forcing it to speak, but by giving it time to show. What changes in the breath when the field opens? Where does the vibration arrive? Which part of the body resists? Which zone seems asleep? Does the patient feel the sound in front of them, around them, inside them, above them, far away, too close? These questions are not accessory. They are instruments of perceptual cartography. They help transform a vague experience into a usable map.

The voice occupies a privileged position in this map. The voice of another human being is sound and relationship in the same act. It carries intention, warmth, history, accent, age, breath, fragility. It can console or expose. It can protect or invade. Many patients have a wounded relationship with voice: voices that commanded, humiliated, abandoned, seduced, threatened; lost voices; voices that can no longer come out. Reconstructing the perceptual world also means understanding how the patient inhabits their own voice and how they react to the voice of another.

MUMEx must not occupy the space of voice. It must prepare it, support it, leave it free. A generative sound field can create a breathing ground over which the patient dares to emit a vowel. It can thin out when the voice appears. It can respond with microvariations that mirror without imitating. It can support the therapist while the therapist uses their own voice as minimal guidance. Voice remains the most immediate proof of presence: when the patient manages to produce even the smallest sound, the internal world has already changed configuration.

Sonic memory is another decisive level. Every person preserves acoustic archives that are rarely explored with enough care. The lullaby, the kitchen radio, the school bell, the engine of a car, the sea of a summer, the sound of cutlery, the television in the next room, the voice of a relative, a song heard in a precise period, the silence of a house after a loss. These elements are not autobiographical decoration. They are constitutive materials of the perceptual world. Sometimes the session must retrieve them; at other times it must respect the fact that they are too charged to be touched immediately.

Perceptual reconstruction therefore requires a form of sonic anamnesis. The therapist can explore which sounds belong to home, mother, father, danger, rest, illness, celebration, school, solitude, spirituality, body, desire. Not to build a sentimental inventory, but to understand which acoustic paths lead toward regulation, opening, memory, defense, pain. One patient may discover that they cannot bear silence because silence coincided with waiting for a family explosion. Another may discover that a natural sound calms them because it reconstructs a childhood place. Another may recognize that their own voice has always been held at the margins of the world.

MUMEx can integrate this anamnesis without turning it into a museum of sound. The danger would be sampling the patient's memories and using them as effects. Serious work is subtler: translating perceptual qualities into generative parameters. If a memory of the sea brings breadth, it is not necessarily necessary to reproduce the sea; one can build a field with wide breath, slow movements, spatial depth, and fluid timbral grain. If a family kitchen brought safety, one need not imitate dishes and domestic noises; one can generate a close, warm, small environment, with delicate and recurrent events. Therapeutic fidelity does not coincide with acoustic realism. It coincides with precision of function.

The session thus becomes a work of perceptual architecture. The therapist observes the state, gathers the sonic history, measures tolerance, proposes a field, listens to the response, corrects, subtracts, reopens. Every choice has weight. A register that is too high can separate the patient from the body. A register that is too low can press them down. Spatialization that is too wide can disperse them. A source that is too close can invade. Repetition can contain or imprison. Variation can liberate or alarm. The professional must become able to think of sound not only as aesthetics, but as ecology.

The concept of perceptual ecology is essential. An organism lives well when its environment is legible, nourishing, sufficiently variable, not chaotic, capable of offering safety and novelty. The internal sound world also needs these conditions. Some patients live in desertified inner environments; others in environments infested with noise; others in rooms without exits; others in spaces that are vast but without orientation. Music therapy can intervene as a practice of reclamation, cultivation, reopening, restoration. Not by returning the person to some presumed original state, but by helping them build a new sensory inhabitability.

Inhabitability is perhaps the most important word in this chapter. Healing, when the term is used seriously, also means being able to inhabit one's own body, memory, voice, and relationship with the world. Many patients do not ask for immediate happiness. They ask for an interior that is less hostile. They ask to be able to stay in a room without being assaulted by the past. They ask to feel the body without fear. They ask to perceive a sound without stiffening. They ask to recover a possibility of pleasure that is not violent. The sound field can become a laboratory of this inhabitability.

Perceptual-sensory reconstruction must nevertheless avoid every automatic promise. Sound is not innocent. It can help and it can wound. It can contain and it can manipulate. It can open and it can disorganize. For this reason rigor is not an ethical ornament; it is the condition of practice. Gradualness is needed. Consent is needed. Observation is needed. Return is needed. The capacity to interrupt an experience is needed even when that experience appears aesthetically successful. The criterion is not the beauty of the field, but the sustainable transformation of the human state.

In MUMEx, this responsibility can be incorporated into design. Every field should have safety parameters, dynamic limits, entry and exit curves, controlled degrees of unpredictability, the possibility of immediate rarefaction, memory of the path, and event tracking. The logbook is not bureaucracy. It is technical consciousness of the process. It allows us to remember: which element produced calm; which produced defense; which favored voice; which generated images; which required return.

This chapter prepares the next part of the book because it shows that the patient is body before being discourse. To reconstruct the patient's perceptual world inevitably means entering vibration, bone resonance, chest, diaphragm, spine, skull, embodied voice. Sound does not merely evoke mental images; it touches living matter. There a vast part of transformation is decided. A body that feels differently begins to think differently. A mind that receives another sensory world may cease, even for an instant, to obey the old organization of pain.

The final question is not which music the patient likes. The question is more exact, more demanding, more therapeutic: what internal sound world does this person inhabit, and what sound world can help them return to inhabiting themselves? From this question arises a music therapy that is neither decorative, consolatory, nor mechanical. It is a music therapy able to work on the place where the human state takes form: the perceptual field, the sensitive body, acoustic memory, and the living relationship with the world.

PART TWO

THE VIBRANT BODY

CHAPTER 6

The Body as Instrument

EPISTEMOLOGICAL LEVEL: *Body-phenomenological model. The body is considered as instrument, resonator, sensor, voice, posture, vibration, and embodied listening.*

The body as instrument is not a poetic metaphor. It is an anatomical, perceptual, and clinical fact. Every human being receives sound through the whole organism: ear, skin, bone, vestibular system, muscles, diaphragm, viscera, breath, posture, and motor memory. Western culture has often narrowed listening to the ear and then to the mind, as if music were an acoustic object to be decoded symbolically. Music therapy knows an older truth: sound reaches the body before it becomes narrative.

A patient may understand very little of what is happening and still change breath, muscle tone, orientation, hand temperature, pelvic position, or the rhythm of the gaze. Transformation often begins there, at a point that language has not yet reached. To say that the body is an instrument means recognizing that it vibrates, filters, amplifies, attenuates, and responds. The human body does not merely undergo the sound wave. It selects the wave according to biological history, psychic history, and present safety.

A low sound may rest against the sternum and become presence; in another person, the same sound may be felt as threatening pressure. A drum may restore grounding to a dispersed body; it may also activate alarm in someone who associates sudden impacts with violence. A bell may open interior space; it may feel cutting to a nervous system that is already overloaded. No frequency is therapeutic in itself. Power arises from the meeting among body, sound field, relationship, and moment.

The body is the first site of measurement. Before asking the patient what they feel, the therapist observes how the patient is. Does the back rest against the chair or remain suspended? Do the hands seek support? Does the breath climb into the chest or descend toward the diaphragm? Is the jaw clenched? Does the throat close when voice appears? Can the gaze remain in the room? Do the feet feel the floor? These observations are not marginal details. They are state data. They reveal how the organism organizes its relationship with the sonic world.

This bodily reading must never become a secret diagnosis. It is an ethics of attention. The therapist does not infer too much from a single gesture and does not impose an interpretation on the body. The therapist gathers converging signs, listens, proposes, waits, and verifies. The MUMEx logbook should register the visible and felt conditions of the session: posture, orientation, breath, tolerance, withdrawal, vocal emergence, movement, and the precise features of the field that accompanied them.

Contemporary neuroscience has restored dignity to the bodily dimension. Interoception—the perception and integration of signals arising from inside the body—is recognized as central to emotional regulation, bodily awareness, and many psychological conditions. Anxiety, depression, somatic disorders, trauma, addictions, and eating disorders often involve altered ways of sensing, interpreting, or fearing internal signals. For music therapy, this is decisive: sound can become a path of interoceptive education, provided it is dosed precisely and placed within a reliable relationship (Craig, 2002, 2009; Khalsa et al., 2018).

When a patient listens to a sound field, one part of the experience concerns external hearing: pitch, timbre, intensity, direction, and distance. Another part concerns the interior body: pressure in the chest, warmth in the face, vibration in the throat, weight in the stomach, release in the shoulders, micromovement in the pelvis, or a perceived change in heartbeat. MUMEx Quantum Music Therapy must learn to treat these two planes as one architecture. Sound is exteroceptive and interoceptive in the same event: it comes from the world and modifies the inner world.

The ear remains decisive, but it belongs to a wider system. The cochlea translates air vibration into neural signals; the vestibular system contributes to balance, orientation, and movement perception; the skin registers pressure and vibration; bone conducts mechanical energy; the chest and skull offer resonance cavities; the musculature prepares, defends, or yields. The listening body is a multimodal system. To reduce it to an acoustic receiver is to lose half of the phenomenon.

Voice occupies an original position because it is both the first instrument and the first bodily field. It arises from breath, meets the vocal folds, resonates in the chest, throat, mouth, and cranial cavities, and reaches the other as embodied presence. When the patient emits even a minimal vowel, they do more than produce sound. They produce evidence of existence. They feel the body from within, listen to the effect of their own vibration in space, and measure the therapist's response.

In shame, trauma, isolation, emotional mutism, or dissociation, a gently sustained vowel can matter more than a long explanation. The therapist's voice, however, requires a specific ethics. A warm voice can contain; a voice that is too close can invade. A whispered instruction can favor gathering but may also activate ambiguous memories. A song can support; a song can occupy. The therapist must know their own voice as they know a delicate instrument: register, attack, vibrato, breath, volume, distance, emotional color, and intention.

In a MUMEx practice, the human voice remains the primary reference. The generative sound field must recede when the patient's voice is born. It must support without covering. It must allow the human body to retain the primacy of presence. In this sense, the most advanced technology is judged by its capacity to leave space for the oldest instrument.

Breath is the second axis. Every sound field produces a relationship with breath, even when the patient does not notice. Regular rhythms, slow pulsations, stable drones, timbral microvariation, and carefully dosed silences can invite the organism toward another respiratory pattern. This invitation must not be confused with imposition. Forced breathing, especially in anxious or traumatized people, can produce control, hypervigilance, and discomfort. Breath should be accompanied indirectly, allowing the body to find its own step.

A well-designed MUMEx field does not order the patient to breathe. It creates conditions in which breath may stop defending itself. The relationship between sound and diaphragm is central. The diaphragm belongs not only to respiratory mechanics but also to postural organization, autonomic tone, and the perception of the bodily center. In chronic anxiety, breath often remains high. In depressive collapse, it may become heavy and low in vitality. In trauma, it may freeze into fragments.

A low, soft sound field without aggressive attacks may help the patient perceive a base. A pulsation that is too marked may feel intrusive. The criterion is not isolated frequency but the body's tolerability in front of the movement proposed. Safety is therefore musical, bodily, relational, and temporal at once.

Bone is a neglected path of listening. Bone conduction shows that sound can reach auditory experience through cranial vibration, in addition to the airborne path. Even without dedicated devices, the patient perceives sound in the bones when they sing, rest the body against a vibrating surface, come near low-frequency instruments, or receive the mechanical energy of a drum or gong. Bone vibration has a particular therapeutic value: it can restore a sense of structure, axis, and density. In highly mentalized patients, work with bone vibration can return weight to the body.

The chest is both symbolic and physical resonance chamber. Voice, affect, fear, courage, grief, and restraint resonate there. Many patients describe psychic pain as a knot in the chest, a weight, an emptiness, armor, or pressure. Music therapy should not treat these words as mere metaphors. They are often accurate descriptions of an interoceptive condition. A sound field can work with the chest without assaulting it: carefully dosed low frequencies, warm drones, sustained voices, strings with soft attack, slow oscillations, and silences that let the patient feel what remains after the sound.

The abdomen is still more delicate. Here sound meets digestion, tension, vulnerability, shame, instinct, and ancient fear. Many people experience the abdomen as blind or threatening territory. Some control it, some dissociate it, and some feel constant alarm there. Abdominal vibration can bring relief, grounding, and warmth; it can also generate discomfort if proposed with too much intensity. Every work on this zone requires consent, graduality, the possibility of interruption, and careful attention to posture. MUMEx can generate low and deep fields, but depth must be dosed like a powerful medicine: with measure, listening, and return.

The spine organizes the experience of sound in relation to axis. A seated, reclining, standing, or walking patient receives the same field differently. Posture modifies resonance, breath perception, availability for movement, and the sensation of safety. A MUMEx session should register at least the principal postural conditions: seated with support, freely seated, reclining, standing, slow walking, and contact with the floor. The same sonic fabric will have different functions in each of these conditions.

Rhythm enters the body through motricity. Even when the subject remains still, rhythm prepares movement. A foot may want to tap, the pelvis may begin to oscillate, a hand may seek a gesture, the neck may release. Research on the relationship among rhythm, movement, and the motor system has shown how deeply music engages anticipatory organization. For music therapy, this means that rhythm is never merely external structure. It is an invitation to bodily organization.

The invitation can heal or invade. A pulse that is too strong can become command. A rhythm that is too complex can fragment attention. A pattern that is too rigid can imprison the body in obedience. A good therapeutic rhythm does not dominate movement; it makes movement thinkable. Sometimes the most effective rhythm is almost absent: a slow recurrence, a distant pulse, a barely perceptible return that allows the body to choose whether to join.

MUMEx can treat rhythm as a field of readiness rather than as a beat. Density, temporal distance, attack softness, and microtiming can be programmed so that the body feels invited rather than driven. This matters especially in anxiety, depression, trauma, neurodivergence, and states of motor inhibition. The aim is not to make the patient move. The aim is to return movement to the realm of possibility.

A body listens differently according to contact. Contact with a chair, floor, wall, mat, therapist, instrument, or vibrating surface changes the field. The back supported by a chair can receive low vibration as containment. A free sitting posture may turn the same vibration into exposure. Lying down can deepen surrender but may reduce agency for some patients. Standing can restore verticality but may increase vigilance. Walking can transform listening into orientation.

For this reason, MUMEx should never record only the sound. It should record the body's situation in the sound. The logbook should include posture, contact points, distance from speakers, volume, duration, patient control, verbal consent, interruption signals, somatic reports, and the therapist's observations. These are not bureaucratic details. They are the grammar through which the body becomes readable without being reduced.

A high-quality MUMEx practice should also distinguish between direct bodily stimulation and environmental sound. A sub-bass transmitted through a couch is not the same as a low drone diffused in the room. A transducer under the back is not the same as a gong across the space. Airborne sound, tactile vibration, and bone conduction have different safety profiles and different meanings. Clinical maturity begins with this distinction.

The body is the first threshold of Quantum Music Therapy. The patient enters with a body before entering with a story. This body may be armored, dispersed, numb, flooded, vigilant, heavy, fragile, ashamed, or ready to sing without knowing it. The therapist meets this body not by forcing it to express itself, but by creating a field in which it can become less defended and more present.

MUMEx becomes meaningful here when it serves the body rather than colonizing it. The system must learn to be precise and humble: to generate, to recede, to leave silence, to support voice, to respect posture, to record context, and to treat vibration as contact. The body is not a passive receiver of therapeutic sound. It is the first instrument, the first sensor, the first resonator, and the first archive of memory.

From this point, the inquiry can move toward a more delicate question: what happens when vibration is considered in relation to the internal organs? The following chapter enters that territory with a strict rule: somatic experience must be respected, but medical claims must be handled only with proportional evidence, professional competence, and clear ethical boundaries.

CHAPTER 7

Stimulating the Internal Organs Through Vibration

EPISTEMOLOGICAL LEVEL: *Theoretical model / frontier territory. Internal organs and vibration are discussed with an obligatory distinction between somatic experience and medical claim.*

To speak of internal organs and vibration requires a severe language. The subject easily attracts two opposite distortions. On one side stands reductionism, which grants sound only an aesthetic, emotional, or distracting function, as if the deeper body remained outside musical experience. On the other side stands pseudocurative rhetoric, which attributes to every frequency a direct power over an organ, reducing the complexity of bodily life to a naive table of correspondences. MUMEx Quantum Music Therapy must avoid both errors.

Sound touches the body in real physical, perceptual, autonomic, and symbolic ways. This reality must be studied precisely, without promising what belongs to medicine and without reducing vibrational experience to subjective suggestion. The liver, heart, stomach, lungs, intestine, pelvis, throat, and head are not abstract organs for the person who lives in them. They are territories of sensation, fear, memory, habit, and meaning.

A patient may say, "I feel it in my stomach," "my chest opens," "the vibration goes to my throat," or "something moves under the ribs." These statements should neither be dismissed nor transformed into diagnosis. They are somatic reports. They tell us how the person's body maps sound. The task of the therapist is to listen, clarify, protect, and document, not to declare that an organ has been treated.

Internal organs are not only anatomical structures. They are experienced through interoception, memory, emotion, and metaphor. The heart is a pump, but the patient also feels it as courage, terror, love, fragility, acceleration, or collapse. The stomach digests, but it is also the site of knots, nausea, hunger, shame, and refusal. The lungs breathe, but they are also room, grief, constriction, and opening. The intestine is physiology, but it is also anxiety, vulnerability, rhythm, and ancient instinct.

Music therapy can work with the felt organ without claiming to cure the medical organ. This distinction is crucial. A sound field may help a person perceive the chest with more safety; that does not mean it treats cardiac disease. A low vibration may make the abdomen feel warmer or less contracted; that does not mean it treats gastrointestinal pathology. A vocal exercise may loosen the throat; that does not mean it treats endocrine or neurological conditions. The clinical value lies in perception, regulation, agency, expression, and reintegration—not in unauthorized medical treatment.

This caution protects both patient and research. It prevents suggestion, dependency, and false bodily narratives. It also allows a real exploration of how sound, vibration, and field design may influence interoceptive awareness, autonomic state, relaxation, tension, and meaning. The path is not closed. It must simply be walked without inflated claims.

The internal body is deeply tied to autonomic regulation. Heartbeat, respiratory rhythm, digestive tone, vascular changes, muscular guarding, and visceral sensation participate in the human state. Sound can modify the temporal environment in which these processes are perceived. It can slow attention, stabilize breath, reduce sensory chaos, or make a hidden tension audible through the body's response.

A MUMEx session can therefore include an interoceptive map. Before the field, the patient may indicate zones of pressure, numbness, warmth, coldness, weight, emptiness, movement, or avoidance. During the field, the therapist observes breath, posture, facial tone, swallowing, hands, and orientation. After the field, the patient describes what changed without being pushed toward a predetermined meaning. The map remains provisional. It is not a medical chart. It is a cartography of experience.

This mapping can be especially useful in patients who live far from the body. Some experience the body only when it hurts. Others experience it as threat. Others inhabit the head and lose the lower body. A carefully designed field can open a path back to sensation without overwhelming the system. The first success is often modest: a patient notices the chest, the back, the belly, the throat, or the feet without fear.

The chest is the primary territory of breath, voice, grief, and courage. Low-frequency fields, warm drones, bowed strings, controlled vocal tones, and gradual dynamic arcs may help the patient perceive the sternum, ribs, and upper back as a container rather than a prison. Yet chest work must remain delicate. People with panic, trauma, respiratory illness, cardiac concerns, or intense somatic anxiety may experience chest sensation as danger. The therapist must give the patient control over volume, distance, duration, and interruption.

The abdomen requires even greater caution. Vibration here may evoke warmth, grounding, digestion, instinct, shame, nausea, or vulnerability. The field should begin with minimal intensity and short duration. It should be accompanied by clear consent and a simple language: "Where do you feel it?" "Is it too much?" "Would you like it farther away?" "Do you want to stop?" Such questions keep the work concrete and prevent symbolic overreach.

The pelvis and lower body concern grounding, support, sexuality, shame, locomotion, and survival. Any direct work in this region demands exceptional sensitivity and, in most contexts, should remain indirect: through the floor, foot contact, low environmental resonance, walking rhythm, or awareness of weight. The cranial field, by contrast, concerns vibration in skull, face, jaw, eyes, and inner hearing. Bells, high harmonics, overtones, and headphones can be powerful but may also be sharp for migraines, sensory sensitivity, trauma, or vestibular problems. The field must fit the person, not the theory.

Work with vibration and internal organs requires explicit contraindication thinking. Pregnancy, acute pain, severe sensory hypersensitivity, complex trauma, active psychosis, severe migraines, vestibular disorders, significant cardiovascular conditions, certain neurological conditions, implanted devices, and medications that alter perception or vigilance require professional evaluation. This does not mean automatic exclusion. It means no improvisation.

Consent must be more than a signature. It must be ongoing, verbal and nonverbal, revisable at any moment. The patient should know what may happen: vibration, pressure, warmth, discomfort, emotional emergence, desire to move, desire to stop. They should have a clear signal to interrupt the field. The therapist should normalize stopping as part of the method. In this work, the right to stop is not a safety detail; it is a therapeutic principle.

Dosage includes intensity, frequency range, duration, spatial distance, contact surface, density, attack profile, and repetition across sessions. A field that is beneficial for three minutes may become intrusive at ten. A low vibration that is grounding while seated may be overwhelming while lying down. MUMEx can help precisely because it can log and reproduce parameters while allowing controlled variation.

An organ-oriented MUMEx field should never be named as a cure for an organ. It should be named by function and experience: chest presence, diaphragmatic softening, abdominal grounding, throat emergence, pelvic support, cranial quieting, or spinal axis. These names describe therapeutic intention without making medical claims. They allow the therapist to design fields that are clear, modest, and usable.

Each field family should specify target experience, contraindications, starting intensity, maximum intensity, duration, entry curve, exit curve, expected somatic reports, interruption criteria, and Reintegration procedure. A chest presence field may use warm low-mid resonance, soft attacks, long releases, and wide temporal spacing. An abdominal grounding field may use very low density, low volume, stable floor contact, and verbal check-ins. A throat emergence field may reduce the generative layer when patient voice appears.

The most mature design will distinguish between airborne sound, vibrotactile contact, voice-led resonance, and movement-mediated resonance. It will also distinguish between individual preference and clinical tolerance. A patient may like a dramatic low sound and still be dysregulated by it. Another may initially dislike a subtle field and later discover that it is more inhabitable. The therapist's task is to keep preference, tolerance, and transformation in dialogue.

The final aim of organ-oriented vibration is not sensation for its own sake. Sensation must become inhabitable. The patient should not leave the session fascinated by an internal event and abandoned inside it. Reintegration is essential: orienting to the room, naming the present, feeling the feet, restoring ordinary breath, speaking if useful, remaining silent if needed, and closing the field gradually.

A person who has felt the chest open may need to return to the chair, the walls, and the present relationship. A person who has felt abdominal warmth may need to stand slowly. A person who has encountered throat emotion may need time before language. The sound field should not vanish abruptly. It should withdraw as a respectful presence, leaving the patient more embodied, not more dependent on the field.

This chapter establishes the discipline needed for deeper vibrational work. The body is real, the organs are real, the sensations are real, and the symbolic meanings are real for the person who lives them. Medical claims require medical evidence. Therapeutic presence requires humility. MUMEx can become a powerful tool in this territory only if it keeps these distinctions alive.

CHAPTER 8

Radionics, Dowsing, and Vibrational Medicine

EPISTEMOLOGICAL LEVEL: *Frontier territory. Radionics, dowsing, and vibrational medicine are treated as controversial, symbolic, or exploratory practices without equivalence to established clinical evidence.*

The territory of radionics, dowsing, and vibrational medicine requires a rare quality: audacity without credulity, rigor without contempt. Here one enters a region charged with promises, testimonies, minority practices, enigmatic instruments, energetic maps, pendulums, dials, devices, personal traditions, intuitive diagnosis, healing stories, accusations of pseudoscience, historical fraud, and intuitions that still lack a shared language. To approach this material seriously means avoiding two poor gestures: naive adherence and arrogant dismissal.

Naive adherence confuses experience, desire, and proof. Arrogant dismissal closes the field before understanding why, at least on the perceptual and symbolic plane, these practices continue to attract practitioners and patients. MUMEx Quantum Music Therapy should not import frontier claims as established evidence. It can, however, study what these practices reveal about human attention, belief, ritual, somatic choice, symbolic resonance, and the need to listen to subtle bodily responses.

The question is not whether a pendulum proves an invisible force. The more useful question is what happens when a person enters a ritual of choice, expectation, attention, microgesture, and meaning. The body responds. The hand moves. The breath changes. The patient feels that something has been indicated. These events deserve description without premature metaphysics.

Radionics historically presents devices that claim to detect or influence subtle energetic states through dials, witnesses, symbolic rates, or nonlocal intention. The clinical problem is obvious: opaque devices can become machines of authority. If the patient does not understand what is being measured and the practitioner claims diagnostic certainty, the device can create dependency, fear, or false belief. A field that cannot be examined risks becoming a theater of power.

For a music therapist, the lesson is decisive. No MUMEx device should become opaque. Parameters must be describable. The patient must know what is being changed: volume, density, register, vibration, spatial distance, duration, or timbral complexity. The therapist must distinguish between subjective report and physiological measurement, between symbolic meaning and clinical inference. Technical sophistication should increase transparency, not mystification.

Radionics can still be studied as a cultural and symbolic phenomenon. It shows how strongly human beings seek maps of invisible suffering. It shows the attraction of personalized frequency, ritual setting, and the belief that each organism has a hidden signature. MUMEx can answer this desire ethically by creating documented sonic profiles rather than secret rates: fields that are heard, logged, adjusted, and discussed.

Dowsing, or radiesthesia, often involves a pendulum, rod, or bodily microresponse used to select an answer, location, or correspondence. Mainstream evidence does not support it as a reliable diagnostic method. Yet the phenomenon can be reinterpreted within a safer frame: as a ritualized form of preverbal choice, attentional concentration, and somatic response. The body often knows preference, avoidance, attraction, or discomfort before the person can explain it.

In MUMEx, this intuition can be translated without occult diagnostic claims. The patient may be invited to choose between two very brief fields without immediate explanation. Field A, field B: which body feels more inhabitable? Which sound do you want farther away? Which one calls you? Words come later. This preserves the radiesthetic intuition of preverbal response and removes it from occult diagnosis. Choice becomes perceptible. The body enters the process. The therapist observes. The system records. A microdecision can become the first gesture of agency.

This practice must remain free of coercion. The patient is not told that the body has revealed the truth. The patient is invited to notice a response. The difference is enormous. One creates authority outside the person. The other strengthens the person's capacity to sense, choose, and revise.

Vibrational medicine is a broad and unstable expression. It may refer to sound, light, electromagnetic fields, homeopathic ideas, subtle energy systems, ritual practices, or body-based resonance. Some areas overlap with measurable physics and regulated devices; others remain symbolic, experiential, or speculative. The first editorial duty is to keep these planes distinct.

A sound wave is physical energy. A symbolic resonance is not the same kind of event. A patient may feel that a tone "cleanses" the chest, "opens" the heart, or "connects" them to a memory. These statements can be honored as subjective, symbolic, or spiritual experiences without being translated into objective claims. The therapist can ask what the experience means, how it feels, whether it is safe, and how the patient returns from it.

MUMEx should therefore develop a vocabulary of levels: physiological, perceptual, emotional, imaginal, symbolic, ritual, spiritual, and experimental. This vocabulary protects the work. It allows the book to speak to frontier material without confusing readers, clinicians, or researchers about its evidential status.

The frontier of vibration also demands an education of language. The music therapist working with MUMEx must know the difference between physical frequency and symbolic frequency, acoustic resonance and emotional resonance, measurable effect and reported experience, energy in the physical sense and energy in the experiential sense. Imprecise language can cause harm. Statements such as "your liver vibrates badly," "your field is blocked," or "this frequency cleared a trauma" can create suggestion, fear, dependency, or false bodily memory.

The right language remains concrete. Does this sound bother you? Where do you feel it? Would you prefer it farther away? Do you want to keep your eyes open? Do you need to move? What changed in the breath? Would you like to stop? The greatness of the practice is not measured by solemn vocabulary. It is measured by the quality of listening. Many vibrational languages become grandiose because they fear simplicity. Music therapy, when it is great, stays close to the real person.

The spiritual dimension should not be expelled. For many human beings, sound has been, and remains, contact with the invisible: prayer, invocation, protection, purification, dialogue with ancestors, nature, subtle forces, and worlds beyond ordinary perception. Radionics and dowsing belong in part to this genealogy of relations with what exceeds the visible.

A secular and rigorous therapeutic practice can recognize this dimension as human experience without transforming it into doctrine. A patient may experience a sound as purification. The therapist can welcome the subjective meaning without declaring that an energetic purification has objectively occurred. The difference is subtle and fundamental. It allows the patient's world to be respected while protecting the work from false claims.

In its mature form, MUMEx should allow different fields for different levels of experience. Bodily fields, with measurable acoustic and vibrotactile parameters. Imaginal fields, intended to support images, memories, and symbols. Ritual fields, built through repetition, entry, duration, silence, and return. Contemplative fields, more rarefied and close to meditation. Experimental fields, used only in protected contexts. Each field should declare its level: physiological, perceptual, symbolic, spiritual, or exploratory.

This taxonomy prevents confusion and strengthens the system. It allows a field to be visionary without pretending to be clinical evidence. It allows a clinical field to remain sober without losing depth. It allows a spiritual experience to be welcomed without being converted into diagnosis. The stronger the frontier, the clearer the labels must be.

The relationship with frontier practices raises a cultural problem. Many institutions defend the already known using the language of rigor, while many countercultures defend confusion using the language of freedom. Both positions are insufficient. Authentic rigor does not guard the museum of the permitted. Authentic freedom does not despise evidence. A revolutionary sound research must escape this false alternative. It must have the courage to explore what the academy avoids and the discipline to reject what enthusiasm deforms.

Observed from this perspective, radionics, dowsing, and vibrational medicine enter not as truths to accept, but as a field of tension. They show the risk of suggestion, opaque devices, excessive promises, and pseudodiagnosis. They also preserve questions that hypertechnical medicine often forgets: how do we listen to the invisible dimension of the body? How do we give form to subjective correspondence? How do intention, ritual, microgesture, and subtle perception matter? How can individual maps of resonance be built without false certainty?

MUMEx can answer with its own language: generative sound field, bodily listening, logbook, perceptual maps, consent, parameters, observation, return, and verification. The pendulum gives way to observed bodily microvariation. The dial gives way to sonic cartography. The miraculous frequency gives way to the documented vibrational profile. Distant treatment gives way to relational presence. Promise gives way to research. Mystery remains, and that is good. Mystery is what drives study. Confusion is what prevents it.

CHAPTER 9

Electromedical Devices and Advanced Vibrational Instrumentation

EPISTEMOLOGICAL LEVEL: *Technical-experimental model. Electromedical devices, vibroacoustics, and biofeedback are considered within criteria of safety, traceability, and validation.*

After the more controversial territory of radionics and dowsing, the inquiry can enter a different region: more measurable, more technical, closer to regulated medicine and instrumental research. Electromedical devices, vibroacoustics, biofeedback, heart rate variability (HRV), lightweight electroencephalography (EEG), neurofeedback, vibrotactile stimulation, and immersive environments give the word vibration a physical parameter: intensity, frequency, amplitude, duration, transduction, bodily contact, and observable physiological response.

The risk changes form. In subtle practices, the principal danger is believing too much in what cannot be verified. In advanced instrumentation, the opposite danger is believing that what is measured coincides with the whole human experience. A machine can register a signal, transform an electrical impulse into a graph, a heart rate into a curve, a respiratory variation into data, a pressure into a number, or a vibration into a calibrated stimulus. This capacity is precious. It reduces arbitrariness and allows repetition, difference, effect, and limit to become visible.

At the same time, no device measures the totality of a human being. An increase in HRV may indicate greater autonomic flexibility, but it does not by itself tell us whether the person feels freer, more heard, or more integrated. An EEG trace may show a change in cortical rhythm, but it does not exhaust the quality of an internal image. A transducer may bring vibration to the sternum, but it cannot decide whether that vibration will become safety, irritation, memory, emotion, or refusal.

MUMEx Quantum Music Therapy must enter advanced instrumentation with a double discipline: welcome measurement and prevent it from becoming idolatry. Data are a window, not the whole body. A graph is a trace, not the person. A sensor is an ally, not a sovereign interpreter. The serious ambition is not to turn the session into a cold laboratory, but to give sonic work a greater capacity to document what happens without impoverishing what happens.

Electromedical devices immediately raise the question of responsibility. Not every device that produces stimulation, detection, or feedback has the same status. It is one thing to use a speaker, subwoofer, vibroacoustic transducer, environmental microphone, or simple respiratory sensor in an experiential context. It is another to use devices presented as diagnostic, therapeutic, neuromodulatory, or clinical instruments. In that case, regulations, certifications, intended use, contraindications, professional competencies, insurance responsibility, and informed consent all become decisive.

Fascination with technology cannot skip these steps. Every clinical promise requires clinical grounding. Every medical device requires its regulatory framework. Every use with vulnerable people requires prudence, traceability, and qualified supervision. This prudence does not weaken research. It makes research inhabitable. It distinguishes nonclinical experimentation, wellness, professional music therapy, medicine, ethics-approved research, and activities that must remain outside the setting when the necessary competence is absent.

Vibroacoustics occupies a central place. It arises from the idea that sound frequencies, often in the low range, can be transmitted to the body through vibrating surfaces, chairs, couches, mattresses, platforms, transducers, or dedicated systems. The subject does not only hear the sound; the subject receives it as mechanical vibration. The body becomes a resonance surface. Muscles, bones, fascia, fluids, thoracic and abdominal cavities, and posture participate differently. Vibration does not remain external. It becomes contact.

This contact must be designed with discipline. The same low frequency can feel grounding, invasive, soothing, oppressive, maternal, mechanical, intimate, or threatening. A couch can create surrender or helplessness. A chair can contain or expose. A transducer under the back can support the spine or become an unwanted force. The therapist must treat physical contact through vibration as seriously as any other form of clinical contact.

A vibroacoustic MUMEx field should specify starting intensity, maximum intensity, frequency range, transducer placement, body position, duration, ramp-in, ramp-out, patient control, and stop signal. It should avoid abrupt attacks, excessive pressure, and extended low-frequency exposure without supervision. The aim is not to impress the body. The aim is to make the body more safely perceptible.

Biofeedback introduces another possibility: the body returns information to the sound field. HRV, breath, movement, muscle tension, skin conductance, and lightweight EEG can become inputs for generative modulation. This does not mean that the machine understands the patient. It means that certain physiological traces can participate in the sonic environment under human responsibility.

A respiratory signal may modulate density. HRV may influence harmonic stability. Movement may open or close spatial distance. EEG should be used with special caution because consumer and lightweight systems can be noisy, context-sensitive, and easily overinterpreted. MUMEx should never convert a weak signal into strong clinical claims. It should use signals as exploratory supports, documented carefully and interpreted modestly.

The most promising form is not biofeedback as spectacle but biofeedback as subtle mirror. The patient hears that breath, movement, or state can influence the field. The therapist observes whether this increases agency, curiosity, calm, frustration, control, or pressure. The signal enters the dialogue. It does not replace dialogue.

Advanced vibrational instrumentation demands a clear safety framework. Pregnancy, acute pain, severe sensory hypersensitivity, complex trauma, active psychosis, severe migraines, vestibular problems, significant cardiovascular conditions, specific neurological conditions, implanted devices, and medications that alter perception or vigilance each require professional evaluation. The point is not permanent exclusion. The point is to avoid improvisation. The power of vibration and immersion must be proportionate to the fragility of the human system that receives it.

The relationship with medicine must be explicit. Music therapy must not present itself as a substitute for diagnosis, pharmacological treatment, physiotherapy, psychotherapy, neurology, cardiology, or psychiatry. It can enter into dialogue with them. It can offer a field of regulation, expression, bodily perception, support, and research. It can participate in teams. It can propose exploratory protocols. Its strength lies in alliance, not in self-sufficient claims.

Data privacy deserves an equally firm place. HRV, EEG, breath, movement, voice, and bodily responses are sensitive data. They cannot be collected without clear purpose, secure storage, informed consent, minimization, and controlled access. Voice is especially personal. A voice sample contains body, age, origin, emotion, and potential identifiability. MUMEx must treat data as part of the therapeutic relationship, not as technical material available for use. Care for data is care for the patient.

Advanced tools also raise an aesthetic question. Many clinical devices sound poor. They produce beeps, crude drones, cold signals, mechanical loops, and functional sounds without musical dignity. For a music therapist, this is serious. Feedback should not be acoustically degrading. A fragile person does not deserve poor sound because a system is medical. Aesthetic quality is part of relational quality. A well-built field communicates respect. Ugly, rigid, repetitive, uncared-for sound can become a form of neglect.

MUMEx can fill this space: to bring compositional quality, generativity, timbral sensitivity, and parametric control into therapeutic instrumentation. An HRV signal does not have to become a beep. It can become harmonic breath. Respiratory data do not have to move a banal cursor. They can modulate a landscape. A movement sensor does not have to trigger demonstrative effects. It can open a sober, necessary, living sonic relationship. Technology becomes therapeutically credible when it stops exhibiting itself.

The immersive and vibroacoustic dimension must eventually face the question of standardization. Research requires comparability; clinical work requires personalization. If every field is completely different, study becomes difficult. If every field is too standardized, the system loses sensitivity toward the patient. The answer may lie in controlled variants: a stable general structure, adaptable parameters, detailed logbooks, and explicit criteria for modification.

MUMEx can generate families of fields: regulation, bodily presence, imaginal suspension, return, vocal work, thoracic vibroacoustics, grounding, and spatial orientation. Each family would have a recognizable nucleus and margins of adaptation. This allows a field to be studied without becoming rigid and personalized without becoming arbitrary.

Advanced instrumentation can help distinguish three levels of work: experience, training, and research. Experience concerns what the person lives in the session: vibration, image, breath, release, discomfort, emotion, or presence. Training concerns the possibility of learning regulation: breathing with a rhythm, recognizing the body, modulating tension, entering and leaving a state. Research concerns the orderly collection of data to better understand relationships between sound fields and responses. Confusing these levels generates errors. Separating them allows them to be used together.

An anxious patient may receive a light vibroacoustic MUMEx field, with a transducer under the back, eight minutes in duration, soft low register, minimal density, slow microvariation, observed respiration, and the possibility of stopping. The subjective experience may be: I feel my back supported; my thinking slows. Training may be: I recognize when breath begins to follow vibration. Research may record: HRV trend, respiratory frequency, field intensity, and post-session words. No level cancels the others. Together, they give thickness.

Another patient with depression may encounter a very sparse immersive field, with a distant frontal sound and minimal thoracic vibration. After a few minutes, the patient asks to increase the low presence slightly. This gesture is clinically meaningful. Not because the low sound cures depression, but because the person exercises choice over a perceived environment, modifies the relationship with space, feels a minimal desire for density, and asks for more world. Instrumentation helps make this gesture audible and documentable.

With children, adolescents, neurodivergent people, or people with disabilities, vibrotactile and gestural interfaces can be particularly valuable. A child who rejects verbal language may discover that movement produces sound. A closed adolescent may control the distance of the field without explaining. A person with motor difficulty may transform a small gesture into a large acoustic event. Here technology does not add complexity. It returns expressive power to minimal gestures. The danger is infantilization. The device must not become a therapeutic toy. It must preserve dignity, beauty, and precision.

Technical advancement also forces a rethinking of the music therapist's training. It will no longer be enough to know acoustic instruments, repertoire, improvisation, and relational psychology. A minimal culture of acoustics, sonic safety, sound pressure, vibration, sensors, physiological signals, data privacy, consent, device regulation, and measurement limits will be necessary. Technology should not turn the music therapist into an engineer. It should, however, prevent naivety. Whoever works with generative sound fields and bodily instruments must know that every parameter has consequences.

The most promising direction is not the machine that decides, but the field that listens under human responsibility. A MUMEx environment may receive signals from the body and return sound, but the therapeutic decision remains with the professional. If a system detects activation, it cannot know by itself whether that activation is fear, enthusiasm, memory, anger, emerging vitality, or sensory discomfort. The therapist must read. The patient must confirm or contradict. Data must enter the dialogue, not replace it.

This framework avoids two deviations. The first is reductionist technicism: more sensors, more data, more control, less listening. The second is antitechnological romanticism: fewer tools, more purity, as if the machine always contaminated the relationship. Both are insufficient. The question is not machine against human. The question is what kind of human is produced by the use of the machine. A device can alienate. It can also restore perception, agency, memory, choice, delicate control, and sonic dignity.

Advanced vibrational instrumentation becomes truly interesting when it stops promising effects and begins building conditions: conditions of bodily listening, regulation, choice, contact with breath, observation, and research. From this perspective, technology is a grammar of environment, not a clinical authority.

MUMEx Quantum Music Therapy can occupy an original position: not electronic medicine, not generic sonic wellness, not an immersive gadget, not spectacular neurotechnology. It can become research on generative sound fields in relation to the human state, capable of integrating bodily vibration, light physiological data, musical quality, improvisation, voice, space, and return. The key word remains integration. A vibroacoustic couch without relationship remains an object. An HRV sensor without listening remains a number. An immersive environment without return remains aesthetic experience. MUMEx must bind these elements into an inhabitable field.

The machine becomes an extension of therapeutic sensitivity only when it knows how to become discreet. It must be able to generate and withdraw, show and fall silent, measure and leave mystery, support and not occupy. Its intelligence does not lie in replacing human judgment, but in offering more precise sonic matter to human judgment. In this sense, advanced instrumentation does not take music therapy away from its origin. It brings it back to the body with new means.

The body, after all, remains the first device. It is the first sensor, the first transducer, the first resonator, and the first recorder of memory. Every serious electromedical instrument should remember this. Every MUMEx field should serve it. Every parameter should ask whether it makes the body more present or more colonized. Technological advancement is worthwhile only if it increases the human being's capacity to inhabit the self.

With electromedical devices and advanced vibrational instrumentation, the first great descent into the vibrating body closes. Sonic matter has become flesh, data, breath, contact, environment, and choice. The next passage will carry sound toward another region: the space of a mind that empties, widens, loses noise, and enters a silent vastness. After measurable vibration, the work must confront the power of sonic emptiness, drone, bell, and suspended harmonic interiority: sound as a path toward a consciousness less contracted and more spacious.

PART THREE

EMPTY INFINITY, TRANCE, AND MEDITATION

CHAPTER 10

Bringing the Mind into Empty Infinity Through Sound

EPISTEMOLOGICAL LEVEL: *Wisdom tradition / phenomenological model. Empty infinity, trance, meditation, and sound are treated as state practices that require containment, consent, and return.*

To bring the mind into a state of empty infinity is to free it, for a guarded span of time, from the saturation that forces it to recognize itself only in its contents. Ordinary mind often resembles a room filled with objects: thoughts, anticipations, fragments of memory, verbal noise, rapid images, judgments, subtle fears, and demands for performance. Many patients enter the session with this inner room already occupied. The therapist meets an organism that breathes, speaks, and listens while an invisible crowd continues to move inside it. The clinical question is therefore concrete: how can a sound field loosen the excess of content without pushing the person into anxious emptiness?

Empty infinity must be defined with precision. It is not annihilation, dissociation, confused trance, emotional anesthesia, or loss of orientation. It is a state of perceptual amplitude in which the mind stops adhering compulsively to its own noise and begins to perceive a space wider than its habitual narrative. The subject remains present. The body remains perceptible. Breath continues to provide an axis. The room does not disappear. What changes is the relationship with what had occupied consciousness. Thought loses its exclusive throne; listening widens; time stretches; the person experiences being larger than mental contraction.

Many contemplative traditions have described similar states in different languages: inner silence, listening to primordial sound, fertile emptiness, the space of consciousness, objectless quiet, open presence. Terminology varies, but a recognizable nucleus remains: the grip of self-referential thought decreases, and a less contracted field of presence emerges. Meditation neuroscience offers partial maps through attention, the default mode network, bodily awareness, emotional regulation, frontal-parietal activity, the insula, the cingulate cortex, and neural oscillations. These maps are useful, but they are correlates. They orient inquiry; they do not replace the living phenomenon.

Mental noise has a sonic structure even when it is not perceived as sound. It has rhythm, intensity, repetition, acceleration, density, interruption, and obsessive return. Anxiety thinks in syncopation. Depressive rumination insists like a figure that repeats without development. Hypercontrol builds tight internal sentences, almost percussive in their pressure. Shame lowers the inner voice and makes it corrosive. Traumatic alarm produces sudden spikes of attention, like dry impacts in a dark room. Music therapy can work on these forms because thought, before becoming argument, is temporal organization of experience.

Sound can empty the mind because it offers the nervous system an alternative temporality. Where thought fragments, the drone holds. Where rumination tightens, sustained tone extends. Where fear anticipates, the bell opens a slower time. Where tension searches for grips, a prepared silence allows the patient to remain without immediately clinging to content. Sound does not abolish thought. It removes thought from sovereignty. It shifts the center of experience from the production of internal sentences to the reception of a temporal, vibratory, bodily field.

This shift is subtle. If the therapist imposes calm, the patient may fight it. If the field is too empty, the patient may fall into the raw exposure of inner noise. If the sound is too beautiful, it may seduce rather than transform. Empty infinity requires a narrow passage: enough continuity to support, enough space to widen, enough bodily center to prevent escape, and enough return to avoid leaving the subject dispersed.

The drone is one of the most powerful forms for this work. Its force arises from stability, duration, and the capacity to generate an acoustic support without compelling the mind to follow a melodic plot. A therapeutic drone, however, must not become an inert mass. Absolute stasis can stiffen, bore, worry, or produce poor hypnosis. It needs a barely perceptible internal life: small spectral shifts, gentle oscillations of amplitude, harmonics that emerge and vanish, and a timbral breath that keeps the field alive. MUMEx can work precisely in this zone: continuity without loop, quiet without immobility, amplitude without dispersion.

The pedal tone, in sacred and modal traditions, has often supported the experience of a center. The tanpura in Indian music, the organ pedal, certain liturgical chants, the low string that remains, the sustained tone of the voice, and the deep hum of archaic instruments have acted for centuries as sonic axes. The ear rests on them, the body tunes itself to them, and the mind gradually stops hunting for novelty. The qualitative repetition of the pedal tone educates attention to remain. In a culture driven toward interruption, remaining is already therapeutic.

The bell works differently. It does not sustain time like the drone; it opens time with a clear gesture and then lets it dissolve. The initial strike gathers attention, the harmonic aura expands it, and the tail of sound leads it toward silence. The bell teaches the mind to follow disappearance without immediately turning it into loss. It is an acoustic form of letting go. For an anxious patient, this process may be precious if carefully dosed: the sound arrives, remains, vanishes, and the world continues. For a traumatized patient, the same bell may be too sudden if the attack is aggressive or spatial distance is not controlled. Therapeutic quality depends on gesture, distance, preparation, volume, and the field that receives the resonance.

The gong has a more ambiguous power. It can generate immensity, body, oceanic vibration, and harmonic density. It can also overwhelm. Its spectral richness and dynamic expansion require competence. Used poorly, a gong produces spectacle, invasion, and confusion. Used with mastery, it may open an immense perceptual field in which the subject feels suspended inside sonic matter that exceeds the ordinary form of thought. Empty infinity does not require great intensity. Often it begins from a gong barely touched, a vibration that does not seek to dominate, a sound that remains near the edge of consciousness and changes its depth.

Harmonics introduce another dimension. Overtone singing, Tibetan bowls, lightly bowed strings, certain analog synthesizers, and extremely delicate filtered voices show the mind that one sound contains several planes at once. Attention may rest on the fundamental and then discover a higher light; it may feel a heavy body and a fine upper thread; it may perceive stability and movement in the same event. This stratification trains consciousness to become less binary. The sound field becomes a school of coexistence: one acoustic body contains many heights, many tensions, and many micro-presences.

Silence is the most difficult material. In wellness rhetoric, it is often treated as calm. In clinical practice, it may be anything: rest, threat, abandonment, vastness, coldness, listening, shame, or waiting. Silence is not therapeutic in itself. It becomes therapeutic when it is prepared, inhabited, and returned to relationship. A silent room may expose the patient violently to inner noise. A silence born after a well-built sound field can become the first experience of a mental space that is not hostile. The therapist must distinguish empty silence from held silence, silence that heals from silence that leaves the person alone.

The most profound silence is usually not the absence of sound, but the trace of sound after withdrawal. The bell has disappeared, yet attention is still shaped by its decay. The drone has stopped, yet the body continues to remember its support. The voice has faded, yet the chest keeps its faint vibration. This residual field can be clinically decisive. The patient discovers that the end of sound is not the end of containment. Absence can be inhabited.

MUMEx can make silence architectural. It can design long decays, rarefactions, intervals, and spaces of listening. It can reduce density when the patient's voice appears. It can allow sonic particles to return after intervals long enough to feel like memory. It can create a silence that is not abandonment, but the extension of a field whose support has become internal.

Electronic sound allows a degree of finesse that acoustic instruments alone cannot always provide. One can sculpt extremely long attacks, almost bodily subharmonics, slow spatialization, rarefied granular fields, microvariation barely available to analytic awareness, bands of colored noise, deep reverberation, and timbral presences without immediate cultural reference. This freedom must be governed. Meditative electronics can easily fall into the generic, the cosmetic, and the ambient carpet without necessity. The criterion remains the human state: every choice must have a perceptual, bodily, or temporal function.

A MUMEx field designed for vastness should not simply sound "large." Large sound can be empty rhetoric. Therapeutic vastness requires proportion. The field must open space while preserving orientation. It must let the mind widen while allowing the body to remain reachable. It must create distance without producing exile. Reverberation, stereo width, spectral height, and low-frequency support must be composed as clinical parameters, not as cinematic effects.

The more abstract the sound, the more important the human setting becomes. A sound without cultural reference may give freedom; it may also remove too many anchors. The therapist's voice, the possibility of eye contact, the right to stop, the clarity of the room, and the final debriefing become structural parts of the field. Empty infinity is not achieved by erasing the world. It is achieved by loosening the compulsive hold of inner content while keeping enough world to return to.

MUMEx can generate empty infinity through three principal movements: reducing saturation, expanding perceptual space, and maintaining a bodily center. Reducing saturation requires low density, no sudden events, legible timbres, slow motion, and few competing streams of information. Expanding perceptual space requires depth, controlled reverberation, broad spatial movement, distant harmonics, and sonic tails able to extend attention beyond the immediate object. Maintaining a bodily center requires a low component, a minimal vocal presence, or a stable tactile reference that prevents the person from dissolving into abstraction.

A basic empty-infinity field may begin with a soft low presence, almost more perceived than heard, followed by a very slow spectral widening. A bell may appear only after the body has found support. A fine harmonic thread may enter at the edge of perception. Silence may not appear as an interruption, but as a gradual rarefaction. The field should not demand mystical experience. It should make room for the possibility of less crowded consciousness.

In the logbook, the therapist should record the density of the field, the presence or absence of low support, the attack profile of bells or gongs, spatial width, average volume, duration, patient position, eyes open or closed, verbal consent, interruption signal, and post-session report. Empty infinity must be studied with the same sobriety as any other state transition. Its delicacy increases the need for documentation.

The word infinity is delicate. In therapeutic practice, it must never become an invitation to flee the world. A fragile consciousness may desire infinity as disappearance. A depressed person may confuse emptiness with annihilation. A dissociative subject may be seduced by states in which the body becomes remote. Empty infinity has value only when it increases presence. After the experience, the person should feel the body more clearly, perceive the room with greater stability, breathe with more freedom, and speak from a more inhabited place.

For this reason, return is not an accessory. It is the ethical seal of the work. Every session that opens vastness must include a path back: lowering spatial extension, simplifying spectrum, reintroducing the body through breath or feet, inviting the patient to name the room, touching an object, hearing the natural voice, and allowing words to reassemble without being forced. Reintegration transforms the experience from altered state into human resource.

In trauma work, the rules become stricter. Eyes closed, long immobility, profound internal attention, or disembodied spaciousness may be difficult or unsafe. Empty infinity may have to be approached through open eyes, clear light, seated posture, brief duration, patient control, and a field that remains connected to the room. The aim is not transcendence. The aim is more freedom inside presence.

A MUMEx protocol for empty infinity should proceed gradually. First, the therapist assesses the patient's relationship with silence, bodily interiority, immobility, and spacious sound. Second, the field begins with a clear bodily anchor. Third, saturation is reduced. Fourth, space is widened only as tolerance appears. Fifth, silence is introduced as a held continuation of the field. Sixth, Reintegration brings the patient back to body, room, and speech. Seventh, the debriefing avoids forcing interpretation and asks simple questions: What changed in the body? What happened to time? Did anything feel too large? What helped you return?

The ethics of vastness is severe. The therapist does not use the infinite to impress, seduce, or display power. The field is successful not when it produces extraordinary visions, but when the patient returns with a more livable relationship to mind, body, and world. Empty infinity is therefore not escape. It is a disciplined expansion that makes ordinary presence less suffocating.

This chapter has moved sound toward a suspended mental amplitude. The next step enters an even more delicate frontier: regression, imaginal memory, and the controversial language of past lives. Here the same principle must become sharper: the experience may be meaningful without being treated as historical proof.

CHAPTER 11

Music Therapy, Regressive Hypnosis, and Past Lives

EPISTEMOLOGICAL LEVEL: *Frontier territory / symbolic practice. Regression and past lives are treated as imaginal, narrative, or transpersonal experiences without presuming historical truth or clinical evidence.*

Regressive hypnosis and past-life material belong to one of the most delicate territories of the whole book. They attract fascination, resistance, ridicule, faith, trauma narratives, spiritual interpretations, and clinical risk. A serious treatment must refuse both credulity and contempt. The fact that a person experiences an image, a voice, a body from another time, or a scene that feels ancient does not establish historical truth. It also does not make the experience meaningless. Human beings live through images. Images shape suffering, identity, fear, longing, and transformation. Music therapy can accompany such material only by adopting exact language.

In this work, past-life imagery is not treated as evidence of reincarnation, nor as a diagnostic source. It is treated as an experience that may appear during altered states, hypnosis, deep listening, dreams, meditative sound, or symbolic exploration. The therapist's task is not to verify the image, embellish it, or give it metaphysical authority. The therapist's task is to protect the person, contain the state, prevent suggestion, and help integrate what the image carries in the present life.

This distinction is crucial for the North American clinical context. The literature on hypnosis, memory, and suggestibility has shown how easily memory can be influenced by expectation, leading questions, authority, group culture, and emotionally charged interpretation. Any practice that works with regression must be vigilant about false memory and narrative contamination. The therapist must never implant content. Sound must never be used to push a patient toward a predetermined story.

Regression, in the most cautious sense, is a shift in experiential time. The subject's present state opens toward earlier forms of feeling, bodily memory, affective pattern, or symbolic scene. This may involve childhood memories, pre-verbal states, family atmospheres, archetypal images, or scenes that the subject interprets as belonging to another life. The difference among these categories matters less at the moment of emergence than the ethical stance used to receive them. The therapist should not rush to classify. The therapist holds the field and asks what the experience is doing now.

Sound can favor this shift because it reorganizes time. A drone weakens ordinary chronological pressure. A bell opens a threshold. A slow descending figure may invite depth. A voice without words can return the subject to preverbal perception. Repetition can make the mind less defended. Silence can allow images to surface. The danger is that these same elements may also intensify suggestibility. This is why regressive work must be framed, consensual, and reversible.

The most mature formulation is this: regressive imagery is a phenomenological event in the field. It can be meaningful, transformative, frightening, beautiful, or confusing. It should be explored through its present function: What does this image allow the patient to feel? What bodily state accompanies it? What fear or desire is organized through it? What does it ask to be integrated? These questions keep the work anchored.

Memory is not a fixed archive that sound simply opens. It is a living, reconstructive process. Music is particularly powerful because it can reactivate implicit memory, bodily atmosphere, autobiographical fragments, and affective states before verbal narration becomes available. A melody may return childhood; a timbre may restore a room; a rhythm may evoke a ritual; a voice may awaken grief without a clear object. In regressive contexts, this power must be handled with extreme care.

MUMEx does not need to create dramatic regressions. Its value lies in constructing a field in which memory-like material may emerge without coercion. A low-density field, a stable center, slow microvariation, and clear opportunities for return can allow images to appear as offerings rather than as forced revelations. If the patient sees a landscape, a face, a corridor, a battlefield, a monastery, a childhood room, or an unknown body, the therapist does not confirm or deny. The therapist asks for the patient's present experience: What happens in the body as you see this? Do you want to stay with it, move away, or return to the room?

Narrative emergence is not always the goal. Sometimes the clinically important event is not the story but the bodily shift: the jaw releases, the breath deepens, the patient feels the back, tears come without panic, a hand opens, or a previously frozen feeling becomes tolerable. The narrative may be symbolic scaffolding for a state transition. The therapist respects it without becoming its historian.

The greatest danger in regressive work is suggestion. Suggestion may be explicit, as when a facilitator asks leading questions: Are you seeing a previous life? Who killed you? What happened in that other time? It may also be implicit: the room, the music, the vocabulary, the therapist's expectation, the promise of revelation, or the prestige of the method may all guide the patient toward a narrative that feels discovered while being partly produced by context. This risk is real and must be acknowledged without ambiguity.

The therapeutic language must therefore remain non-leading. Instead of asking, "What past life are you seeing?" the therapist may ask, "What image is present?" Instead of asking, "Who harmed you?" the therapist may ask, "Is there anything in this image that feels important or difficult?" Instead of saying, "This explains your current fear," the therapist may say, "Let us notice what this experience brings into the body now." The difference is not stylistic. It is ethical.

Sound design must also avoid suggestion. If the field uses stereotyped "ancient," "ritual," "Eastern," or "funerary" signals, it may steer imagery too strongly. A MUMEx field for regressive imagery should avoid cinematic coding unless the explicit purpose is symbolic theater and the patient knows it. For clinical and research purposes, the more neutral and precisely documented the sound field, the more trustworthy the process becomes.

A MUMEx regressive field should have several layers of protection. First, it must contain a stable bodily anchor: a low support, a soft pulse, a gentle vocal reference, or a clear spatial center. Second, it must allow the patient to remain oriented in the room. Third, it must avoid abrupt dynamic expansion. Fourth, it must include planned points of return. Fifth, it must be documented in the logbook with duration, density, timbre, spatialization, volume, patient posture, consent, and debriefing notes.

The sound should not claim to retrieve. It should permit. Retrieval language is dangerous because it implies that the past exists intact behind a door and that the field opens it. A more disciplined language says: the field creates conditions under which images, sensations, memories, and symbolic forms may emerge. Some will be autobiographical. Some will be imaginal. Some will be culturally shaped. Some may have transpersonal meaning for the patient. The clinical task is not to establish their origin, but to integrate their effect.

The field may work through Suspension. The ordinary narrative loosens, the mind moves into a less crowded temporality, and images gain space. Gentle Perturbation may introduce a slight difference, enough to move a fixed state without overwhelming it. Perceptual Collapse may occur when a diffuse image becomes a scene, word, gesture, or feeling. Reintegration is essential: without it, the experience remains open and may become disturbing.

Past-life experiences can be profound for those who live them. They may provide symbolic organization, relief, mourning, explanation, or a sense of continuity larger than ordinary biography. Some traditions accept reincarnation as metaphysical truth. Some patients arrive with that belief, and it must be respected without being clinically imposed. The therapist does not need to argue metaphysics in the session. The therapist must protect the patient's freedom of meaning while maintaining professional accuracy.

The safest formulation is this: the session may receive the experience as subjectively real without declaring it historically verified. The patient may say, "I felt as if I were in another life." The therapist can respond, "Let us stay with what this brings into your present body and present life." This respects the experience and avoids the claim. It allows spiritual meaning without losing clinical ground.

This position is not timid. It is strong. It allows the frontier to remain open without selling certainty. It prevents the therapist from becoming an oracle. It protects the patient from dependency on exceptional narratives. It keeps the work oriented toward transformation of state, not accumulation of spectacular stories.

Debriefing after regressive imagery must be slow and grounded. The patient should be invited to return to the room, feel the feet or hands, orient to light and objects, drink water if useful, and describe the experience without pressure. The therapist should avoid premature interpretation. The first questions should concern safety, body, time, and the present: Where are you now? What is most alive in the body? Is anything unfinished? What would help you return more fully?

Clinical boundaries must remain explicit. This work is not a substitute for trauma therapy, psychiatry, medical care, or psychotherapy when those are indicated. It is not appropriate for every patient. People with severe dissociation, psychosis, unstable trauma symptoms, high suggestibility, or acute crisis require particular caution and often exclusion from regressive practices. If such material emerges spontaneously, the therapist should prioritize stabilization and referral rather than exploration.

In a mature MUMEx framework, regressive and past-life material remains a frontier chapter, not the center of the method. It teaches that sound can open imaginal time, but it also teaches humility. The deeper the state, the stricter the ethics. The more powerful the image, the more necessary the return. Music therapy does not become a metaphysical tribunal. It remains a field where human experience can be held, named, and reintegrated.

CHAPTER 12

Nada Yoga and the Eastern Paths of Sound

EPISTEMOLOGICAL LEVEL: *Wisdom tradition. Nada Yoga, mantra, drone, raga, tala, and inner listening are situated within their cultural and spiritual genealogies before any clinical translation.*

Nada Yoga places sound at the center of the path. Nada means sound, vibration, resonance, or subtle sonic current. Yoga indicates union, discipline, integration, or the path by which consciousness is gathered and transformed. The core intuition is immense: sound is not merely an object of hearing. It can become a vehicle of consciousness. It can lead the practitioner from external listening toward internal listening, from scattered attention toward vibratory presence, from ordinary mental dispersion toward a more unified state.

For Quantum Music Therapy, the importance of Nada Yoga is not exotic decoration. It is methodological. The tradition teaches that sound can be practiced, repeated, inhabited, and followed inward. It teaches that continuity can transform attention. It teaches that the body is not separated from consciousness: breath, mouth, chest, spine, skull, and inner ear participate in the path. These principles speak directly to MUMEx, provided that they are translated with respect and not appropriated superficially.

The first lesson is that sound needs duration. A culture of immediate effect misunderstands contemplative sound. A mantra repeated for three seconds is not the same as a mantra inhabited. A drone heard as background is not the same as a drone followed with the whole organism. A field is not therapeutic because it contains a sign of spirituality; it becomes meaningful when it changes the listener's capacity to remain.

Mantra is one of the most refined technologies of sonic repetition. Whether understood theologically, spiritually, psychologically, or phenomenologically, a mantra gives the mind a vibratory form to inhabit. The repetition does not only occupy thought. It reorganizes breath, articulation, attention, and bodily resonance. The mouth repeats; the chest vibrates; the ear receives; the breath adapts; the mind gradually stops producing competing language.

In clinical translation, mantra requires consent, cultural respect, and careful framing. Some patients may belong to traditions for which specific mantras are sacred. Others may prefer a secular syllable, a vowel, a word of safety, or a simple vocal tone. The therapist must not use sacred material as neutral decoration. When a traditional mantra is used, its source and dignity should be acknowledged. When the context is secular, a nonreligious vocal form may be more appropriate.

MUMEx can support mantra or vocal repetition by creating an environment that holds without covering. A discreet generative drone, subtle timbral microvariation, slow spatial breathing, or a soft harmonic field can transform a fragile vocalization into an experience of presence. The field should amplify the patient's own vibration symbolically and acoustically. It should not turn the voice into performance.

The tanpura offers an extraordinary model for thinking the sound field. In the context of Indian music, it does not accompany in the Western sense. It does not produce harmonic progressions, narrate an autonomous melody, or push toward resolution. It creates a tonal womb. It maintains a center. It repeats without becoming mechanical because every string, resonance, and fluctuation produces microdifference. Its sound teaches that stability is not immobility. A field may remain faithful to a center while continuously changing within it.

Many contemporary sound environments fail because they confuse calm with staticity. A flat drone without micro-life becomes anesthesia or irritation after a few minutes. The tanpura, by contrast, lives through vibrating continuity. The center remains; the matter breathes. Quantum Music Therapy can translate this principle generatively: maintain a stable tonal or timbral reference without fixedness; introduce noninvasive microvariation; build harmonics that do not saturate; let the field suggest duration without imposing decorative hypnosis; and protect orientation while attention deepens.

For MUMEx, the living center is not only a pitch. It may be a timbre, a low bodily presence, a breath-like oscillation, a spatial point, or a vocal memory. The center says to the patient: you may widen because there is something to which you can return. This is the difference between therapeutic vastness and dispersal.

The raga introduces another lesson. In Indian tradition, a raga is not simply a scale. It is a melodic organism, a form of time, a way of coloring attention, a constellation of privileged notes, movements, accents, directions, affects, hours of the day, and interior seasons. Its structure teaches that sonic material has behavior, not merely pitch content. Every raga has a character, a breath, a quality of appearance. This idea speaks directly to the design of MUMEx fields: a therapeutic field should not be defined only by acoustic parameters but by a quality of behavior. How does it enter? How does it insist? How does it withdraw? How does it allow the body to emerge? How does it prepare silence? What internal time does it produce?

Tala, the cyclic rhythmic system of Indian music, shows that repetition can be circular, complex, and alive. Modern Western culture has often transformed rhythm into productive pulse: drive, acceleration, control. Eastern traditions offer a more subtle notion: rhythm as return, memory of the cycle, waiting for the point of reconnection, and walking inside a form that allows freedom. In music therapy, this quality can help patients who are fragmented, dispersed, or deprived of temporal center. A gentle rhythmic cycle, perceptible without becoming oppressive, can reconstruct prediction, support, and continuity.

MUMEx can translate these lessons without imitating the tradition. A field may have a cyclic memory, a privileged return, a nonmechanical drone, a melodic behavior that opens at certain thresholds, and rhythmic recurrences that create orientation. The purpose is not to generate ersatz Indian music. The purpose is to learn from a tradition that understands sound as state, time, and presence.

The boundary between contemplative practice and therapeutic practice must remain clear. The music therapist does not become a guru. The session does not become a disguised spiritual ceremony. The therapist does not take mantras, ragas, bowls, bells, or Eastern drums as exotic objects to be grafted onto an impoverished Western setting. Respect passes through competence and sobriety. Using a Tibetan bowl, mantra, or tanpura-inspired drone without understanding the cultural body from which it comes creates a double risk: aesthetic superficiality and improper suggestion. The patient does not need Orientalist scenery. The patient needs an ethically constructed sound field.

The Eastern path of sound becomes fertile when it is heard in its principles, not stolen in its surfaces. The first principle is continuity. Sound educates attention when it allows the mind to remain long enough to see its own agitation. The second is bodily resonance. Contemplative sound does not belong to the head alone; it belongs to breath, mouth, chest, spine, skin, and posture. The third is transformative repetition. To repeat is not to duplicate; it is to travel the same form several times until every return changes the practitioner. The fourth is relationship with silence. Sound is valuable for the silence it makes possible. The fifth is intention. Without intention, repetition becomes automatism; with intention, it becomes orientation of state.

A generative field inspired by Nada Yoga should not imitate India, Tibet, Japan, or any other tradition. It should generate conditions of deep listening: timbral continuity, tonal center, microvariation, breath, space, controlled decline of events, and a measured relationship between presence and emptiness. It may use pure electronic sounds, processed acoustic material, natural samples, voices, harmonics, and slow pulsations. What matters is the function: to move perception from consumption of stimuli toward vibratory presence.

This distinction protects both the tradition and the clinical field. If MUMEx uses an Eastern sign only to make the session feel spiritual, it becomes decoration. If it studies how a tradition organizes attention, breath, repetition, center, and silence, it becomes research. The difference is decisive. A premium North American edition must make that difference visible because readers will rightly be sensitive to appropriation, evidence, and clinical boundaries.

In work with anxiety, the principles of Nada Yoga suggest that activation should not be fought with imposed calm. The sound field should offer a center stable enough to be followed, a repetition predictable enough not to generate alarm, and an implicit breathing quality capable of slowing without command. Voice may enter as simple vibration, not as performance. An anxious patient might be invited to sustain a vowel over a soft drone, listening to where the sound vibrates and where it breaks. The aim is not to sing well. The aim is to discover that the body can produce a continuity more reliable than thought.

In work with depression, contemplative sound teaches that transformation may be poor, minimal, and almost invisible. A field that is too luminous may feel offensive. A rhythm that is too vital may increase the distance between the patient and the world. What is often needed is sonic matter that accepts grayness without confirming it as destiny: a warm drone, a low resonance, a distant bell, a harmonic that appears rarely, a timbral breath that restores depth to time. Mantra, whether secular or traditional according to context and consent, may give the mind an anchor when thought repeatedly falls into the same groove.

In trauma, greater caution is required. Many meditative practices invite the person to close the eyes, remain still, and observe internal sensation. For some traumatized subjects, this can become threatening. Inner listening is not always safe. The body may be experienced as the place where danger returns. Sound must therefore maintain a clear relationship with the room, orientation, and the possibility of interruption. A field inspired by Nada Yoga should not dissolve perceptual boundaries in these cases. It should make them gentle and present. The therapist's voice, light, movement, volume choice, and the right to stop become essential parts of practice.

Eastern sound traditions also offer another conception of silence. In the West, silence is often understood as the absence of sound. In contemplative traditions, silence is a full quality, a presence without explicit sonic form, a field in which listening does not end. After a bell, decay is not the end of the event; it is its subtle continuation. After mantra, the body continues to vibrate. After drone, the inner ear retains a trace of resonance. Music therapy can work precisely on this invisible tail. Many patients discover themselves not while the sound is full but as it begins to withdraw.

Inner listening should be received without pathologizing and without mythologizing. Some patients report ringing, buzzing, pulses, currents, vibrations, or acoustic images. Others perceive only bodily qualities: weight, warmth, openness, or pressure. Some phenomena require audiological or medical attention, such as tinnitus or hyperacusis. Some belong to imagination and meditation. Some are subtle bodily perceptions that can become therapeutic material. Distinguishing them is essential.

Reintegration translates contemplative sound into clinical maturity. The patient does not remain in a sacred aura. The patient returns to feet, chair, light, hands, room, and speech. The value of the experience is tested by return: more presence, more body, more breath, more freedom, more dignity in ordinary life. Nada Yoga gives Quantum Music Therapy a great lesson: sound may lead inward, but it must not imprison the listener inside inwardness. The path of sound is complete only when inner listening becomes a more inhabited world.

CHAPTER 13

Sacred Song, Western Meditation, and Sound Healing

EPISTEMOLOGICAL LEVEL: *Wisdom tradition / history of sacred practice. Liturgical chant, Western meditation, and sound healing are distinguished from clinical evidence, while their phenomenological value is retained.*

Sacred song is one of the oldest forms through which human communities have organized breath, fear, mourning, gratitude, and the relation with the invisible. Before being doctrine, chant is collective physiology. Bodies breathe together. Voices align. Time becomes ritual. The individual's inner noise is placed inside a form that exceeds personal agitation. A chorus, a psalm, a responsorial chant, a hymn, a lament, or a simple repeated invocation can give the nervous system a larger container.

For music therapy, sacred song matters even when the clinical setting is secular. Its power does not lie only in belief, but in the organization of time, voice, repetition, resonance, and communal containment. A patient who cannot bear solitary silence may be able to enter a shared vocal field. A group that feels fragmented may recover cohesion through a repeated tone. A grieving person may discover that sorrow can be carried when breath is supported by others. Sacred song teaches that voice can become shelter.

This does not mean importing religious practice into clinical work without consent. Sacred material carries identity, memory, trauma, belonging, exclusion, and devotion. For some, it heals; for others, it wounds. The therapist must know the difference. In the North American context especially, spiritual diversity and religious trauma require precision. A clinical session cannot presume a shared faith. It can study and use the structural wisdom of sacred song only through consent, context, and respect.

Western contemplative sound has produced forms of extraordinary discipline. Gregorian chant, Byzantine chant, Ambrosian chant, psalmody, monastic recitation, organ pedal, responsorial forms, sacred polyphony, and later meditative choral traditions all organize the relationship among breath, word, resonance, and vertical time. They do not simply decorate belief. They create an acoustic architecture in which the subject can inhabit a more ordered interior.

Chant often reduces rhythmic agitation and places the body inside a long line. The melody does not behave like modern song. It floats, turns, returns, and follows breath-shaped phrase. The word becomes elongated until semantic meaning and vibration become inseparable. For a patient caught in fragmented thought, this kind of line can be profoundly organizing. It gives duration without pressure. It lets the body breathe phrase by phrase.

Liturgy adds another element: form before the individual. The subject does not invent the sequence; the form holds them. This can relieve performance anxiety and narcissistic control. It can also be problematic if authority, dogma, or past religious injury are active. In music therapy, liturgical wisdom must be translated into noncoercive form: predictable sequence, shared response, repetition, return, and solemnity without authoritarian pressure.

Hildegard of Bingen offers a luminous example of sacred sound as visionary amplitude. Her chants stretch melodic space upward, often with a sense of flame, ascent, and ecstatic contour. They remind us that sacred song is not always quiet or static. It can be vast, radiant, intense, and embodied. The therapeutic lesson is not to imitate Hildegard as style, but to recognize how a melodic line can pull the body toward vertical imagination and expanded breath.

Gregorian chant offers another teaching: modal space without harmonic hurry. The absence of functional progression frees attention from the expectation of modern resolution. The line moves in a field rather than through a chordal plot. This can be particularly useful for MUMEx. A generative field may sustain modal gravity without becoming a song; it may allow melodic fragments to appear like breath-forms rather than themes; it may produce a space where time is not pushed toward climax.

Modal sound can be therapeutic when it creates inhabitable ambiguity. It is neither tonal drive nor formless atmosphere. It gives a center, but not a closed destiny. It allows sorrow without collapse, openness without sentimental brightness, solemnity without heaviness. The MUMEx Sound Field can learn from modal traditions how to create a perceptual room large enough for the patient's state to move without being forced into emotional resolution.

The contemporary expression "sound healing" is powerful and problematic. It names a wide range of practices—bowls, gongs, tuning forks, voice, drums, overtone singing, vibroacoustic sessions, meditation concerts, and ritual sound environments. Some are practiced with great sensitivity. Others are surrounded by exaggerated promises, frequency myths, medical overclaims, and commercial mystification. A super-premium edition of this book must speak clearly: subjective benefit, relaxation, spiritual experience, and bodily resonance are real phenomena; they are not the same as evidence of disease treatment.

The language of healing should be used with care. In some contexts, healing means cure; in others, it means integration, meaning, comfort, mourning, regulation, or return to self. The ambiguity can mislead. Quantum Music Therapy should prefer precise verbs: regulate, support, contain, orient, invite, deepen, accompany, widen, integrate, and help the patient return. When clinical claims are made, they must be proportionate to research. When spiritual or symbolic meanings are present, they should be named as such.

This discipline does not weaken the field. It strengthens it. A practice that can distinguish experience from evidence is more credible than one that promises everything. Sound may change a person's state profoundly without curing a medical condition. It may open grief, restore breath, reduce perceived tension, support attention, or make silence bearable. These are not small outcomes. They deserve to be studied without being inflated.

The voice becomes sacred when it is treated as more than expression. In ritual, voice carries the individual into a form shared with others. Even a single patient may experience this if the therapist's voice is steady, respectful, and noninvasive. A humming line, a simple repeated tone, a soft responsorial pattern, or a held vowel can create a ritual frame without requiring religious content. The body feels that it is not alone in time.

Group music therapy can draw particular strength from this dimension. A group that sings together may experience synchronization, shared breath, mutual listening, and a reduction of isolation. Yet group voice also requires protection. Some people fear being heard. Some carry shame around singing. Some associate sacred song with coercion. The therapist must build a frame in which participation can be partial, silent, or purely listening. Ritual containment must never become pressure to join.

MUMEx can support collective voice by creating a harmonic ground that holds without dictating. It can maintain a low center, subtle spatial movement, or a resonant field that lets voices enter and withdraw. The technology should not replace the group's living sound. It should create a room in which fragile voices can risk being present.

A central challenge is how to work with the sacred without imposing confession. The sacred, in a clinical context, may be understood as depth, reverence, threshold, humility, vastness, gratitude, mourning, or contact with what exceeds the ego. It does not need to be tied to one doctrine. Many patients need experiences of reverence even when they do not belong to a religious tradition. Others need protection from religious language. MUMEx can offer a secular architecture of sacred attention: slowness, resonance, silence, breath, and return.

This secular sacredness must not become vague spirituality. It needs form. The field may begin with orientation, enter a resonant center, allow a long suspension, support a vocal or silent act, and return through body and room. The therapist explains the process in clinical language: we will work with attention, breath, resonance, and a sense of space. If spiritual meaning arises, it belongs to the patient. The system does not define it.

The sacred without confession is especially important for a plural North American audience. The book must be open enough to honor the spiritual dimension of sound and precise enough to protect readers from confusion between ritual, therapy, and medical evidence. MUMEx does not sell sanctity. It builds conditions in which human experience may become more reverent toward itself.

A secular clinical translation of sacred song involves several operations. First, remove doctrinal compulsion while preserving form: repetition, response, breath, resonance, and solemn time. Second, keep consent explicit. Third, use vocal material appropriate to the patient's history and culture. Fourth, avoid exotic or ecclesiastical signs when they are not clinically necessary. Fifth, document the field in the logbook. Sixth, always include Reintegration.

The therapist may use a single vowel, a humming tone, a neutral syllable, a patient-chosen word, a short poetic phrase, or a traditional chant when the patient asks for it and the context supports it. The field may be acoustic, electronic, or hybrid. What matters is that the practice does not pretend to be neutral when it carries symbolic force. Sacred sound is never empty of history. Clinical maturity lies in acknowledging that history while constructing a safe present.

In this translation, the five operators gain a particular color. Resonance establishes bodily and relational compatibility. Suspension opens a solemn interval. Gentle Perturbation may introduce a slight harmonic or vocal movement. Perceptual Collapse may occur when an inner image, prayer, grief, or word takes form. Reintegration returns the patient to ordinary life with the experience held rather than dramatized.

Sacred song, meditation, and sound healing all risk one error: confusing depth with distance from the world. A session may feel profound because it suspends ordinary life. Yet the true test is return. Does the patient leave more embodied or more dependent on exceptional atmosphere? Does the voice become more available in daily life? Does breath become less defended? Does grief become more speakable? Does silence become less hostile? Does the person carry a trace of dignity into ordinary action?

MUMEx Quantum Music Therapy must be judged by this return. The field may open Suspension, but Reintegration completes the work. The sonic sacred is not an escape from the body. It is a way of giving the body more space, more resonance, and more meaning. It does not ask the patient to vanish into sound. It helps the patient re-enter the world with a different interior acoustics.

PART FOUR

VIBRANT NATURE

CHAPTER 14

The Garden as a Living Vibrant Organism

EPISTEMOLOGICAL LEVEL: *Ecopsychological model. The garden is treated as a multisensory field and relational organism, not as generic scenery or decorative wellness content.*

The garden is one of the oldest forms of sonic intelligence. Modern culture has often reduced it to green space, urban ornament, architectural pause, or a pleasant resting zone for tired bodies. This reduction prevents us from hearing what a garden actually is: a perceptual organism, a living engine of microvariation, and a biological composition in which water, leaves, wind, insects, birds, stone, footsteps, shadow, temperature, scent, and silence construct a field of experience. A garden does not merely accompany care from the outside. It can become part of care when it is understood as an environment that modulates state, attention, breath, and the patient's relationship with the world.

Every garden has a score without a score. In the morning it speaks differently from the afternoon. After rain, it changes resonance. In wind, it produces grains, rustlings, interruptions, small frictions, and sudden openings. Water draws continuity, droplets, falls, flows, and acoustic reflections. Insects introduce subtle pulsations, often registered by the nervous system before conscious listening notices them. Birds bring signals, calls, territorial gestures, distances, and small theaters of response. Gravel underfoot organizes the body in space. A bench, wall, pergola, or tree canopy modifies the perception of safety. The garden acts because it does not give the subject one signal. It immerses the subject in a living plurality that remains legible without ever becoming identical to itself.

This is why the garden stands so close to generative sound fields. Nature does not produce loops. It repeats, varies, reappears, deviates, suspends, intensifies, and thins. The rustling of leaves preserves a recognizable identity, yet never returns as an exact copy. A bird call has species, function, and context, yet each emission contains microdifference. Water repeats its own continuity while producing local events. The sonic life of the garden teaches a grammar that MUMEx can study closely: continuity without rigidity, variation without chaos, identity without fixation, and unpredictability without aggression.

The notion of soundscape is fundamental here. A soundscape is not a sum of sounds. It is the way an environment is heard, interpreted, inhabited, remembered, and bodily negotiated. In a garden, geophony, biophony, and anthropophony coexist: nonbiological natural sounds, sounds of living organisms, and human-made sounds. Therapeutic quality depends on the balance among these layers and on the relationship they establish with the patient's present state. Birdsong may support opening and orientation. Water may provide continuity and masking. Wind may evoke spaciousness or unease. Distant voices may reassure or disturb. Near-silence may calm one person and frighten another.

Anthropogenic noise profoundly alters the garden's effect. A park exposed to continuous traffic may preserve visual value while losing much of its regulatory function. The nervous system does not easily separate green image from acoustic threat. Leaves can be covered by engines; birdsong can become a residual fragment; water can be used as sonic masking rather than as living continuity. A music-therapeutic approach to the garden must therefore listen before adding. Where does the noise fall? From which direction does it arrive? Which frequencies dominate? Which natural elements resist? Which zones allow the body to lower its guard? Before a MUMEx intervention is designed, the real acoustic ecology must be understood (Buxton et al., 2021).

A therapeutic garden is not simply a beautiful garden. Beauty matters, sometimes decisively, yet it is not enough. A garden designed for care must offer readability, safety, accessibility, choice, resting points, shade, protection, clear paths, tactile materials, seasonal variation, water when appropriate, reduction of invasive noise, zones of intimacy, and zones of openness. It must be inhabitable by different bodies: children, older adults, fragile patients, wheelchair users, sensory-sensitive subjects, people who need movement, and people who need stillness. Its sonic dimension deserves the same dignity as light, planting, and form.

For MUMEx, the garden must be mapped as a living partner. Each garden has a signature: a hospital courtyard, a therapeutic vegetable garden, a cloister, a domestic garden, a botanical garden, a small urban green space, a school park, a terrace with aromatic plants, a night garden, or a winter garden. Each creates a different relationship between body and world. A MUMEx garden map should describe zones of rest, zones of acoustic exposure, dominant natural sounds, intrusive noises, resonant surfaces, surfaces for walking, possible vocal positions, access to shade, proximity of water, and available paths of return.

This mapping is not technical bureaucracy. It is the first ethical act. The therapist does not impose a field on the garden. The therapist learns what the garden already says, where the patient's body can hear safely, and where a generative sound field may support rather than colonize the ecology already present.

A first practice is static listening. The patient is invited to remain in one point of the garden and let the sonic field arrive without immediately searching for meaning. Breath is observed. Posture is observed. The spontaneous orientation of the head is observed. Which sounds open the body? Which sounds make it defend? Which remain background? Which become figure? The question is not aesthetic preference. It is the relationship between environment and state. A person may declare love for water and discover that, today, the water agitates them. Another may not notice insects, yet their subtle carpet may support diffuse calm. The body often listens before declared preference.

A second practice comes from walking. Walking in a garden modifies listening because it introduces rhythm, weight, alternation, and spatial orientation. The step becomes a bodily metronome. Gravel answers. Soil absorbs. Wood resonates. Grass attenuates. Each surface gives the patient a different perception of presence. For dissociation or bodily estrangement, the sound of the step can become an anchor. For anxiety, walking can transform excess energy into motor sequence. For depression, progress through space can offer a minimal form of future: a point to reach, a curve, a plant, a bench, and a return.

A third practice concerns voice in the garden. The voice outdoors behaves differently from the voice in a room. It disperses, rests less on walls, meets vegetation, and changes intimacy. A whisper near an aromatic plant differs from a tone under a pergola or a sustained vowel in front of water. The patient's voice can be invited not to dominate the environment, but to enter it delicately: a brief note toward a tree, a murmur with the wind, a syllable after a bird call, a sounded breath while the hand touches a leaf. Voice ceases to be performance and becomes ecological relation.

The garden also works through smell. Music therapy cannot ignore this dimension because the human state never changes through one channel alone. Rosemary, wet earth, cut grass, flowers, wood, humidity, dry leaves, compost, warm stone, and night air all carry mnemonic and bodily force. A sound field in the garden always meets these elements. Water heard beside wet soil is not the same sound heard in headphones. A very light electronic drone among aromatic plants may be perceived as the environment's breath; the same drone in a neutral room may feel abstract. Sensory context changes the nature of sonic intervention.

Season is equally important. A spring garden may invite emergence; a summer garden may produce fullness or sensory overload; an autumn garden may support grief, decline, and transformation; a winter garden may reveal structure, silence, and endurance. The super-premium clinical language of this book must avoid simplistic symbolism, yet it should not deny seasonal intelligence. Human states often seek a season capable of holding them. MUMEx can learn from seasonal variation how to design fields that change without losing identity.

For depressed patients, the garden can restore perceptual relief. Depression often flattens the world, reduces the attractive force of objects, and makes the future opaque. The garden does not have to make the patient happy. It can offer microdifferences: a leaf edge, a bird far away, a change in light, a slightly warmer stone, a water rhythm that continues without demanding emotion. These small differences may return a minimal contour to the world. That is already state work.

For anxious patients, the garden can become a training ground for boundary and orientation. Anxiety often converts the environment into an alert system. The therapist must help distinguish signal from threat, movement from danger, variation from catastrophe. A MUMEx field should never add excessive complexity to an already vigilant body. It should provide a stable center, predictable low density, and the possibility of reducing intensity. The patient learns that a living field can change without becoming hostile.

With trauma, ecological safety is essential. Open space may feel exposed; sudden birds may startle; hidden movement in vegetation may activate hypervigilance; closing the eyes outdoors may be unsafe. Garden work can begin with open eyes, seated posture, clear exits, short duration, and patient control. The goal is not to force contact with nature. It is to find one environmental element that the body can meet without being overtaken.

A MUMEx garden field should not imitate a garden already present. It should dialogue with it. If the garden has water, the field may not need water; it may need a low resonance that lets the water become figure. If birds are present, the field may remain sparse to avoid competing. If traffic dominates, MUMEx may provide a warm layer that gives the body support without pretending to erase the city. The design principle is complementarity, not duplication.

The logbook should record location, weather, time of day, dominant sounds, intrusive sounds, patient position, walking or stillness, vocal use, volume, spatial arrangement, density, field duration, interruption signal, and debriefing. Garden fields must become documentable without losing delicacy. The more alive the environment, the more precise the record must be.

The garden's deepest therapeutic power lies in its capacity to return the patient to the world without overwhelming them. It offers reality in a softened form: not social demand, not abstraction, not spectacle, but living presence. A patient who has been trapped in mental noise can perceive that the world continues outside thought. A patient who has felt cut off from the body can find breath again through air, step, scent, and sound. A patient who has lost trust can encounter a field that changes gently and still holds together.

The garden teaches MUMEx that a field must be alive enough to interest the nervous system and coherent enough to contain it. In this sense, the garden is not scenery. It is a model of generative care. It shows how an environment can support transformation without declaring itself therapeutic at every moment. It simply lives, and the patient's state learns again how to live among variations.

CHAPTER 15

Trees, Forests, Woods, and Music Therapy

EPISTEMOLOGICAL LEVEL: *Environmental evidence / ecopsychological model. Forests, woods, and trees are considered in relation to perceptual regulation, walking, orientation, attention, and embodied sound.*

The forest is not a backdrop. It is a collective body, a breathing mass, and an acoustic organism formed by trunks, bark, canopy, roots, cavities, dry leaves, hidden animals, wind, humidity, shade, paths, slopes, absorptions, short reverberations, cracks, and sudden openings of light. Whoever enters a forest does not simply enter green space. They enter a complex perceptual structure that modifies gait, sight, hearing, breathing, the sense of distance, the posture of the head, and the quality of attention. The forest does not regulate because of sentimental naturalism. It regulates because it removes the body from the rigid geometry of the artificial environment and returns it to a web of living signals.

The city often produces frontal, rapid, defensive perception. The gaze is captured by hard surfaces, signs, vehicles, corners, crossings, hazards, screens, and mechanical noise. The ear must select, filter, and protect itself. The nervous system remains in continuous vigilance, even when the person does not name it. In the forest something different happens. The perceptual field distributes itself. There is no single center. A rustle may arrive from the left, a branch may move above the head, a bird may answer from far away, and the ground may change texture under the foot. Attention ceases to be pointed like a blade and becomes diffuse, circular, and less aggressive. This transformation of attention is already a music-therapeutic event.

Contemporary research on forest bathing, forest therapy, restorative environments, and natural soundscapes has increased interest in the effect of forests on stress, mood, anxiety, heart rate, blood pressure, cortisol, perceived well-being, and attention recovery. These findings must be read precisely: studies are heterogeneous, protocols vary, and the forest cannot be turned into a generic medicine. Yet the overall direction is strong. Intentional contact with forest environments can support psychophysiological regulation, reduce mental load, improve mood, and increase bodily presence.

For music therapy, the crucial point is not to prove that the forest "cures" in the abstract. The point is to understand how forest environments modulate sonic, respiratory, and perceptual state. The forest changes listening. It changes the distance between sound and body. It changes the patient's sense of being watched, held, exposed, or accompanied. These changes can become clinical material when the therapist documents them and designs the sound field around them.

A forest is built by vertical and horizontal acoustics. Trunks interrupt, reflect, and hide. Canopies filter wind, rain, and bird calls. The ground absorbs or cracks depending on leaves, needles, mud, stone, root, and slope. Unlike a cathedral, the forest does not produce grand reverberation; it produces countless short responses, nearby absorptions, and small depths. This is a therapeutic lesson. Not every state needs vastness. Some states need near complexity: a living density that does not engulf.

MUMEx can translate these features into field design. A forest-inspired field may use multiple small events rather than one large gesture; diffused spatial points rather than a central source; soft attacks rather than shocks; and variable absorption instead of continuous reverb. The aim is not to play a forest sample. The aim is to understand forest behavior: concealment, response, filtered distance, grounded movement, and the living alternation between figure and background.

Walking in the forest is a sonic intervention. The ground answers every step. Dry leaves crack; moss absorbs; gravel scatters; roots interrupt; mud slows; wood bridges resonate. For patients who are dissociated, depressed, anxious, or overmentalized, the sound of walking can restore bodily location. The patient hears themselves as a body in space. They are not only thinking. They are making contact.

A therapist can build a forest session around walking without turning it into exercise. The patient may be invited to listen to two steps, then stop; to notice the difference between one surface and another; to choose a slower rhythm; to let breath change with terrain; to hear how silence changes when the body is still. MUMEx, if used outdoors or in a forest-like indoor environment, should support this motor listening rather than covering it. The step is already music.

A MUMEx forest field can be designed through layers: a low earthen support, a middle layer of porous movement, rare high events, distant calls, close crackles, and a silence that contains microtraces. The field should never become a cinematic forest. Its value lies in proportionality. Too many insects, too many birds, too much reverb, or too much lushness will turn the clinical room into an immersive attraction. A therapeutic forest field must breathe, leave gaps, and allow the patient to orient.

The field may be organized by cycles rather than loops. A wind layer can increase and recede; a branch-like granular event can appear on one side, then vanish; a distant call may return irregularly; a low resonance may remain stable enough to protect the body. Gentle Perturbation becomes the leading operator: the field moves, but it does not assault; it varies, but it does not disorganize.

Forest fields may support patients who need grounding, distributed attention, sensory richness without social demand, and a more organic sense of time. They may be useful in anxiety when the field is slow, legible, and nonstartling; in depression when it restores subtle world-contour; in grief when it allows continuity and decline to coexist; in rehabilitation when walking and listening can be joined; and in older adults when forest sounds awaken environmental memory.

Contraindications must be taken seriously. Forests can also evoke fear, abandonment, darkness, vulnerability, childhood danger, hunting, storms, insects, or loss of control. A patient with trauma may not tolerate hidden sounds. A sensory-sensitive person may be overwhelmed by high microevents. A person with paranoia may not tolerate ambiguous distance. The therapist should begin with sparse fields, clear orientation, patient control, and explicit permission to stop.

The forest introduces the nonhuman witness. Trees do not respond like people, yet their presence changes the patient's experience of being alone. Many patients who feel threatened by human intimacy can tolerate the companionship of trees, wind, and distance. This is not sentimental symbolism. It is a different relational field. The patient feels accompanied without being interrogated. Presence exists without demand.

MUMEx should preserve this quality. A forest-derived field should not speak too directly. It should not interpret. It should allow the patient to be with a world that does not ask for performance. For highly defended patients, this may be crucial. The first therapeutic relationship may be with an environment that holds without looking back.

The forest must return to the room. Whether the session happens outdoors or through a MUMEx field indoors, Reintegration is necessary. The patient names the chair, floor, breath, therapist, and present time. The forest field thins; the low support becomes ordinary room resonance; distant calls disappear; the step returns to the floor. What matters is not to leave the patient enchanted by a simulated nature. What matters is to let the forest teach the body a form of attention that can survive after the field ends.

The forest gives Quantum Music Therapy a severe lesson: the most powerful environment is often the one that does not insist. It surrounds, filters, absorbs, interrupts, and renews. It lets the organism remember that life is not flat, that attention can widen, and that the body can belong to a field larger than its symptoms.

CHAPTER 16

Birdsong as a Replicable Sonic Model

EPISTEMOLOGICAL LEVEL: *Bioacoustic model. Birdsong is considered as a matrix of microvariation, call-and-response, spatial behavior, vocal learning, and generative form.*

Birdsong obliges music therapy to think generativity with finer precision. Few natural phenomena reveal so clearly the coexistence of biological necessity, musical form, variation, call, response, territory, learning, memory, and sudden beauty. Birds sing for reasons that precede human aesthetics: they defend space, attract partners, coordinate presence, signal, learn, recognize, mark distance, and participate in an ecological fabric. Yet the human ear receives that singing as something that exceeds function. It hears phrase, timbre, rhythm, attack, suspension, return, surprise, and fragile architecture of air.

This ambiguity is precious. Birdsong was not created to console human beings, and for that reason it can educate therapeutic listening. It is not music engineered to produce a psychological effect. It is living behavior, inscribed in a body, species, environment, season, hour of day, and field of relations. When it enters music therapy, it should not become naturalistic decoration. It should become a model of organization: how a microphrase is born, how it repeats, how it varies, how it occupies space, how it answers another sound, and how it leaves air around itself.

Bioacoustics has shown how structured birdsong can be. Many species organize their repertoire into syllables, motifs, sequences, phrases, and transitions. Some songs follow ordering rules; others show probabilistic variation; others reveal local dialects, social learning, auditory feedback, practice, and consolidation. Songbirds have become an important model for vocal learning because they show sensitive periods, tutors, motor practice, correction, memory, and specialized neural circuits. Nature here offers a double lesson: singing is a body that learns, and learning is sound that stabilizes without losing vitality (Bolhuis et al., 2010; Jarvis, 2004).

For MUMEx, the essential feature is microvariation. A therapeutic field can learn from birdsong how to remain recognizable without becoming mechanical. A motif may return, but not as a copied loop. It may change interval, position, density, contour, or spatial distance. The patient receives continuity and novelty at once. This is precisely the grammar needed for Gentle Perturbation: small enough to be tolerated, alive enough to move the state.

Birdsong is often spatial before it is musical. A call marks distance. Another answers. Territory is drawn through air. A sound high in the canopy differs from one close to the ground. A solitary call differs from a dense chorus. A distant call differs from a near one. A clean recording differs from a soundscape contaminated by traffic. Active listening differs from background ambience. Music therapy must bring these distinctions into practice instead of settling for the generic category of natural sounds.

Call-and-response has immediate clinical value. A patient may listen to a brief call and answer with voice, whistle, hand drum, breath, or silence. The answer does not need to imitate. It only needs to establish relation. This can be especially useful when direct speech is difficult. A bird-like exchange allows contact without full verbal exposure. The field becomes a safe distance where communication can begin as signal before becoming statement.

Artificial generation raises ethical and aesthetic questions. To replicate birdsong through synthesis, sampling, or generative models is to touch material belonging to living species, ecosystems, and territories. Technical quality is not enough. Respect is required. Birdsong should not become acoustic merchandise emptied of its environment. A recording should be used with awareness of context. A synthesis should acknowledge the distance between model and organism. MUMEx may create fields inspired by birds while avoiding the pretense of replacing the living world. Nature remains teacher, not archive to be plundered.

The difference between imitation and transfiguration is decisive. Imitation copies surface. Transfiguration grasps a principle and carries it into another domain. A MUMEx field may use quick melodic contours without sounding like a bird, spatial alternations without realistic samples, or granular microattacks that evoke life without naturalism. This path is often more powerful. It frees the patient from postcard nature and brings them toward new perception. The avian model becomes an archetype of light, mobile, breathing generativity.

In trauma work, avian sounds require extreme measure. High pitch, sudden attack, and unpredictability may activate alarm. At the same time, a distant, stable, rare call placed in a soft field can help the patient orient to the present. The clinical question is always the window of tolerance. Birdsong must not surprise the body as an uncontrollable event. It must enter with a quantity of life compatible with the state. In some cases it is better to begin with lower registers, less acute timbres, and wide intervals, allowing the avian profile to appear only at the edge.

In depression, birdsong can work on the relief of the world. Depressive suffering often flattens the environment. Everything seems equal, distant, and without attraction. A well-dosed avian microevent can create a small but precise difference. It does not demand joy. It indicates that something is happening. One distant call, another answer, a lateral response, an interval of waiting: the field begins to show margins and directions again. The patient may not feel happy, yet the world stops being an opaque wall for a moment.

In anxiety, the main value may be orientation. Anxiety often hears the world as diffuse threat. Birdsong teaches the nervous system to distinguish signals without catastrophizing them: high, far, near, brief, repeated, stable, harmless. A MUMEx field can transform this distinction into practice. The patient learns to follow a sound, let it vanish, wait for return, and perceive that minimal unpredictability does not equal danger.

With children on the autism spectrum or with delicate sensory profiles, caution must be high. Some children may be drawn to short recognizable sequences; others may be overloaded by acute or irregular sounds. Avian models should offer control: volume, distance, call type, pause, interruption, imitation, response, and reduction. The brief form can be an advantage because it allows clear turns. A child can hear a call and answer with a gesture, syllable, instrument, or movement. The field becomes regulated dialogue.

With older adults, especially in cognitive fragility, birdsong may reopen environmental memory. Before narrative memory, a climate returns: a summer morning, a window, a courtyard, countryside, a journey, a house. Birdsong can act as an index of world. It must be dosed delicately, avoiding dense environments that confuse. A simple, recognizable texture with few spatial events can support orientation and affection without requiring explanation. Memory does not always return as a sentence. Sometimes it returns as a posture of listening.

A MUMEx field based on birdsong should begin with mapping. First the therapist listens to the patient. Then the profile is defined: more realistic or more abstract, nearer or farther, denser or rarer, more diurnal or crepuscular, more social or solitary, more vocal or timbral. Then the trajectory is established: entry, first calls, possible dialogue with voice or instrument, spatial expansion, reduction, and return. Avian material permits extraordinary delicacy if it is not used to fill the field.

Replicability must be understood seriously. To replicate birdsong does not mean to reproduce identical audio files. It means to make the principles observable: number of events per minute, average cell duration, prevailing register, dynamic range, spatial position, variation among repetitions, sound-silence ratio, response to patient gesture, and progression over time. This replicability is compatible with generativity. Indeed, it strengthens it. Two sessions may not produce the same sounds while sharing the same formal and therapeutic logic.

Birdsong teaches the value of incompletion. Many calls seem to open without closing according to Western tonal expectations. They are arrows, flashes, curves, not completed periods. This quality can help patients trapped in the need for formal control. A brief fragment permits not knowing immediately where the field will go. It allows curiosity. In an age saturated by overproduced music, the imperfect call of the bird returns a nonindustrial freshness to listening. The sound seems born before composition, and for that reason it touches a primary zone of perception.

Quantum Music Therapy should treat birdsong as a school of proportion. No element should be too large for the listening body. No beauty should become invasion. No naturalness should become disguise. The task is to create fields that are light but incisive, capable of awakening orientation, curiosity, response, memory, and presence without forcing the experience into pastoral rhetoric. Birdsong is powerful because it remains minute. Its greatness lies in the precision of the small.

CHAPTER 17

The Sonic World of Animals

EPISTEMOLOGICAL LEVEL: *Bioacoustic and ethological model. Animal sound is considered as a repertoire of body, voice, instinct, territory, care, alarm, and nonhuman alterity.*

The sonic world of animals returns music therapy to a region before articulated language, before the sentence, and before the social policing of voice. Growls, breaths, calls, howls, whistles, bellows, buzzes, cries, murmurs, guttural vibrations, and group signals compose an immense atlas of bodies that communicate without separating sound from posture, territory, hunger, fear, desire, care, alarm, and play. The animal emits sound with the whole organism. Voice is not content to be interpreted; it is muscle, breath, orientation, distance, and contact.

For MUMEx Quantum Music Therapy, this evidence is decisive. The human being retains vocal and motor strata that culture has educated, refined, compressed, and sometimes imprisoned. Many patients arrive in therapy with a domesticated voice: thin, controlled, socially correct, and poorly breathed. They can describe discomfort while failing to emit a full sound. They can name anger while being unable to give it body. They can speak of fear while freezing before an elemental vocal gesture. The animal layer of voice, when excluded, can become symptom: tight throat, rigid jaw, mute chest, contracted diaphragm, and a body that thinks too much while vibrating too little.

Animality here does not mean crude regression, loss of dignity, or theatrical instinct. It means biological wisdom before the mental mask. A dog that growls establishes a boundary. A cat that hisses declares distance. A wolf howl links individual presence with group field. A whale sends long modulated signals through marine space. Dolphins work with whistles and clicks of orientation. Horses communicate through breath, whinny, weight shift, and muscular tension. Primates call, warn, gather, and organize social life. Each species builds a specific relationship among sound, body, and environment.

Therapy can learn from this unity: no sound is separate from the body that emits it and the field in which it takes meaning. A patient's voice cannot be treated as an isolated expressive channel. It carries territory: how close the other may come, where the body feels defended, what distance is safe, whether contact is desired or feared. Animal models remind the music therapist that voice is not only beauty. It is boundary, appetite, mourning, attachment, alarm, and play.

Animal sounds must not be used as decorative effects. The animal world is not a cabinet of exotic timbres for human self-care. It is a field of other lives. Ethical use begins with humility. A whale call is not a mystical wallpaper. A wolf howl is not automatically a symbol of freedom. Insects are not simply texture. Each sound comes from an organism, a species, an ecological function, and a territory. MUMEx may learn from animal sonics, but it must avoid appropriating the living world as a theatrical resource.

Alterity is clinically important. Many patients suffer from an excessively humanized field: too many words, too many evaluations, too much social self-monitoring. Animal sound can introduce another order of presence. It can remind the body that communication may be breath, signal, distance, rhythm, posture, and intensity before it becomes explanation. This can be liberating, especially when verbal therapy has become a cage of polished self-description.

Work with animal vocality can begin without imitation. The patient may explore a breath, a hum, a low vibration, a brief call, a soft growl, a protective exhalation, a playful whistle, or a syllable without semantic burden. The therapist must protect dignity. The aim is not to make the patient "act like an animal." The aim is to release a layer of voice that is still human because it belongs to the human body, yet it is freer than social speech.

This practice can be especially useful when shame has captured the voice. A person may find it impossible to sing but possible to make a small nonverbal sound. A person who cannot say "no" may discover a boundary through a low tone. A person who cannot express grief may find a long exhaled sound. A child may communicate through call before phrase. The clinical value lies in the restoration of sonic agency: the body learns that it can emit, mark, answer, and withdraw.

MUMEx can translate animal sound worlds through principles rather than mimicry. Herd animals teach group regulation, proximity, and subtle contact signals. Predators teach silence, tension, and sudden event. Marine mammals teach long-distance resonance and spatial depth. Insects teach microdensity and pulse fields. Amphibians teach night chorus, periodicity, and humidity of sound. Domestic animals teach attachment, familiarity, and cross-species listening. These are not ready-made therapeutic recipes; they are models of sonic behavior.

An animal-derived MUMEx field might therefore be organized around breath, low bodily presence, call-and-response, group density, or territorial spacing without presenting recognizable animal samples. In other cases, carefully chosen recordings may be used when their context and clinical purpose are clear. The distinction matters. A realistic animal sound can be powerful, but it can also become too literal, triggering fear, nostalgia, grief, or distraction. Abstracted principles often allow a safer and more refined transformation.

The animal layer touches aggression and boundary. This makes it clinically precious and clinically risky. A growl can restore strength; it can also unleash shame or fear. A howl can open grief; it can also feel ridiculous. A roar can organize energy; it can also overwhelm. The therapist must dose intensity with precision, provide alternatives, and keep the patient in control. No one should be pushed into animal sound because the therapist finds it expressive. The patient's dignity is the first container.

With trauma, the therapist should avoid sudden predatory, high-alert, or hidden sounds unless the patient has prepared for them and requested that territory. With anxiety, animal sound may require low volume and clear distance. With depression, small living signals may help restore vitality without demanding emotional display. With children, animal vocality can be playful, but play must still be regulated. With older adults, domestic animal sounds may evoke attachment or loss and should be introduced gently.

Where real animals are involved, the work enters another ethical domain. Animal-assisted interventions require training, consent, hygiene, safety, welfare, and clear professional boundaries. The animal is not a tool. It is a participant with needs and limits. The patient's comfort and the animal's welfare must both be protected. A music-therapeutic approach that includes live animals must collaborate with qualified handlers and avoid improvising clinical procedures from affection alone.

Even without live animals, ethical respect remains. Recordings should be sourced responsibly when possible. Species context should be known. Cultural meanings should not be imposed lazily. The animal world deserves more than symbolic consumption. It teaches humans because it remains other. The therapeutic value lies precisely in that otherness: a sound that does not flatter the human ego, yet returns the human body to its own living basis.

The wild body is not the opposite of the civilized person. It is the living basis that civilization needs in order not to become sterile. Quantum Music Therapy can help patients recover parts of voice, breath, boundary, and movement that have been overcontrolled or exiled. Yet every opening must return. After a session involving animal vocality or animal-derived fields, the patient should come back to human speech, ordinary posture, room orientation, and social dignity. Reintegration prevents the work from becoming theatrical release without clinical meaning.

The sonic world of animals teaches that sound is action. It marks, protects, calls, bonds, warns, and plays. MUMEx can translate this insight into generative fields that restore the body's right to signal. The aim is not to become animal. The aim is to become more fully embodied as human beings who still remember that voice begins in life before it becomes language.

CHAPTER 18

Natural Soundscapes and Perceptual Healing

EPISTEMOLOGICAL LEVEL: *Soundscape evidence / perceptual model. Natural soundscapes are treated through an ecological and contextual approach to perceptual healing, not as generic relaxation loops.*

A natural soundscape is not a pleasant recording to be used as relaxing background. It is a living fabric of presences, distances, materials, rhythms, signals, gaps, cycles, returns, and sudden appearances. Water, wind, insects, fire, stone, sea, caves, storms, canopies, steps on earth, cracks, distant calls, and minute vibrations of undergrowth compose a perceptual order that precedes composed music and also instructs it. Before any instrument, the world produced sound fields. Before any scale, it organized pitch, density, resonance, periodicity, colored noise, and active silence. Before any sound therapy, human beings were already being cared for or wounded by the way the world resonated around them.

The term soundscape transformed contemporary acoustic thought because it shifted attention from isolated sound to the environment in which sound becomes meaningful. A stream is not merely flowing water. It is proximity, continuity, imagined freshness, microvariation, orientation, moving surface, and promise of life. Wind is not merely rustling. It is moving air that makes audible what is usually invisible: leaves, cracks, branches, grasses, and distance. Thunder is not merely loud noise. It is atmospheric dramaturgy: pressure, waiting, impact, water, altered light, smell of earth, and the return of quiet.

Soundscape ecology distinguishes three major components: geophony, biophony, and anthropophony. Geophony includes the nonbiological sounds of the earth: water, wind, rain, waves, ice, fire, and material movement. Biophony gathers the sounds of living organisms: birds, insects, mammals, amphibians, fish, vegetation in motion, and acoustic communities. Anthropophony concerns the human soundprint: motors, traffic, machines, systems, amplified voices, industrial noise, and artificial signals.

This tripartition has therapeutic value because it reveals a decisive fact: the modern patient often lives in an impoverished acoustic world, saturated with anthropophony and poor in geophony and biophony. The body loses contact with sonic cycles that accompanied waking, resting, hunting, walking, orientation, protection, fear, desire, and belonging for millennia. Perceptual healing may require not only quieter spaces, but richer sonic ecologies.

Music therapy must rescue natural sounds from the market of standardized wellness. App-based rain, ocean loops, birdsong used as acoustic wallpaper, and synthetic forests repeating identically for hours may be pleasant, yet they often betray the strength of the soundscape. Nature is not a loop. It does not repeat the same phrase without transforming it. Its order arises from variation, relation, event, density, withdrawal, measured unpredictability, and cycles. A therapeutic natural soundscape must preserve this life or honestly declare that it is only a background.

MUMEx can offer a more refined path because it works generatively. Instead of reproducing a rain file, it can generate evolving aquatic fields. Instead of overlaying random birds, it can build logics of call and response. Instead of simulating a forest like a postcard, it can model layers: geophonic base, peripheral biophony, distance, orientation, seasonal variation, rare appearances, and silence. Instead of using nature as ornamental content, it can translate natural principles: cyclicity, microvariation, stratification, coexistence, emergent events, proportion, and return.

Perceptual work should begin with a biographical sound map. Which natural sounds belong to the patient's life? What water do they know: sea, river, rain, fountain, well, lake? What wind have they inhabited: countryside, mountain, city, childhood home? Which animals have mattered? Which sounds generate safety, nostalgia, irritation, fear, or longing? Which silences are tolerable? Which landscapes are culturally familiar? The natural soundscape is not universal. Every person carries an acoustic geography of memory.

A session based on natural soundscapes can begin very simply: an almost empty field, distant water, few microevents, low volume, therapist presence, and the possibility of choosing distance and density. The patient should not be immersed immediately. They must be able to enter the field, modify it, refuse it, name it, or ignore it. Therapy does not consist in bringing the patient into idealized nature. It consists in allowing sonic nature to meet the present state without violating it.

In individual work, natural soundscapes can become mirrors of state. One patient always chooses strong wind: perhaps they seek movement, perhaps they only know instability, perhaps they want to erase inner voice. Another chooses caves: perhaps they seek protection, perhaps they fear openness, perhaps they desire a return inward. Another refuses water: perhaps flow feels too emotional, perhaps liquid continuity destabilizes. The therapist listens to these choices as subtle clinical data without interpreting too soon.

In group work, the natural soundscape can create nonverbal belonging. Participants may contribute voice, objects, small percussion, breath, imitations of wind, water, animals, or steps. MUMEx can sustain the generative ground while the group produces human biophony. The room becomes a temporary ecosystem. Each participant hears that they influence the common climate. A sound too strong changes the balance; a sudden silence alters the landscape; a distant voice creates orientation. The group learns relational ecology through sonic ecology.

Spatial dimension is essential. Natural sounds should not all come from the same point. Nature does not speak from a central loudspeaker. It surrounds, answers, withdraws, appears behind, above, below, at the edge, and in depth. Immersive spatialization can restore part of this complexity if it remains sober. A spectacular field turns the session into a sensory attraction. A well-designed field allows the body to orient. Orientation is already care: knowing where a sound is helps the patient know where the body is.

Silence must also be rethought. In natural soundscapes, absolute silence is rare. There are silences full of microevents: air, distance, far insects, minimal water, crackles, and the body listening. Many patients fear silence because they associate it with mental emptiness, abandonment, or lack of response. A natural silence can be inhabited. MUMEx can generate porous silences, with almost imperceptible traces, able to support those who cannot tolerate complete acoustic void.

Realistic recording and symbolic generation are two different paths. Field recording carries the memory of place: impurity, accidents, real life, and unplanned events. MUMEx generation offers control, adaptation, trajectory, and safety. The most fertile practice may arise from their encounter: real recordings analyzed, decomposed, and transformed into generative principles. Do not copy the forest; understand how it breathes. Do not imitate the sea; study its alternation. Do not use insects as an effect; translate their microstructure into inhabitable density.

Natural soundscape work introduces ecological responsibility. To listen to the world is to recognize that many environments are losing voice. The reduction of biodiversity also produces acoustic impoverishment: fewer birds, fewer insects, less complexity, more human noise. Perceptual care cannot be separated entirely from care for the sonic planet. A patient who regains sensitivity toward water, wind, birds, insects, and forests may also develop a different alliance with the living world.

In this perspective, music therapy does not work only on the interior. It repairs the relationship between the human organism and the world. This statement should not be romanticized. It should be operationalized. Each soundscape field should document geophonic, biophonic, and anthropophonic composition; density; distance; predictability; rare events; maximum intensity; duration; spatial behavior; patient choice; and signals of return. Description does not impoverish the poetry of the field. It makes it shareable.

A MUMEx natural soundscape protocol should proceed by assessment, mapping, field design, patient choice, gradual exposure, modulation, and Reintegration. The therapist first identifies the patient's biographical sound map and tolerance. Then the field is selected or generated with a clear ratio among stability, variation, and event. The patient chooses distance or density when possible. The therapist observes breath, posture, gaze, startle, curiosity, and withdrawal. The field is modified rather than imposed. Finally, the soundscape returns to room, body, and speech.

After a field of sea, cave, wind, or storm, the patient must recover the room, body, breath, therapist, and possible word. Water may diminish until it becomes breath. Wind may transform into voice. Thunder may dissolve into warm silence. Animal presence may withdraw and leave feet on the floor. Reintegration is the difference between suggestive experience and responsible therapeutic work.

Natural soundscapes teach that life can heal through complexity—not chaotic complexity, but living order made of variations, signals, returns, distances, bodies, and materials. Contemporary human beings often suffer in acoustic environments that are poor or violent: noises without depth, functional music, alerts, notifications, engines, compression, and breathless spaces. To restore a natural soundscape is not to flee reality. It is to remind the perceptual system that the world can still be articulated, breathing, and inhabitable. Part Four therefore completes a crucial turn: after inner vastness, the work returns to the living world. The next movement will enter MUMEx itself as an architecture of generative fields.

PART FIVE

MUMEx AND GENERATIVE SOUND FIELDS

CHAPTER 19

MUMEx: Generative Architecture and Philosophy

EPISTEMOLOGICAL LEVEL: *Technological-generative model. This chapter defines MUMEx as an architecture of memory, density, variation, nonlinearity, adaptivity, and clinical governability.*

MUMEx—MUSIC MULTIVERSE EXPLORATION—enters the center of Quantum Music Therapy at the moment sound ceases to be treated as a completed object and begins to be understood as an environment in birth. A musical work has a fixed contour. A recording preserves its own destiny. A playlist arranges materials whose forms have already been decided. A Generative Sound Field operates differently: it emerges from rules, memory, variation, density, orientation, and the possibility of transformation. It does not hand the patient a closed form. It creates a temporal space in which body, attention, breath, and imagination may reorganize themselves.

The word generative must be rescued from fashion. It does not mean producing abundant material, nor does it mean allowing an algorithm to manufacture sonic events without responsibility. To generate, in the strongest sense, is to create conditions of birth. A MUMEx field has value only when change preserves internal necessity. Variation must be related to the human state, the therapeutic relationship, the trajectory of the session, and the quality of return. A therapeutic generative system becomes poor when it merely surprises. It becomes powerful when it creates living continuity.

The first architectural quality is memory. Without memory, generation becomes organized noise or mutable decoration. Memory allows the field to preserve a relationship with what has already occurred: a rhythmic cell, a timbral curve, a previous density, a pause, a figure, or a register. The patient is not exposed to a succession of unrelated events. They inhabit an environment that recognizes its own history. The formal continuity of the field may support psychic continuity, especially in people who are dispersed, fragmented, hyperactivated, or invaded by mental noise.

Memory in MUMEx must not be confused with repetition. Repetition may reassure, yet it may also imprison. To remember is to transform without losing identity. A material returns in another light, with lower density, a different register, a softer dynamic profile, or a more distant spatial position. The body perceives something familiar and renewed at the same time. In that delicate interval, a therapeutic possibility opens: the person encounters continuity without immobility.

The second architectural quality is variation. Every living organism varies. The heartbeat is not a metronome. Breath is not a machine. Human walking is not a perfect grid. Variation brings life into the field, provided that it remains legible. A microvariation of timbre can make a drone breathe; a minimal oscillation of density can prevent saturation; a slight rhythmic deviation can keep the body from falling into automaticity. The therapist must distinguish nourishing variation from invasive variation. In MUMEx this distinction becomes a design question: how much movement can this state support now without losing safety?

The third quality is nonlinearity. The human state does not respond proportionally to stimulus. A minimal change can produce a major transition; an intense event may pass without effect; a pause may carry more weight than a complex sequence. MUMEx generation must accept this logic. The task is not to increase energy in order to obtain response, nor to reduce sound in order to obtain calm. The task is to design conditions. The field works on internal probabilities, not on emotional buttons.

The most useful image is therefore that of a sonic organism. An organism breathes, contracts, expands, reacts, conserves memory, spends energy, and alternates activity with rest. The image does not replace technical description; it gives the architecture a criterion. A field without breath sounds artificial even when built from natural samples. A field saturated with detail suffocates. Excessive predictability anesthetizes. Excessive mutability disperses. Vitality emerges from the proportion between stability and transformation.

MUMEx gives technical body to a severe intuition: music can be described as a system of states, and each sonic state can act on a human state. The operational nucleus may be kept in the formula already introduced in the theoretical section: rho_H(t + Delta t) = E_{S,C}(rho_H(t)). The human state evolves through the joint action of the sound field S and the context C. There is no isolated frequency, no magic formula, and no therapeutic automatism. Sound operates within a living context: room, body, therapist, history, consent, intensity, silence, duration, voice, and the possibility of interruption.

Technically, this means that MUMEx does not merely generate sequences. It organizes fields with duration, edge, density, depth, direction, memory, and temporal character. A field may be rarefied or compact, pulsating or granular, material or transparent, unstable or breathing. It may orient perception toward the body, an image, silence, movement, landscape, or Reintegration. A parameter becomes meaningful only when it answers a question about state: what does this register support, what does this density expose, what does this distance protect, what does this silence make possible?

Timbre is perhaps the most delicate material. Before pitch, rhythm, or form are named, the body recognizes matter: rough, warm, metallic, opaque, luminous, wooden, liquid, granular, vocal, animal, organic, or electric. Timbre touches memories that precede narrative. A low band may provide support; a metallic sound may evoke alarm; an air grain may open breath; a vocal component may activate attachment; badly dosed white noise may erase instead of contain. MUMEx architecture must treat timbre as a primary clinical element.

Density determines how much sonic matter occupies the field. High density means many events, many relationships, and a high level of acoustic information. Low density means space, waiting, and greater exposure of the subject to themselves. Both can help and both can harm. A depressed patient may need minimal density to avoid invasion, or a richer thread to avoid falling into emptiness. An anxious patient may be soothed by ordered structure or irritated by excessive detail. Density must become a therapeutic control, not an aesthetic preference.

Silence inside MUMEx is a positive parameter. It is not the absence of field; it is part of the field. A mature generative system must know how to create conditions for silence: rarefaction, suspension of events, waiting, decay, and listening space. Silence allows the patient to perceive the residual effect of sound in the body. It allows the therapist to observe. It allows voice to emerge. It prevents the field from becoming dependency. The power of the system is measured also by the quality of the voids it can leave.

Time must be designed with equal precision. MUMEx can construct linear time, circular time, suspended time, pulsating time, granular time, and the time of return. Human distress often deforms temporality: anxiety accelerates and anticipates; depression slows and empties; trauma fractures the present; dissociation increases distance; trance concentrates;

meditation dilates. The field should be able to meet these temporal distortions without merely reproducing them. A decisive perceptual change may begin when a person discovers that another duration can be inhabited.

The fourth quality is adaptivity. A therapeutic Generative Sound Field should be able to change in relation to the session. Adaptation may occur directly through the therapist's gesture; it may occur through preset parameters; it may be oriented by light physiological signals such as breath, heart rate variability, or movement; it may derive from patient choice. The highest adaptivity is not maximum automation. Often the most clinical adaptation is the one decided by a human presence observing a body and modifying a parameter with restraint.

MUMEx must remain governable. A technology that produces complexity without control produces fascination and risk. The music therapist must know which dimensions are active, which limits are set, which transitions are possible, and which events are excluded. The field must not surprise the therapist beyond the therapist's capacity to contain it. Therapeutic generativity requires an ethical perimeter: no unplanned sudden peak, no dynamic invasion, no instability that prevents return, and no decision-making opacity when the patient is vulnerable.

From this requirement emerges the role of the logbook. Every field should leave a trace. Not sterile bureaucracy, but a memory of the process: duration, average density, dominant register, dynamics, variation type, emergent events, silences, transitions, therapist modifications, physiological signals when present, phenomenological notes, and the patient's words after the session. The logbook makes the field discussable. It allows the therapist to return to what happened, compare experiences, identify patterns, correct errors, and build research. A practice without trace remains impression. A trace without listening becomes a dead archive. MUMEx must hold both dimensions together.

The logbook also protects against mythologizing the session. If a field produced a powerful experience, the question must be asked with precision: what was the density? what was the maximum level? what was the temporal curve? when did the patient's breath change? what was removed? when did silence arrive? how did the patient return? This discipline does not diminish mystery. It gives mystery a body capable of being examined.

The philosophy of MUMEx requires a discipline of sonic matter. Every parameter should be justifiable. Why this register? Why this density? Why this duration? Why this spatial distance? Why this degree of unpredictability? Why this absence of pulse? Why this return? The criterion is neither the isolated taste of the composer nor the technical fascination of the system. The criterion is the relationship between sound field and human state.

The music therapist of the generative field is not reduced to operator. The therapist becomes custodian, composer of conditions, reader of microstates, and ethical governor of intensity. They must know when to support and when to remove; when to let the field continue and when to stop it; when to allow the system to breathe and when to bring in the human voice. The more powerful the field becomes, the more necessary human responsibility becomes.

Within this hierarchy, the human voice remains sovereign. The patient's voice carries identity, risk, body, and history; the therapist's voice carries presence, containment, and orientation. MUMEx must be able to lower its density, clear the midrange, suspend events, or withdraw altogether when a voice enters. A system that covers the human voice has failed, however sophisticated its generation may be. The same principle governs improvisation: the field may provide continuity and memory, while the human gesture retains precedence, uncertainty, and the right to change the course of the session.

This discipline does not impoverish creativity. It sharpens it. A composer trained to think form can enter MUMEx with enormous advantage, provided they renounce the temptation to dominate the patient with the beauty of the work. A session is not a concert. Aesthetic quality remains decisive because poorly designed sound assaults the perceptual field. Yet therapeutic beauty is not identical to beauty for pure listening. It is responsible beauty: capable of sustaining, withdrawing, waiting, simplifying, and returning.

The composer's posture changes accordingly. In a closed work, form is shaped for the listener. In a therapeutic generative field, form must leave room for another person to exist inside it. This requires a composition of hospitality. Greatness lies less in displaying invention than in creating an environment capable of receiving a fragile, contradictory, changing presence. The field becomes an architecture of welcome: rigorous enough to hold, porous enough to be altered by the person who enters it.

MUMEx therefore proposes a grammar of state. It teaches the therapist to think through density, register, spectrum, dynamics, time, unpredictability, morphology, memory, spatiality, and energetic curve. This literacy must not turn the therapist into an engineer. It must offer a more precise language for governing the field. The next step is to examine electronic and spatialized sound as a clinical material rather than as spectacle.

One fertile extension of this architecture is fractal memory. Natural systems often show kinship across scales—branches, coastlines, clouds, flows, veins, waves, flocks, distributions of events. MUMEx can use related logics to create structures that feel alive without imitating nature superficially. A figure may return at another scale, density, register, or temporal span. The value is not that a pattern is fractal. The value lies in whether scale-dependent repetition creates complexity the body can inhabit rather than complexity that merely demonstrates itself.

Physiological adaptation must remain subordinate to the same discipline. Breath, heart rate variability, movement, or other light signals may inform the field and may allow a participant to hear that bodily action changes the environment. Yet no physiological signal is the truth of the person. HRV can inform; it cannot interpret. Breath can guide; it cannot command. Data enters the therapeutic relation as evidence to be considered, never as an oracle. The highest level of adaptivity is not maximum automation. It is the capacity to use information without surrendering judgment.

CHAPTER 20

Immersive and Spatialized Electronic Sound in Music-Therapy Practice

EPISTEMOLOGICAL LEVEL: *Technical-operational model. Immersive and spatialized electronic sound are considered as clinical materials only when level, duration, consent, orientation, and return are precisely governed.*

Electronic sound is often misunderstood in therapeutic contexts. It is either treated as technological novelty or rejected as artificial. Both reactions are too simple. Electronic sound is not less embodied because it is produced by circuits, synthesis, sampling, code, or digital processing. The body does not ask whether a vibration began in wood, metal, string, membrane, voltage, oscillator, or algorithm. The body asks how the vibration arrives, how it behaves, how it relates to breath, how it occupies space, and whether it respects the threshold of the person who receives it.

The power of electronic sound lies in its capacity to create materials unavailable to conventional acoustic instruments: infinitely slow morphologies, sustained spectral bands, sub-audible pressure, granular clouds, spatial trajectories, microtonal fields, decays that extend beyond human gesture, and timbral forms that are neither instrumental nor natural. These possibilities are not automatically therapeutic. They become therapeutic only when governed by clinical intention, aesthetic intelligence, and ethical containment.

Binaural reproduction, multichannel diffusion, and Ambisonics address the same fundamental problem through different architectures: how to give sound a credible place. Binaural work, usually through headphones, relies on interaural differences and filtering to create intimacy, motion, and apparent externalization. Multichannel systems distribute real sources through a physical room. Ambisonics represents the field spherically and can be decoded for different loudspeaker arrays. None of these techniques has therapeutic value by itself. Their value begins only when technical precision is subordinated to orientation, consent, body, and setting.

Immersion is not spectacle. A room filled with sound may impress the listener and still fail therapeutically. Contemporary culture often confuses immersive experience with intensity, surround sound, visual wow, and technological display. Quantum Music Therapy must move in the opposite direction. Immersion means that the patient is placed within a field that can be inhabited. The field surrounds, supports, orients, and transforms without demanding submission. Its purpose is not to overwhelm consciousness, but to give consciousness a new acoustic world in which to reorganize.

The therapist must therefore ask sober questions. Does the patient know where they are? Do they retain the possibility of stopping? Is the sound near enough to support or too near and invasive? Is movement around the body calming or threatening? Does the field produce depth or loss of orientation? Is the patient curious, absorbed, frozen, dissociated, or seduced? Immersion must always be assessed by state, not by technical achievement.

Spatialization is one of the most powerful variables in MUMEx because sound is never only heard. It locates the body. A sound in front of the patient may offer direction. A sound behind may activate vigilance. A sound above may open vertical imagination. A sound at the side may stimulate peripheral awareness. A distant source may create landscape. A near source may create intimacy or invasion. Spatial movement can organize attention, yet it can also destabilize patients who need stable boundaries.

The clinical value of spatialization lies in orientation. A patient who has lost bodily location may hear a stable low field beneath or in front of them and regain a sense of ground. A patient trapped in frontal cognitive control may benefit from gentle peripheral events. A patient in grief may encounter distant sound as a form of continuing world. A patient with trauma may require spatial stability before any movement is introduced. Spatialization is therefore not an effect. It is a therapeutic geometry.

Proximity and distance deserve separate attention because they carry different relational meanings. A very near sound can communicate intimacy, support, or containment; the same nearness can become invasion. A distant sound can open internal space, memory, or desire for movement; it can also intensify abandonment or isolation. MUMEx can modulate apparent distance slowly, almost respiratorily, allowing a sound to approach without assault, remain at the perceptual edge, become a lateral support, then withdraw. Such microdramaturgy can teach the body that contact need not equal attack and distance need not equal loss.

Loudspeakers and headphones create different therapeutic realities. Loudspeakers allow the sound to enter the room, meet the body, and become part of shared space. The therapist hears what the patient hears, though each body receives differently. There is distance, air, and the possibility of spatial relation. Headphones create intimacy and isolation. They can help when external distraction must be reduced, yet they may also intensify vulnerability, reduce therapist containment, or produce a sense of being sealed inside the field.

The room is never neutral. Walls, floor, ceiling, furniture, curtains, windows, resonant corners, and patient position all modify the sound field. A low frequency in one corner may become overwhelming. A beautiful drone may turn muddy in a small room. A granular texture may become brittle through a specific speaker. A clinical room must be listened to before the session. The therapist should know where the patient sits, how the field behaves at that point, and where volume limits must be set.

The field must therefore be verified bodily in the actual room. The therapist should walk the space, sit where the patient will sit, listen standing and seated, test the lowest practical level, examine corners, reflections, and low-frequency accumulation, and hear how the system changes when a body is present. Spatial design created only on a computer is incomplete. The room is part of the instrument, and the body is the final measurement surface.

Sub-bass and low-frequency materials require particular care. They may create ground, weight, containment, and bodily presence. They may also produce discomfort, anxiety, pressure, nausea, or the sense of being invaded. No claim should be made that low frequencies act on organs in a deterministic way. What matters clinically is felt resonance, tolerance, duration, level, and context. The patient's report, posture, breath, and possible stop signal are more important than any theoretical frequency association.

Movement and reverberation create another layer of architecture. Rapid rotation around the body may produce fascination, vertigo, or destabilization; slow movement can support orientation with far greater precision. Reverberation changes the felt size of the world. A dry field can feel concrete and controllable. A long decay can open depth, suspension, or sacred distance. Too much reverberation erases boundaries; too little can expose the listener harshly. In MUMEx, speed and reverberant depth should be treated as state variables, with drier, clearer conditions for orientation and broader, slower spaces only when the body can tolerate them.

Drones can sustain continuity, yet they may also trap the patient in sameness. Granular textures can introduce life and microvariation, yet they may irritate sensory-sensitive subjects. Metallic spectra may awaken attention, yet they may activate alarm. Bright high material can open space or become painful. Electronic sound makes these parameters finely adjustable. This precision is a gift and a responsibility. Every increase in control creates an equal obligation to use control with restraint.

A super-premium clinical edition must speak clearly about sound level. Volume should never be left to intuition alone. Sessions should define maximum sound pressure level when possible, document subjective comfort, avoid sudden peaks, and use gradual onset and offset. The field should be tested in the room before the patient enters. If sub-bass or strong vibration is involved, contraindications, consent, and duration must be especially clear. The purpose is not fear. The purpose is professionalism.

Documentation should include playback system, speaker configuration, headphone model when used, approximate listening level, patient position, room notes, duration, peak events, silence periods, spatial movement, patient choices, interruptions, physiological observations when relevant, and debriefing. Immersive sound becomes credible when its conditions are not hidden. A vague claim about an immersive field is weak. A documented field can be discussed, repeated, modified, and studied.

A minimum spatial design vocabulary should include center, periphery, apparent distance, height, movement, diffusion, reverberant depth, and source density. These variables interact with attack, decay, grain, unpredictability, silence, spectrum, and intensity. Their clinical meaning is relational rather than universal. A dispersed patient may need center and edge. An overcontrolled patient may benefit from a gradual opening of the periphery. A highly vigilant patient may need a broad but predictable field with almost no sudden event. Spatial design becomes credible when these choices can be named and revised.

Every immersive session requires return. The field must not simply stop. It should move from density to simplicity, from spatial depth to room orientation, from altered attention to ordinary presence. The patient may be invited to feel the chair, floor, hands, breath, and the therapist's voice. If eyes were closed, reopening should be gradual. If the field was wide, the final sound may become near, warm, and stable. If the field was bodily, the final phase may restore language.

Spatialization can also enlarge the patient's own voice, but only with consent and restraint. A vocalization may be allowed to remain naked, or it may receive a slight halo, a delayed reflection, or a wider placement that makes presence audible without converting the person into an effect. The transformation of a voice is never a neutral technical act. Hearing one's own sound in front, around, behind, or above can alter self-perception intensely. The system must always preserve the source as human and the patient's right to ask for the unprocessed voice back.

The ethical difference between immersive attraction and music therapy lies here. Attraction leaves the subject impressed. Therapy returns the subject more inhabitable to themselves. MUMEx must be designed from the end backward: no field is complete until its Reintegration has been composed.

CHAPTER 21

The Five Sonic Operators

EPISTEMOLOGICAL LEVEL: *Central operational model. The five operators are design functions for Generative Sound Fields. They are not rigid stages, clinical guarantees, or mechanical treatments.*

The five sonic operators form the operational grammar of MUMEx Quantum Music Therapy: Resonance, Suspension, Gentle Perturbation, Perceptual Collapse, and Reintegration. They are not techniques to be applied in a fixed order. They are functions of a field. A single session may use all five, only two, or one dominant operator with traces of the others. Their value lies in giving the therapist a language for designing and observing the relationship between sound and state.

No operator corresponds to one privileged sound. Resonance may arise from a voice, a drone, a drum, a low-density electronic field, or a distant bell. Suspension may be carried by a stable harmonic band, inhabited silence, long reverberation, or a nearly immobile acoustic texture. Gentle Perturbation may be rhythmic, timbral, spatial, or dynamic. Perceptual Collapse may be supported by convergence, subtraction, a newly focused voice, or a figure becoming recognizable. Reintegration may use simplification, bodily orientation, speech, pulse, room sound, or silence. The function matters more than the object that carries it.

An operator does not cause a result in a simple way. It changes the probability that certain configurations of the human state may become accessible. Resonance may make safety more available. Suspension may make ambiguity tolerable. Gentle Perturbation may allow movement without rupture. Perceptual Collapse may support the emergence of form from diffuse experience. Reintegration may return body, speech, and orientation. The operator is a map, not a command.

Resonance is the operator of compatibility. It seeks a first agreement between body and field. This agreement may be rhythmic, timbral, respiratory, spatial, or energetic. Resonance does not mean that the sound must be pleasant. It means that the field can be received without immediate defense. The patient's body recognizes enough continuity to remain present. Breath may settle, posture may soften, attention may gather, and the room may become less hostile.

Resonance is built through proportion: moderate intensity, stable or slowly moving materials, readable timbres, sufficient space, and an absence of aggressive surprise. In practice, Resonance may use low warmth, vocal hum, slow pulse, continuous textures, gentle instrumental support, or a room tone that gives the patient somewhere to rest. The danger is overidentification. A field that resonates too completely with a closed or depressed state may confirm it. Resonance must hold the present state while leaving a path beyond it.

Rhythmic entrainment offers one physiological reference for Resonance, yet the operator is broader than synchronization. Regularity can support movement, breath, and autonomic organization, but Resonance also includes timbre, posture, memory, culture, and relationship. Its failure mode is capture. A field can become so compatible with the initial state that it confirms depression, freezes trauma, or turns reassurance into dependence. The field must say, in effect: I recognize where you are, and I am preserving enough life for movement to remain possible.

Suspension is the operator of possibility. It reduces premature closure and opens an interval in which the patient can remain with ambiguity without needing immediate explanation. The field becomes less goal-directed, less narrative, and more spacious. Time stretches. The mind does not yet choose. The body is allowed to stay with what is emerging. Suspension is especially important when verbal interpretation would arrive too early or when the patient needs to experience not-knowing without collapse.

Sound can create Suspension through drones, long decays, sparse events, slow harmonic ambiguity, hovering spatial layers, porous silence, and absence of strong cadence. The risk is dissociation. A suspended field must be anchored enough to prevent disappearance. A patient with trauma or psychotic vulnerability may need clear orientation, open eyes, shorter duration, and explicit control. Suspension is not escape from the world. It is a temporary widening of the field of possibility.

Suspension acts directly on the felt structure of time. It can interrupt the demand to know, decide, speak, or defend immediately. Yet quiet appearance is not sufficient evidence of therapeutic suspension. The therapist must distinguish presence from withdrawal by observing breath, color, muscle tone, feet, gaze, responsiveness, and the capacity to return to a word or gesture. A suspended field remains connected to the room. If the patient becomes unreachable, the operator has crossed into a failure mode and Reintegration should begin.

Gentle Perturbation is the operator of movement. It introduces difference without violence. Many human states are trapped not because they are empty, but because they are too stable: the anxious loop, the depressive flatness, the rigid defense, the frozen posture, the repetitive thought. Gentle Perturbation creates a small deviation. Something changes, yet the field remains safe enough to be inhabited. The patient discovers that change does not have to mean rupture.

Musically, Gentle Perturbation may appear as slight rhythmic displacement, microvariation in timbre, a small spatial event, a new register at low density, a brief interruption, or a subtle shift in pulse. Its measure is clinical: enough to be perceived, not enough to invade. In nature, this operator is everywhere: leaves move, water changes, birds answer, wind rises and falls. MUMEx can translate this living instability into a field that invites the nervous system to move again.

The operator can also be understood through the relation between expectation and deviation. Total confirmation risks dead repetition; excessive violation can trigger alarm or disorganization. A proportionate deviation recruits attention and invites the internal model to update. The clinical art lies in locating that narrow zone where difference is unmistakable and still survivable. Gentle Perturbation is therefore not weak stimulation. It is exact dosing of novelty.

Perceptual Collapse is the operator of emergence. The term is used psychologically and phenomenologically, not as a physical claim about the brain. It names the moment in which a diffuse configuration becomes a felt form: an image, word, memory, gesture, tear, breath, decision, or bodily recognition. Before the moment, many possibilities coexist. After it, something has become available to consciousness or to embodied experience.

MUMEx cannot force Perceptual Collapse, and it must never attempt to dramatize it. The field can prepare conditions: enough Suspension for possibility, enough Gentle Perturbation for movement, enough Resonance for safety, and enough silence for emergence. When the patient says, "I see something," "I feel my chest," "I remember," or simply changes presence, the therapist must avoid interpretive capture. The field should converge and then recede. Human experience must be given room to speak or to remain silent.

When a form does emerge, the field should usually do less. Density can fall, spatial movement can narrow, and unnecessary harmonic information can recede. The therapist may ask whether the patient wants to remain with the image, name it, sound it, move with it, or let it pass. The threshold is crossed only when the experience belongs to the participant. If the system or therapist rushes to interpret, amplify, or reproduce the moment, emergence becomes capture. Perceptual Collapse is clinically meaningful only when agency survives it.

Reintegration is the operator of return. It is the ethical seal of the entire model. A session may open states, modify perception, awaken body, touch memory, or produce images, but the patient must return to the room, to breath, to posture, to relationship, to language when appropriate, and to ordinary agency. Reintegration is not an afterthought. It should be designed from the beginning.

Reintegration may use tonal simplification, reduction of density, grounding pulse, stable low register, therapist voice, naming of the room, bodily orientation, small movement, verbal debriefing, and a closing silence that is warm rather than empty. The patient should leave more present, not more dispersed; more capable of choice, not more dependent on the field. In MUMEx, every opening must include its path of return.

The operators often overlap. A field of Resonance may contain small Gentle Perturbations. Suspension may prepare Perceptual Collapse. Reintegration may preserve a trace of Resonance. A session with an anxious patient may begin with Resonance, introduce minimal Gentle Perturbation, avoid deep Suspension, and close with extended Reintegration. A session with a creatively blocked subject may need Suspension and Gentle Perturbation before any strong emergent form appears. A session involving grief may require long Resonance, careful Suspension, and exceptionally tender Reintegration.

Combination requires listening. The operator model is not a staircase. It is a set of forces. The therapist must feel which operator is active, which is excessive, which is missing, and which should be withdrawn. A field that remains in Suspension too long may dissolve orientation. A field that overuses Gentle Perturbation may become anxious. A field that seeks Perceptual Collapse too directly may become manipulative. A field without Reintegration is ethically incomplete.

Each operator has a shadow. Resonance can become stagnation. Suspension can become dissociation. Gentle Perturbation can become irritation. Perceptual Collapse can become dramatized suggestion. Reintegration can become premature closure. The therapist must recognize these distortions immediately. Operator literacy exists to protect the patient from the therapist's fascination with the field.

The five operators are powerful because they make the work discussable. A practitioner can say: the field produced too much Suspension; Reintegration was too short; Gentle Perturbation began before Resonance; Perceptual Collapse was interpreted too quickly. This language transforms vision into method. It also prepares the transition to actual session design.

CHAPTER 22

Designing a MUMEx Sound Field for the Session

EPISTEMOLOGICAL LEVEL: *Design model. This chapter translates the MUMEx field into clinical planning: assessment, intention, sonic prescription, adaptive control, contraindications, documentation, and revision.*

A MUMEx field should never be designed in the abstract. The first question is not what sound is beautiful, nor what technology is available, but what human state is present. Assessment includes clinical context, goals, sensory tolerance, trauma history, medical cautions, musical biography, cultural background, relationship to silence, voice, rhythm, and bodily vibration, as well as the patient's present breath, posture, attention, and capacity for choice. Design begins by listening before sound begins.

The relevant profile is a perceptual ecology, not a diagnostic label. Which sounds calm this person, and which invade? What brings them back into the body? What removes orientation? What is their relationship to the human voice, rhythm, low frequencies, childhood music, natural sound, silence, and spatial depth? Conscious preference may contradict bodily response. Someone may say they love the sea and tense at the sound of waves; another may reject electronic music and settle inside an almost imperceptible drone. Design begins when the therapist allows the body's response to correct the questionnaire.

This assessment does not replace clinical evaluation. It refines the sonic conditions of the session. A patient with high auditory sensitivity may require low density and predictable events. A patient who is disconnected from the body may require grounded resonance. A patient in grief may need fields that allow continuity without forcing consolation. A patient who dissociates may need short fields, open eyes, clear stop signals, and strong Reintegration. The field is designed for this person, this moment, and this therapeutic frame.

A field intention is a concise statement of what the sound field is meant to support. It may be: establish bodily safety; widen attention; support vocal emergence; provide gentle movement; prepare memory work; contain grief; restore orientation; or close a session. The intention must be humble. It should not promise healing. It should name a direction in state.

From this intention emerges the sonic prescription: density, register, timbre, rhythm, spatial behavior, duration, variation rate, silence, and operator dominance.

Parameters should be conceived as an interdependent architecture rather than a checklist. Lowering density changes the exposure of silence. Moving a source farther away changes the emotional meaning of timbre. Increasing reverberation changes temporal perception. A darker spectrum can make a field feel supportive in one body and oppressive in another. The designer should therefore ask not only what each parameter does alone, but what configuration the parameters create together and whether that configuration can still be simplified quickly if the state changes.

A sonic prescription is not a formula. It is a disciplined starting point. For Resonance, the field may use stable low-mid warmth, moderate volume, slow movement, and clear predictability. For Suspension, it may use sparse long tones, ambiguous harmonic support, and porous silence. For Gentle Perturbation, it may introduce small deviations and rare events. For Perceptual Collapse, it may gradually converge and then leave space. For Reintegration, it may simplify, ground, and return to voice.

The session arc matters as much as the material. A MUMEx field may be designed in phases: entry, first Resonance, widening, controlled perturbation, possible emergence, simplification, and return. These phases should not be rigid. They provide orientation for therapist and system. The field must be able to pause, shorten, extend, or change course according to the patient's state. A planned arc is not a cage. It is a responsible path through an uncertain territory.

The decisive skill is listening to the transition. One patient may need far more Resonance than planned because trust in time has not yet formed. Another may need an early difference because absolute stability resembles depressive immobility. Another may require short, recognizable repetitions because unpredictability is still coded as threat. A field should arrive with a plan and remain free to abandon the plan. The best form is produced by the meeting between design and correction.

Timing is clinical. Five minutes can be too long for a patient in high vigilance and too short for a patient who needs time to cross the threshold of listening. A change introduced after thirty seconds may feel invasive; the same change after ten minutes may be welcome. The therapist should treat duration as a living parameter. A generative field is useful precisely because it can preserve identity while adapting time.

Adaptive control can be manual, semi-automated, or data-informed. Manual control preserves direct therapeutic judgment: the therapist reduces density, changes register, or opens silence after observing the body. Semi-automated control uses preset pathways and safe limits. Data-informed control may consider breath, movement, HRV, or other noninvasive signals. None of these approaches should be fetishized. The most important adaptive system remains trained human presence.

A mature system must make simplification easier than escalation. The therapist should be able to reduce event probability, narrow spatial width, stabilize register, shorten reverberation, remove sub-bass, clear the voice range, and enter a return state without navigating a complex interface. Manual override and emergency stop are not technical accessories; they are part of the clinical architecture. The most dangerous field is not necessarily the loudest one. It is the field that cannot be made simple fast enough.

The patient can also participate. Choice may be simple: closer or farther, more or less dense, warmer or brighter, still or moving, continue or stop. These choices restore agency. The patient hears the field change because of their decision. This can be profound for people who feel that their inner state has no effect on the world. MUMEx should make agency audible without turning the patient into a technician.

Every MUMEx session must include a stop signal. The patient should know that the field can be reduced or stopped without failure. Contraindications may include acute psychosis, severe dissociation, high sensory defensiveness, recent trauma activation, neurological sensitivity, migraine vulnerability, unstable medical conditions, severe panic, or any clinical situation in which altered state work would be inappropriate without specialist containment. These cautions do not negate the model. They make it credible.

The therapist should watch for signs of overload: shallow or frozen breath, sudden pallor, rigid posture, loss of orientation, excessive startle, dissociative gaze, agitation, pressured speech, nausea, pain, or inability to respond. In such cases the field should simplify, lower, stabilize, or stop. Reintegration begins immediately. No theoretical commitment to a field is more important than the patient's state.

After the session, the logbook should record not only what was intended but what actually happened. Which operator dominated? Which transition worked? Where did the patient change breath? Which moment caused difficulty? What did the patient report? Was the field too dense, too empty, too long, too beautiful, too suggestive, too distant, too near? The revision of future fields depends on this honesty.

Documentation also protects research language. If MUMEx is to become more than a visionary framework, it must produce fields that can be described, compared, and iteratively refined. The logbook is the bridge between art, clinical practice, and study design. It allows a therapist or researcher to say exactly what was done, how it was changed, and why.

Design also includes explicit decisions about what to avoid. For one patient, the exclusions may be posterior spatial events, long reverberation, marked pulse, metallic timbre, or extended silence. For another, some of those same materials may later become useful. No sonic material is pure in itself. The task is to distinguish function from superstition: a sound does not heal because it carries a special number or frequency label. It acts within a responsible relation among state, setting, dose, meaning, and return. Silence belongs to the same design discipline; a field that cannot generate its own subtraction remains immature.

A Resonance prototype may begin with three minutes of low, warm, stable material, almost no spatial motion, and a therapist seated within clear sight. The patient is invited only to notice breath and bodily support. A Gentle Perturbation prototype may add very small timbral events after initial safety is established. A Suspension prototype may use long decays and wide silence, but only for patients who can tolerate ambiguity. A Perceptual Collapse prototype must be extremely restrained, allowing emergence rather than seeking it. A Reintegration prototype should be used after every field, regardless of intensity.

These prototypes are not recipes. They are disciplined examples. The patient, therapist, room, culture, diagnosis, biography, and moment all change the design. MUMEx does not replace clinical judgment; it makes judgment audible, recordable, and revisable.

CHAPTER 23

MUMEx, Voice, and Improvisation

EPISTEMOLOGICAL LEVEL: *Clinical-musical model. Voice, improvisation, and the Generative Sound Field are treated as embodied relational processes, not as performance or automatic expression.*

The voice is the first sound field inhabited by a human being. Before instrument, scale, chord, or composition, there is a body moving air through diaphragm, larynx, cavities, tongue, jaw, skull, and chest. Voice carries breath, identity, modesty, aggression, desire for contact, fear of being heard, maternal trace, childhood memory, cultural belonging, wound, prayer, and call. No sonic device possesses comparable human density. The voice does not merely accompany the person. It exposes them.

The human voice remains sovereign. MUMEx may generate complex fields, but it must always yield before the patient's sound. The voice contains breath, identity, risk, shame, memory, desire, and bodily truth. A small vocal emission may carry more clinical significance than a sophisticated field. When the patient's voice appears, the system should support, thin, listen, or withdraw. If the field covers the voice, it has misunderstood its role.

The voice is not only melody. It may be sigh, hum, murmur, cry, vowel, consonant, whisper, broken tone, spoken word, laugh, or refusal. A patient who cannot sing may still voice. A patient who speaks constantly may be unable to voice. MUMEx should create conditions in which the voice can arrive without being forced into performance. The first therapeutic sound may be almost nothing. That almost nothing must be respected.

For this reason, murmur is often more important than song. Singing may evoke judgment, school, church, family, stage, failure, or the demand to be beautiful. Murmur stays closer to the body. It can begin with the mouth closed, inside the skull, chest, nose, or throat, and allows vibration without full declaration. Sounded breath is even more primordial. An audible exhalation may be the first gesture of presence. A trembling breath may disclose fear before words can name it. MUMEx can support these beginnings with an almost imperceptible floor, leaving irregularity intact rather than correcting the breath into an ideal pattern.

A field designed around voice should leave spectral room. Dense midrange material may mask the human voice. Strong rhythmic patterns may pressure it. Too much harmonic beauty may seduce the patient into imitation instead of expression. A supportive field may use low ground, airy high traces, soft spatial depth, and responsive reduction when the patient emits sound. The field behaves like an accompanist who knows when not to play.

Voice clearance should therefore be built into the system. When a patient or therapist vocalizes, MUMEx should be able to reduce midrange density, soften attacks, suspend sudden events, simplify rhythm, and stabilize register. This is more than good mixing. It is an ethical hierarchy: the field must know how to make room for human presence. The most advanced generative behavior may sometimes be withdrawal.

The patient may be invited to choose whether the field follows, holds, or ignores the voice. Following can validate. Holding can contain. Ignoring can liberate the patient from the pressure of being mirrored. Each option changes the relational field. The therapist should avoid assuming that responsiveness is always therapeutic. Some patients need the world to answer; others need a world that remains steady while they risk a sound.

The therapist's voice is also part of the field. It gives orientation, warmth, boundary, permission, and return. In a generative session, verbal guidance should be sparse, precise, and embodied. Too much language can pull the patient out of the field; too little can leave them alone inside it. The therapist's tone, pace, volume, and distance matter as much as semantic content. A single calm sentence can function as Reintegration.

Vocal containment may be sung or spoken. A low hum can offer Resonance. A soft repeated syllable can stabilize breath. A spoken naming of the room can return the patient from altered attention. The therapist's voice must never compete with MUMEx. It should govern the field by presence. The machine generates; the human voice certifies that someone is there.

Improvisation is not surpassed by generativity. It is transformed by it. A therapist improvising within a MUMEx field enters a triadic relation: patient, therapist, and field. The field offers continuity, memory, atmosphere, and nonhuman movement. The therapist offers immediate listening, risk, timing, gesture, and clinical judgment. The patient offers signs, sounds, silence, choices, and state transitions. The session becomes a living ecology.

A responsive system must also know how not to respond. If MUMEx answers every gesture, it steals the center. If it beautifies every irregularity, it converts clinical information into aesthetic reward. If it anticipates too quickly, improvisation becomes interaction with a clever machine. Responsible response needs delay, inhibition, and the possibility of silence. The system should react because a response serves the field, not because a transformation is technically available.

This ecology requires restraint. The therapist should not fill the field simply because there is space. Improvisation may consist in one note, one drum stroke, one breath, one answered rhythm, or one deliberate silence. MUMEx can sustain the background so that the therapist can play less and listen more. The quality of improvisation is measured by appropriateness, not virtuosity.

Acoustic instruments bring human gesture into the generative environment. A drum introduces hand, skin, impact, and pulse. A bell introduces attack, decay, and shimmer. A string instrument introduces friction, breath-like bowing, and tactile continuity. A flute introduces air. A piano introduces weight and resonance. These instruments should not be used as decorative additions. Each must have a function in the field.

Gesture matters because the patient sees sound being made. In electronic fields, sources may be hidden. Acoustic gesture returns causality to the room. For some patients, this is grounding. They can see the hand, hear the sound, and connect event with origin. For others, visible gesture may create performance pressure. MUMEx allows the therapist to balance visible and invisible sound, human action and environmental continuity.

Electronic transformation of the voice requires a stricter consent threshold than transformation of an instrumental sound. Transposition, granulation, multiplication, long reverberation, or spatial diffusion can produce powerful experiences of enlargement and estrangement. They can also create shame, loss of boundary, or fear of no longer recognizing one's own sound. In many sessions the best choice will be the unprocessed voice, barely supported. Clinical truth does not increase with the number of effects.

Voice and improvisation introduce risk. The patient may fear sounding foolish, exposed, primitive, childish, aggressive, ugly, or too emotional. The field must protect risk without smothering it. Silence is often the safest companion. A patient may need long intervals before a sound. The therapist should not rush. The absence of vocal response may itself be meaningful. Silence can be a chosen sound when it is held, not abandoned.

The same restraint applies to error. A cracked note, broken rhythm, failed entrance, abrupt silence, or sound that is too strong may be state information. If the system automatically corrects every deviation into seamless beauty, the field loses evidence. MUMEx should be able to receive irregularity without humiliating it and without erasing it. The therapeutic task is not to make what emerges aesthetically perfect. It is to make it recognizable and inhabitable.

Embodied choice should be simple. Do you want the field to continue? Do you want it lower? Do you want to add a sound or listen? Do you want your sound answered or left alone? These questions restore agency and reduce suggestion. The patient becomes co-designer of the field. In this sense, improvisation is not only musical. It is existential: the patient experiments with making a mark in the world.

After vocal or instrumental emergence, Reintegration must be delicate. The field should not immediately interpret what happened. The therapist may ask where the sound was felt, whether another sound is needed, or whether silence should follow. If a memory or image arose, it should be received without colonization. The patient's own language must lead.

MUMEx can help by preserving a trace of the improvisation: a softened contour, a transformed resonance, a lower-density echo, or a final stable ground. The patient hears that their gesture has entered the field, but also that the field can return safely. This is the deep clinical promise of voice and generativity together: the patient's sound changes the environment and then returns to the body as experience.

A voice-centered MUMEx field should therefore possess four qualities: porosity, responsiveness, sobriety, and memory. Porosity leaves real space for human sound. Responsiveness allows relation without saturation. Sobriety prevents the system from admiring its own effects. Memory preserves traces of the process so that the next session need not begin from zero. These qualities make the technology a companion of the field rather than its protagonist.

CHAPTER 24

The Experiential Laboratory and Musical Instruments

EPISTEMOLOGICAL LEVEL: *Laboratory model. This chapter describes supervised experiential practice, instrument-based exploration, group field work, and the transition from workshop knowledge to documented method.*

Quantum Music Therapy cannot remain only a theory. It needs a laboratory. The laboratory is not a spectacle room, not a concert studio, and not a place for uncontrolled experimentation on vulnerable people. It is a supervised environment where therapists, researchers, artists, and trained participants learn how sound fields affect state, body, attention, voice, movement, and return. The laboratory translates intuition into disciplined experience.

The room itself is already part of the experiment. Temperature, light, the number of visible objects, the possibility of sitting on the floor, the distance from a loudspeaker, the presence of a microphone, a resonant corner, a fluorescent hum, or an open window can alter state before the first deliberate sound occurs. A mature laboratory begins when the therapist enters the empty room and recognizes that no element is perceptually innocent.

A MUMEx laboratory should train listening at multiple levels. Participants learn to hear the field, their own body, the room, the group, and the transitions between operators. They learn how density changes attention, how low register changes posture, how silence exposes, how spatial movement orients or disturbs, and how a field can be stopped without failure. This training is essential before clinical application.

Musical instruments can function as probes of state. A drum reveals relationship to pulse, impact, boundary, and motor force. A bell reveals tolerance for attack and decay. A singing bowl reveals response to continuous resonance. A string instrument reveals pressure, friction, and sustained line. A wind instrument reveals breath and exposure. Small percussion reveals agency and timing. The instrument does not diagnose in a medical sense. It reveals how the state meets sound, gesture, and choice.

Four qualities should govern instrument choice: accessibility, graduality, reversibility, and bodily resonance. Accessibility means that a meaningful event can be produced without technical examination. Graduality means that power can be approached rather than imposed. Reversibility means that the participant can stop, move away, lower, or choose another object. Bodily resonance means understanding what kind of gesture and what kind of body the instrument calls forth. These criteria matter more than prestige, rarity, or sonic beauty.

In the laboratory, instruments should be introduced one at a time and documented carefully. What happens when the patient strikes? What happens when they only listen? Do they prefer control or reception? Do they need predictable sound or unexpected response? Does rhythm organize or accelerate? Does resonance ground or blur? These observations become the foundation for later MUMEx design.

Touch is a sonic dimension. The hand touching a frame drum, the finger on a string, the mallet on wood, the palm on a resonant surface, and the foot on the floor all create motor listening. The body hears what it does. This is crucial for patients who live too far from bodily agency. Producing sound can restore causality: I act, the world responds, and I can modulate the response.

Material also matters. Wood, metal, skin, stone, glass, water, paper, and electronic controllers produce different relationships with force and sensitivity. A fragile patient may need a material that responds to minimal touch. An overcontrolled patient may need a surface that permits stronger impact. A dissociated patient may need tactile feedback before symbolic interpretation. MUMEx can surround these materials with fields that support, expand, or soften the motor event.

Different instrument families invite different state behaviors. The drum couples gesture, impact, and boundary; it can organize force or turn into coercion if pulse becomes too insistent. Shakers and granular objects distribute energy more diffusely and may permit fine regulation without frontal attack. Bells, cymbals, and gongs place emphasis on decay: the gesture is brief while listening continues, teaching the body to remain after the action. Strings introduce tension, friction, continuity, and visible vibration. Wind instruments expose breath and therefore require caution when panic, respiratory anxiety, or bodily control are central themes.

The group laboratory introduces relational ecology. Each participant's sound changes the common field. Too much force dominates. Too little presence disappears. A repeated pattern can hold the group or imprison it. Silence can feel respectful or rejecting. MUMEx can provide a generative ground while participants learn how their gestures affect a shared environment. This is music therapy as social field.

Microphones, sensors, and controllers need equally clear ethics. A microphone changes behavior simply by being present; for one person it makes a fragile voice audible without effort, for another it creates performance anxiety. Recording requires transparency, consent, and control over the material. Sensors and controllers should enter only when they increase agency: a movement can alter density, a pedal can reduce the field, a simple control can change distance or register. The participant needs to feel the relation between gesture and consequence, not understand the software architecture behind it.

Group protocols must protect boundaries. Participants should know that they may listen without playing, stop at any time, and choose distance from the sound. The facilitator must monitor not only musical balance, but also relational pressure: who leads, who vanishes, who imitates, who resists, who floods, who withdraws. The sound field becomes a mirror of group state, but the facilitator must avoid simplistic interpretation.

Supervision is necessary because powerful sound experiences can seduce practitioners. A trainee may confuse intensity with depth, emotion with integration, beauty with therapeutic value, or altered attention with healing. The laboratory must repeatedly teach the same principle: no opening without return, no field without consent, no interpretation without humility, no technology without human containment.

Instrument choice is also biographical and cultural. A frame drum, guitar, piano, shell, synthesizer, microphone, or sampler carries worlds of family, territory, religion, school, celebration, embarrassment, and memory. A sample is not equivalent to the body that plays the original instrument. The laboratory must preserve the genealogy of materials instead of flattening everything into abstract sound. Self-built instruments can be especially powerful because the participant helps bring the object into existence; a simple resonant box, seed rattle, string frame, or water-and-stone object can become an extension of agency and biography.

Training should include adverse responses. Participants must learn how to recognize overload, reduce density, reorient the body, stop the field, speak simply, and document what occurred. The laboratory is successful not when every experience feels profound, but when practitioners learn to govern both depth and limit.

Silence and failure must also be trained. After a gong, drum stroke, vocalization, or MUMEx event, immediate filling can destroy the information carried by decay. The laboratory should teach the sequence of event, absorption, and possible response. It should also allow an instrument to remain untouched, a prepared field to be rejected, or a supposedly regulating practice to irritate. These outcomes are not embarrassing deviations from the method. They are data about the field and the person.

The MUMEx workbench is the practical interface where fields are designed, stored, modified, and compared. It should allow control over density, register, timbre, dynamics, spatial movement, rhythmic behavior, randomness, memory, silence, duration, and operator dominance. It should also include safe ranges, preset clinical templates, manual override, emergency stop, and logbook export. The interface must be musical enough for artists and clear enough for clinicians.

The most fertile ecology is dialectical. Acoustic instruments bring resistance, friction, error, contact, and the visible craft of gesture. The generative field brings continuity, variation, memory, spatiality, and adaptive behavior. Acoustic-only work can lack environmental depth or precise traceability. Generative-only work can lose hand, weight, sweat, and the risk of material action. The laboratory becomes distinctly MUMEx when drum, voice, string, object, room, and electronic field listen to one another rather than compete for centrality.

A workbench that is too technical will alienate therapists. A workbench that is too simplified will conceal risk. The design challenge is to make complexity governable. Each control should answer a clinical question: what does this parameter do to the field and to the possible human state? MUMEx becomes useful when technology becomes transparent to care.

Every laboratory session should produce a structured logbook entry. Who participated? What field was used? Which instruments entered? Which operators were active? What changed in breath, posture, voice, attention, movement, and group balance? What was difficult? How did Reintegration occur? What should be modified next time? These entries build a corpus of experience.

The laboratory is therefore the bridge between artistic research and formal protocol. Before SMP-001 or any controlled study, the field must be trained through supervised practice. The book's vision becomes credible when its laboratory produces methods that other practitioners can understand, reproduce, critique, and improve.

CHAPTER 25

Practices, Exercises, and Experiential Protocols

EPISTEMOLOGICAL LEVEL: *Experiential protocol. The practices in this chapter are exploratory, educational, and research-oriented. They require consent, screening, professional judgment, and appropriate clinical boundaries.*

The value of an experiential practice is measured by the quality of presence it changes, not by the complexity of its apparatus. A breath, a low-intensity vowel, one careful drum stroke, a hand near a transducer, or a minute of silence after a MUMEx field may be enough. The practice becomes serious when its entrance is clean, its function is intelligible, its duration is proportionate, interruption remains possible, observation is precise, and return restores orientation.

Every experiential MUMEx practice begins with consent, safety, and orientation. The participant must know what will happen, how long it may last, how to stop it, what choices are available, and that no particular response is expected. The facilitator should explain that experiences may include bodily sensation, imagery, emotion, boredom, resistance, or no noticeable change. All responses are valid. The purpose is not performance. The purpose is observation of state in relation to sound.

Orientation includes the room, chair, exit, therapist or facilitator, stop signal, volume, and return procedure. For vulnerable participants, orientation should be repeated at the end. The field should begin below the threshold of spectacle. MUMEx practice must earn depth through trust, not through force.

The Resonance practice begins with a short field of low to moderate density, stable timbre, and minimal spatial movement. The participant is invited to feel contact with the chair or floor, notice breath, and listen without searching. After several minutes, the facilitator may ask one simple question: where does the sound meet the body? The answer may be verbal, gestural, or silent. The field remains steady enough to support recognition.

A useful first variation is postural listening. No emotional story is requested. The participant notices where sound seems to occur in the body —chest, throat, neck, abdomen, hands, feet, or back. The question is not what the sound means, but where it happens. From this map, a micropercussion exercise may follow: one small strike, a pause, a second strike, one slight variation. The aim is to experience an effective gesture and its consequence. For people who doubt their impact on the world or fear their own intensity, such minimal causality can be more informative than an elaborate musical task.

Afterward, the logbook records perceived body location, comfort, resistance, breath, imagery, and tolerance. The practice should not seek relaxation as its only success. Resonance is present when the participant can remain with the field without immediate defense and without losing orientation.

The Suspension practice introduces spaciousness, long decays, slow morphologies, and porous silence. It is appropriate only when the participant can tolerate ambiguity. The instruction should be minimal: allow the field to remain unfinished. The facilitator observes whether the participant becomes calm, curious, restless, dissociated, sleepy, or anxious. If orientation weakens, the practice is shortened and Reintegration begins.

Dialoguc with a drone offers another precise practice. A well-designed drone is not dead monotony; it is a surface with internal life. The participant may listen, breathe with it, hum above it, oppose it, introduce an alien note, or remain silent. The continuity allows duration to be experienced rather than filled. For fragmented states, duration itself may be corrective; for anxiety, it can test reliability; for depression, it can provide a minimal support within flattened time. The facilitator observes whether continuity holds, traps, or invites movement.

Debriefing should avoid asking for dramatic content. Better questions are: did time change? did the body feel near or far? did the field open or empty? was silence tolerable? These questions respect the operator without turning it into suggestion.

The Gentle Perturbation practice begins after sufficient Resonance. A stable field receives small deviations: a slight timbral shimmer, a distant event, a rhythmic displacement, a low-density spatial movement, or a new color that appears and withdraws. The participant is invited to notice the difference between change and threat. This practice can be useful for states that are rigid, overcontrolled, or fearful of movement.

Vibroacoustic practice requires a separate language of caution. External listening should precede proximity, and proximity should precede optional contact. The participant describes the vibration as pleasant, neutral, irritating, localized, diffuse, heavy, light, warm, cold, near, or distant. These words form a somatic map. The purpose is perception, regulation, presence, and orientation—not claims that a frequency directly treats an organ or pathology. A controlled field may accompany the process, but the body's report determines the pace.

The facilitator must calibrate carefully. If the participant startles, tightens, or becomes irritated, the perturbation was not gentle enough or not correctly timed. The goal is not surprise. The goal is the discovery that a field can change and remain safe.

The Perceptual Collapse practice is the most delicate and should be used only in appropriate conditions. It begins with Resonance and Suspension, then allows a gradual convergence: the field simplifies around a possible image, bodily sensation, vocal impulse, or remembered trace. The facilitator does not tell the participant what to experience. The field creates enough coherence for something to become form if it is ready.

When emergence occurs, the field should reduce density. The facilitator may ask, "Would you like to stay with it, name it, sound it, or let it pass?" The participant's choice governs the next step. If no emergence occurs, the practice is still valid. Perceptual Collapse cannot be forced. Its ethical condition is freedom from expectation.

The Reintegration practice should be trained independently, not only after intense experiences. A field gradually simplifies, lowers density, stabilizes pulse or warmth, reduces spatial depth, and returns attention to room and body. The facilitator names present time, chair, floor, breath, hands, and the possibility of speech. The participant may move fingers, open eyes, drink water, or speak a few words.

This practice teaches the nervous system that every opening has a path of return. It also teaches practitioners not to abandon participants after altered attention. Reintegration is not administrative closure. It is therapeutic architecture.

Every complete experiential protocol should contain four movements: reading the state, proposing sound, observing transformation, and returning. Observation includes more than verbal report; it includes breath, posture, vocal color, gaze, movement, and the quality of silence. Return may take many forms: feet on the floor, hands on the thighs, naming the room, one short word, a small rhythm, water, three written lines, a quick drawing, a final therapist tone, or a MUMEx field that reduces density, returns to the middle register, narrows space, and lowers unpredictability. Return is not administrative closure. It is the ethical completion of the journey.

Group protocols should be shorter, clearer, and more structured than individual work. The group may begin with shared Resonance, then each participant contributes one sound, gesture, or silence. MUMEx sustains a low-density field while the facilitator monitors balance. No participant should be required to perform. Listening is full participation.

Debriefing should separate experience from interpretation. Participants may describe body, time, sound, image, emotion, or difficulty. The facilitator records common patterns and divergent responses. A field that calms one participant may irritate another. This is not failure. It is data. Group work teaches that the sound field is never universal; it becomes meaningful through bodies, histories, and relationships.

Measurement must remain plural and modest. HRV, breath, heart rate, subjective scales, phenomenological description, and behavioral observation may enrich the record, yet no single measure contains the whole state. A participant can show a favorable physiological change and still feel exposed; can report calm while the body remains vigilant; can appear still while undergoing intense internal movement. The protocol should cross data, words, body, and field rather than enthrone any one of them.

The experiential practices prepare the ground for the Q-MUMEx State Modulation Protocol, SMP-001. They identify tolerable durations, safe densities, effective return procedures, vocabulary for debriefing, and field parameters worth studying. Before a formal protocol measures anything, the field must be ethically and experientially understood.

Imagination must be held with the same restraint. An image that emerges—a house, animal, face, childhood room, light, landscape, or symbolic body—does not require immediate interpretation. The more mature questions concern its bodily quality, the sound that sustains it, the distance it needs, and whether it should remain or pass. Some practices may later become brief daily exercises: one minute of sounded breathing, three vowels in the morning, a micropercussion for boundary, a simple evening field, or a sonic perception diary. Their purpose is autonomy, not dependence on the system.

The practitioner must undergo the same experiential discipline. No one should guide deep fields without knowing, in their own body, Resonance, Suspension, Gentle Perturbation, Perceptual Collapse, and Reintegration. The therapist should know which timbres invade them, which silences create discomfort, which rhythms trigger control, which kinds of voice expose them, and where fascination with intensity begins. Self-experience reduces the risk of turning the patient into the practitioner's first laboratory.

Guided parameter choice is one of the most fertile ways to connect practice with agency. The participant is not burdened with technical categories. They may choose closer or farther, lower or higher, more still or more mobile, fuller or more rarefied, darker or brighter. Each choice changes the field. The inner state alters the environment, the environment responds, and the response is heard. Over time, these choices can build individual response maps rather than rigid diagnoses: lower density may favor voice, greater spatial width may disorient, a microperturbation may open imagination, a return to a stable drone may support integration.

Part Five therefore completes the operational turn of the book. MUMEx is no longer only a concept or a promise. It becomes an architecture, a grammar, a workbench, a set of operators, and a disciplined practice. The next movement will bring this architecture into dialogue with neuroscience, depth psychology, interoception, and archetypal life.

PART SIX

NEUROSCIENCE AND DEPTH PSYCHOLOGY

CHAPTER 26

Neuroscience and Music Therapy

EPISTEMOLOGICAL LEVEL: *Established evidence / neuroscientific model. This chapter addresses music, rhythm, memory, autonomic regulation, HRV, plasticity, reward, neuroaesthetics, and measurement while avoiding reductionist claims.*

The neuroscience of music begins with a fertile paradox. The more precise the instruments of measurement become, the clearer it becomes that music cannot be confined to a single cerebral place. Musical sound engages auditory pathways, motor systems, memory, emotion, prediction, reward, attention, autonomic regulation, and social cognition. It moves through the nervous system as a distributed event. To ask where music is in the brain is already too small a question. A more useful question is how music organizes a living system over time (Chanda & Levitin, 2013; Koelsch, 2014).

Music therapy has much to gain from this evidence, provided neuroscience is not used as decorative authority. Saying that a practice "activates the brain" explains almost nothing. Every living experience activates the brain. The clinical question is more rigorous: which musical parameters, in which context, for which person, under which conditions, seem to change breath, attention, movement, memory, emotional tone, orientation, and relationship? Neuroscience becomes useful when it sharpens clinical questions instead of replacing them with images of neural illumination.

Listening begins in the auditory system, yet it never remains there. Acoustic pressure becomes nervous information: pitch, intensity, timbre, localization, duration, contour, attack, decay, pulse, and pattern. Almost immediately, these elements become predictions. The brain expects continuations, closures, variations, returns, and surprises. A cadence gives completion because expectation has been formed. A syncopation acts because the body has already anticipated another place of arrival. A silence matters because the system keeps listening into absence.

This predictive architecture is crucial for MUMEx. A Generative Sound Field does not simply present sounds. It shapes expectation. It can make the future feel reliable, ambiguous, porous, alive, or threatening. A patient with anxiety may live in a nervous system that overpredicts danger. A patient with depression may lose the sense that the future contains possibility. A traumatized patient may hear the present through the prediction of past threat. Sound can participate in the reeducation of expectation when it is gradual, legible, and contained.

Rhythm occupies a central place because it connects brain and body with rare immediacy. Human beings do not hear rhythm only as abstract structure. Even when visible movement is absent, motor systems participate in listening. The body anticipates the beat, prepares movement, resists it, aligns with it, or is disturbed by it. Rhythm is time made bodily. For this reason, rhythmic work in music therapy must be treated as a clinical force, not as a simple background pattern.

The concept of entrainment is useful and often misunderstood. It indicates the tendency of oscillatory systems to coordinate. In musical experience, this coordination may involve foot, breath, attention, expectation, vocal impulse, and interpersonal timing. It should not be imagined as an automatic hypnosis of rhythm. A pulse may help one patient stabilize and make another feel trapped. A repeated pattern may support motor timing and, in another context, intensify obsessive control. Entrainment must be designed, observed, and revised.

MUMEx is especially valuable because it can separate pulse from mechanical repetition. A field can offer rhythmic ground while retaining microvariation. It can create a sense of time that is reliable without being rigid. It can hold a low pulse for orientation, introduce small perturbations after safety is established, or dissolve pulse gradually when Suspension is needed. This makes rhythm a flexible clinical material rather than a metronomic command.

Prediction also explains why timing matters. A sound introduced too early may invade; the same sound introduced after Resonance may open movement. A silence at the beginning may feel like abandonment; a silence after containment may become integration. Neuroscience confirms what experienced therapists already know: the nervous system responds to sequence, not isolated events. MUMEx design must therefore be temporal architecture. The field before prepares the field after.

The relationship between music and the autonomic nervous system is one of the most important clinical bridges. Heart rate, breath, skin conductance, muscular tone, and heart rate variability (HRV) can offer valuable clues about regulation. They do not tell the whole story. They do not replace the patient's report, the therapist's observation, or the complexity of meaning. They provide a physiological window into part of the state.

HRV is often treated as a marker of flexibility in autonomic regulation. This can be useful, yet it must be kept in proportion. Higher HRV is not automatically well-being. Lower HRV is not automatically pathology. Context, age, health status, breathing pattern, posture, medication, arousal, fatigue, and measurement conditions all matter. A book that proposes a serious model of sound and state must resist simplistic claims. Physiological data should be read as part of a larger clinical ecology.

A MUMEx session can be designed with autonomic regulation in mind. Stable low-density fields may support downshifting when the patient remains oriented. Slow breath-compatible pulses may help some people notice respiratory rhythm. Warm timbres may reduce defensive attention. Sudden dynamic shifts, excessive sub-bass, intense spatial motion, or high spectral brightness may overload vulnerable systems. The task is to design conditions for regulation, not to force calm.

Clinical caution is part of scientific credibility. When a field changes autonomic state, the change can feel powerful. Power does not equal safety. A person may become calm because they are regulated; another may become quiet because they are dissociating. A decrease in movement may mean rest or collapse. MUMEx practice requires trained observation, simple stop signals, debriefing, and Reintegration. The nervous system must be respected as living intelligence, not treated as a machine to be tuned.

Musical memory reveals one of the most moving relationships between brain and identity. A song from childhood, a religious melody, a lullaby, a festival rhythm, or the timbre of an instrument can return entire worlds: faces, rooms, smells, gestures, losses, and belonging. Memory is not a storage cabinet opened by sound. It is a living reconstruction in which music can give shape to time. This power can orient and heal, yet it can also reopen pain.

For this reason, biographical music must be used with delicacy. A beloved song may contain grief. A sacred melody may support one patient and wound another. A familiar rhythm may restore identity in dementia or intensify longing in bereavement. The therapeutic value of memory lies in the relationship between sound, person, and moment. MUMEx adds another possibility: rather than using only fixed autobiographical music, it can generate fields that carry the quality of memory without forcing specific content.

Emotion in music is never only pleasure. Music can move, agitate, excite, soften, anger, console, awaken tenderness, evoke nostalgia, or bring fear to the surface. Reward systems participate in musical pleasure and anticipation, yet they are only one layer of the event. A therapeutic field may be beautiful and useful, beautiful and useless, neutral and profound, or initially uncomfortable and necessary. The criterion is not pleasure. The criterion is transformation with safety.

Plasticity is another key word that must be protected from inflation. The brain changes with experience, repetition, training, environment, and meaningful engagement. Music is especially potent because it is multimodal, temporal, motoric, emotional, and social. Yet not every musical exposure produces stable change. Plasticity can be adaptive or maladaptive. Trauma is plasticity as well: the system learns threat too well. Anxiety is plasticity as well: the system rehearses danger. MUMEx must seek forms of repetition and variation that invite reorganization without hardening defenses.

Neuroscience helps reframe listening as action. Listening is not passive reception. It is orientation. The patient listens with the head, skin, memory, expectations, defenses, posture, and breath. In anxiety, attention tends to scan for threat. In depression, attention may flatten or withdraw. In trauma, attention may jump between hypervigilance and dissociation. In neurodevelopmental conditions, sound may arrive with unusual intensity, fascination, or overload. To design sound responsibly means to ask how listening itself is organized.

A Generative Sound Field can invite active listening without demanding performance. It can give the patient a field to inhabit, explore, resist, choose, and eventually influence. The patient may discover that attention can move from danger to vibration, from mental noise to breath, from scattered vigilance to a boundary in the room. This is not entertainment. It is a reorganization of perception.

The social brain is equally important. Music is synchronized relation. In shared voice, rhythm, improvisation, call and response, and co-listening, the nervous system regulates itself with another nervous system. The therapist is not an external operator. The therapist's body, timing, voice, gaze, and silence are part of the field. The more we know about neural systems, the more obvious the human center of music therapy becomes.

Measurement should enter this model with discipline. Electroencephalography (EEG), HRV, respiratory measures, skin conductance, movement analysis, vocal analysis, subjective scales, and structured debriefing can all provide valuable information. The danger begins when data become idols. A graph can indicate change without explaining meaning. A physiological shift may look impressive while the patient feels invaded. A subjective report may be modest while the clinical transition is profound.

MUMEx offers a distinctive advantage because the field itself can leave a trace. Parameters, density, duration, transitions, register, spatial behavior, silence, therapist intervention, patient choice, and reported experience can all enter the logbook. This makes the field discussable. It allows a practitioner to compare not only outcomes but conditions. The question becomes: what field was generated, how did it evolve, what state markers changed, what was reported, and what should be modified next time?

Measurement without reductionism means accepting multiple levels. Physiological data, subjective report, therapist observation, audio analysis, session notes, and follow-up each reveal a different slice of the event. No single measure owns truth. The human state is not a number, yet numbers can help when they remain accountable to experience.

MUMEx can be understood as an embodied neuroscience of generative sound. It does not produce neuroscience by itself. It does not guarantee outcomes. It has no independent clinical wisdom. It offers a new material: Generative Sound Fields that are plastic enough to be designed and stable enough to be documented. This is the bridge between vision and verification.

The neuroscientific perspective strengthens rather than diminishes the role of the music therapist. Choosing a sound means intervening in prediction, attention, breath, memory, reward, movement, and social regulation. This is too complex to be left to automation. The therapist remains the custodian of timing, intensity, consent, meaning, and return. MUMEx can generate the field; the human professional must govern its clinical use.

At the end of this chapter, the brain is not the enemy of vision. It is one of vision's embodied forms. Speaking of networks, plasticity, HRV, entrainment, memory, and reward does not remove mystery from music. It prevents mystery from becoming vagueness. Sound remains greater than every explanation, yet explanation helps the field become responsible.

CHAPTER 27

Jung, Symbol, and Sonic Imagination

EPISTEMOLOGICAL LEVEL: *Depth-psychological model. Jungian concepts are used as symbolic and phenomenological tools, not as established neuroscientific or diagnostic claims.*

Jung enters Quantum Music Therapy because he offers a language for inner image that does not reduce it to private fantasy, perceptual error, or simple narrative content. The image, in depth psychology, is an event. It comes with force. It organizes attention, emotion, memory, and body. It may arise before interpretation and often resists explanation. Sound has a natural affinity with this territory because it can summon image without naming it.

Music therapy knows this phenomenon intimately. A patient hears a low tone and sees a cave. Another hears a bell and remembers a church from childhood. A slow string field evokes a feminine presence without any spoken story. A drumbeat brings an animal feeling into the body. None of these experiences should be treated as proof of metaphysical reality, nor dismissed as meaningless fantasy. They are events in the psyche. They matter because they change state.

The symbol differs from the sign. A sign points to something already known. A symbol gathers more meaning than consciousness can immediately hold. In a MUMEx session, a field may become symbolic when it carries a density of meaning that exceeds description: sea, night, mother, threshold, stone, descent, flight, wound, animal, star, house, or voice. The therapist should receive such material without rushing to decode it. The symbol must be allowed to breathe.

Jung's theory of archetypes and the collective unconscious remains one of the great twentieth-century attempts to think the continuity between personal experience and inherited symbolic patterns. It has been influential, criticized, reinterpreted, and often misused. In this book it is approached with respect and caution. Archetype is not used as a rigid template, nor as a license to impose mythological labels on the patient. It is used to describe recurring forms of psychic organization that may appear through image, affect, body, and sound.

A sound may evoke the maternal without naming a mother. It may make the shadow perceptible before any moral language arises. It may call forth the heroic without narrating a quest. It may open the feeling of death, rebirth, descent, protection, exile, or return. These are not universal mechanical effects. They are possible symbolic resonances. Culture, biography, religion, trauma, and personal imagination shape every encounter.

MUMEx must therefore avoid archetypal kitsch. A "mother field," "shadow field," or "hero field" would risk reducing the symbol to a preset aesthetic. The more serious task is to design fields capable of supporting symbolic emergence without dictating content. The field prepares depth; the patient's psyche provides form.

The shadow is especially relevant because sound can approach rejected material without the immediate defenses triggered by direct explanation. Anger, shame, envy, dependence, hunger for love, aggression, grief, and forbidden desire may appear first as timbre, pressure, rhythm, darkness, heaviness, or bodily resistance. The therapist must protect the patient from both avoidance and invasion. Shadow work in sound requires grounding, consent, and careful return.

Anima and animus, in Jungian language, point toward inner figures of otherness, mediation, and psychic complementarity. In contemporary work these concepts must be handled without gender essentialism. Their value for this model lies in the experience of encountering an inner presence that is both intimate and other. Sound can support such encounters through distance, timbre, call, echo, and suspended response. The field should never tell the patient what the figure means. It should allow the encounter to remain alive until the patient can find their own language.

The Self, understood as an organizing totality rather than the everyday ego, has a natural relation to music. A musical field can hold multiplicity without immediate contradiction: low and high, stable and moving, familiar and strange, personal and transpersonal. MUMEx may become a sonic environment in which scattered fragments begin to orbit a center. This does not mean the field produces individuation. It means the field can support experiences in which the psyche feels more organized, spacious, and whole.

Active imagination provides a bridge between Jungian practice and MUMEx. In active imagination, the person enters into relationship with an image, figure, scene, or affect rather than merely interpreting it from outside. Listening can become an acoustic form of active imagination. The patient does not chase images; the patient listens until something becomes present. The field provides time, containment, and atmosphere.

This form of listening requires restraint. The therapist should not say, "Now imagine a cave," or "Let the shadow appear." Such instructions overdetermine the field. Better is to offer a clear frame: notice whether the sound has body, place, distance, color, movement, or image. If nothing appears, nothing has failed. The absence of image may itself be meaningful. In depth work, forcing the symbol destroys it.

MUMEx can support active imagination through slow morphologies, controllable density, extended decays, subtle returns, and quiet spatial depth. The field should feel alive enough to invite relationship and stable enough to prevent disorientation. It is not a cinematic soundtrack for the unconscious. It is a disciplined environment for inner listening.

Symbolic material can be powerful and destabilizing. A patient may encounter grief, memory, fear, religious imagery, erotic charge, ancestral feeling, or archetypal intensity. The therapist must avoid interpretation that colonizes the experience. The safest first questions are phenomenological: where did you feel it, what changed in the body, did the image have distance, did it want anything, do you want to stay with it or return?

Clinical boundaries are essential. Jungian language should not be used to bypass trauma work, impose spiritual meaning, or romanticize distress. Not every image is deep. Not every intense experience is therapeutic. Not every archetypal resonance should be pursued. If the patient becomes flooded, confused, grandiose, dissociated, or frightened, the work returns to body, room, breath, and relationship. Reintegration is the ethical law of symbolic depth.

MUMEx should include symbolic work only when the patient can tolerate ambiguity and the therapist can hold the frame. The field must remain subordinate to the living person. No beautiful symbol matters more than the patient's capacity to return.

Archetypal Resonance in MUMEx does not mean programming universal symbols. It means designing sound fields that can carry depth without deciding meaning. Low sustained matter may support descent. Wide silence may support threshold. Cyclical pulse may support ritual time. Distant bells may support memory, calling, or passage. Granular textures may suggest dissolution. Warm harmonic ground may support holding. Each of these possibilities remains contextual.

The logbook becomes important here. If symbolic material emerges, the therapist records the field parameters and the patient's language without turning it into theory too quickly. Over time, patterns may appear: certain timbral ranges, densities, or temporal arcs may support imagery in some populations or states. This is where depth psychology can enter dialogue with disciplined observation.

The aim is not to prove Jung with sound. The aim is to use Jungian sensitivity to protect the symbolic dimension of music therapy from reduction. Neuroscience can describe networks and regulation; Jung helps name the fact that human beings do not suffer only as organisms. They suffer and heal as image-bearing creatures.

Symbolic emergence is incomplete until it returns to life. A patient may see a river, an animal, a door, a child, a figure of light, or a dark room. The therapeutic question is not only what it means. The question is what relation the patient can now have with the body, the world, and choice. Reintegration translates symbolic event into grounded presence.

MUMEx can assist this return by simplifying the field, reducing spatial depth, restoring warmth, softening motion, and bringing attention to breath, hands, feet, and present time. The therapist may ask whether one word, gesture, tone, or drawing should preserve the symbol. The goal is not closure. The goal is carrying the symbol without being carried away by it.

In this sense, Jungian depth strengthens Quantum Music Therapy by reminding it that sound does not act only on physiology. It acts on the imaginative life of the person. The human state includes symbol. A complete model must make room for it.

CHAPTER 28

Roberto Assagioli, Psychosynthesis, and the Inner Orchestra

EPISTEMOLOGICAL LEVEL: *Depth-psychological / integrative model. Assagioli is used to frame plurality, will, center, subpersonalities, and synthesis as therapeutic concepts compatible with sound-field practice.*

Roberto Assagioli's psychosynthesis offers Quantum Music Therapy a language of plurality and integration. The person is not a single block. Within each human being live tendencies, roles, wounds, ambitions, fears, protective structures, creative impulses, childish parts, disciplined parts, spiritual aspirations, and defensive formations. These parts may cooperate, conflict, ignore each other, or compete for control of the state.

Music is uniquely suited to this model because music already knows how plurality can become form. A chord contains different notes. A polyphony contains independent lines. An orchestra contains distinct timbres that can collide or converge. A rhythm section can support a melody without becoming it. Dissonance may need resolution or may hold necessary truth. Psychosynthesis and music meet around one central insight: unity is not sameness. It is organized multiplicity.

The patient who enters a session may say, "I want to change," while another part resists. One part wants exposure; another wants hiding. One part longs for tenderness; another protects through contempt. One part wants silence; another fears what silence will reveal. A sound field can help the person hear this plurality without immediately turning it into pathology.

Assagioli's concept of subpersonalities can be translated sonically with great precision, provided the translation remains sober. A subpersonality is not a theatrical character invented for effect. It is a relatively coherent pattern of feeling, posture, memory, belief, and action. It may have a voice, rhythm, weight, and spatial position in experience. The inner critic may be sharp, high, dry, or repetitive. The abandoned child may be quiet, low, distant, or breathless. The controlling part may be metronomic and rigid. The creative part may arrive in irregular bursts.

MUMEx can create short fields that allow these patterns to be sensed without caricature. The therapist might invite the patient to notice whether a part has sound, distance, density, or movement. The field may mirror very lightly, contrast gently, or hold a neutral ground. The patient should never be pushed into dramatization. The work is one of recognition, not performance.

The metaphor of the inner orchestra is powerful because it preserves both difference and relationship. The aim is not to silence difficult instruments. The aim is to hear what each part is trying to protect, express, or avoid. An aggressive brass-like energy may contain boundary. A fragile flute-like impulse may contain tenderness. A heavy drum may contain survival. Synthesis begins when the person can listen from a position larger than any single part.

Assagioli placed great emphasis on will. In contemporary therapeutic language, will is sometimes treated with suspicion because it can sound moralistic: as if suffering people simply needed to try harder. That is not the will required here. The will in psychosynthesis is closer to a capacity for direction, choice, and coordination. It is the possibility of taking a position within one's plurality.

Sound can strengthen this capacity without preaching. A field can give the body a line of movement, a pulse of continuation, a stable center, or a gentle direction forward. A patient may feel, perhaps for the first time, that an inner act is possible. The act may be small: breathe, stay, say no, stand, sound, return, choose, wait. Such acts matter because they restore agency in a state that has felt automatic.

The center is equally important. In psychosynthesis, the person is not identical with any subpersonality. There is an observing and choosing center capable of relating to the parts. In sound terms, this center is not a loud solo voice dominating the orchestra. It may be a quiet axis that allows the whole ensemble to become audible. MUMEx can support this experience through fields that do not overwhelm the patient with content yet create enough organization for inner listening.

Synthesis is not fusion. It is not the erasure of conflict. It is the emergence of a larger organization in which parts can relate. Musically, synthesis may happen when a rhythm that felt oppressive becomes grounding, when a fragile tone is supported by a warm field, when a harsh sound finds a place in the texture, or when silence allows several inner voices to remain present without collapsing into chaos.

The five operators provide a precise path. Resonance gives the person a ground. Suspension allows the plurality to appear without immediate solution. Gentle Perturbation helps rigid arrangements move. Perceptual Collapse may allow one inner configuration to become clear. Reintegration returns the person to center, body, and ordinary life. This does not make psychosynthesis automatic. It gives the therapist a musical grammar for integrative work.

A synthesis-oriented field should avoid excessive beauty. Beauty can seduce the patient into premature harmony. Some parts of the psyche need to remain rough before they can be integrated. The therapist must allow dissonance, unevenness, and uncertainty while protecting the patient from fragmentation. The goal is not a pleasant sound. The goal is a more truthful organization of the state.

MUMEx can function as a field of inner coordination. It can hold several layers simultaneously: a stable low ground, a distant irregular figure, a soft vocal trace, a pulsed element, and a long harmonic field. These layers may become analogues of inner parts. The patient does not need to assign labels immediately. The field allows complexity to be perceived as inhabitable.

This is particularly useful for people who experience inner life as noise, conflict, or fragmentation. When complexity is presented musically with enough structure, the person may feel that multiplicity itself can be held. The session becomes an experience of organization before it becomes an explanation of organization.

The logbook should record which layers were used, which felt supportive or intrusive, which part of the body responded, which images appeared, and whether the patient experienced more agency after the field. This creates a bridge between depth work and practical research. Inner plurality remains subjective, yet the field conditions that supported it can be described.

Working with parts, will, and synthesis requires ethical restraint. The therapist must not decide which part should dominate or which should disappear. Integration cannot be imposed. A defensive part may be protecting the patient from overwhelming material. A silent part may need respect rather than activation. A resistant part may be preserving dignity. The sound field should invite relationship among parts, never force confession or harmony.

Part work can become suggestive if handled carelessly. The therapist's language should remain open: "Does this sound connect with any part of you?" is safer than "This is your wounded child." The patient's own terms must lead. If a part becomes too intense, the work returns to orientation and body. Reintegration is not an afterthought; it is the condition that makes depth work responsible.

MUMEx should also distinguish educational exercises from clinical treatment. In training or artistic research, the language of inner parts can be explored lightly. In clinical settings, it requires competence, supervision, and awareness of trauma, dissociation, and diagnosis. A Super Premium edition for North America must state this clearly: the model is powerful because it is bounded.

Assagioli helps Quantum Music Therapy avoid two errors. The first is reducing the person to a symptom. The second is dissolving the person into endless fragments. The mature aim is centered plurality: a state in which the person can recognize inner parts without being possessed by them, can hear conflict without losing center, and can choose a direction without denying complexity.

When a session reaches this level, the patient is not made simpler. The patient becomes more organized. The inner orchestra does not become uniform. It becomes listenable. MUMEx offers a field in which this listening may begin: not as doctrine, not as cure by sound, but as an architecture for the gradual synthesis of state.

CHAPTER 29

Barry Simmons, Phil Stutz, and Sonic Inner Tools

EPISTEMOLOGICAL LEVEL: *Practical-transformative model. The references to Barry Simmons and Phil Stutz are used for their operational interest in inner tools, visualization, will, and state transition. They are not presented as established music-therapy evidence.*

Contemporary psychology has often separated what experience keeps together: image, gesture, breath, will, sound, and decision. One tradition privileges analysis; another privileges action. One asks for understanding; another asks for practice. Quantum Music Therapy is interested in the place where understanding becomes act. The patient does not need only an interpretation of the block. The patient often needs a tool that can be used when the state returns.

The line that brings Barry Simmons and Phil Stutz into this discussion is practical. Phil Stutz's Tools, known widely through clinical and public work, are active procedures built from image, gesture, intention, and repetition. Barry Simmons is invoked here within a broader frontier of inner practice and transformative method. Both references are used cautiously: they are not cited as music-therapy authorities, nor as substitutes for evidence-based care. They are useful because they force the question of operative transformation. How does a person move from being trapped in a state to having an act within that state?

Music understands tools because music is practice. A scale, a breathing pattern, a rhythm, a motif, a cadence, a warm-up, and a return phrase are all tools. They do not merely explain. They train access. A sonic inner tool is a short, repeatable, embodied field that helps a person recognize a state and perform a small act of transition.

A sonic inner tool requires several elements. First, it must identify a state: avoidance, anger, insecurity, shame, collapse, dissociation, stagnation, or creative block. Second, it must create a sound form that makes the state recognizable without intensifying it beyond tolerance. Third, it must introduce an act: step forward, breathe, voice, contain, soften, stand, choose, or return. Fourth, it must close with a clear word, gesture, or silence that seals the transition. Without closure, the tool remains atmospheric rather than operative.

The tool should be brief. A three-minute field may be more effective than a long immersive journey. The patient should be able to remember it in the body. The field may have a stable opening, a small challenge, a decision point, and Reintegration. In this sense, the sonic inner tool is closer to a ritual microform than to a composition. It is designed for use, not contemplation alone.

MUMEx is well suited to this because it can generate controlled microforms. The same tool can be personalized across density, timbre, register, tempo, and spatial depth. It can remain recognizable while adapting to different days. The patient learns: when this state returns, I have a sound-path, a breath-path, an act-path. This is where technology becomes practical psychology.

Every block has a temporal signature. Avoidance has stagnant, viscous, circular time. Anxiety has accelerated, anticipatory, fragmented time. Anger held inside has contracted, pulsing time. Insecurity has hesitant time, interrupted before action. A sonic tool must address this temporal architecture. It cannot apply generic calm to every difficulty.

For avoidance, the field may begin with stable low ground and then introduce a discreet forward pulse. The sound does not push violently. It makes movement possible. A small sonic threshold appears, and the patient practices crossing it with breath, voice, or gesture. The therapeutic act is not heroic conquest. It is a contained step.

For anger, the sound must neither anesthetize nor inflame. Anger often contains boundary, dignity, protest, and energy. A field may provide firm rhythmic containment, low impact, and a safe channel for vocal or percussive expression. The goal is to give anger shape without allowing it to become domination. Reintegration returns the patient from charge to choice.

For insecurity, sound must touch posture and inner volume. Insecurity is not only negative thought. It is a reduced internal amplitude, a voice asking permission to exist. A sonic tool may build a simple ascending line, a warm harmonic support, or a steady pulse under a spoken phrase. The patient practices occupying slightly more space. The act may be one word said with breath.

Shadow work requires even greater care. The tool should allow the rejected part to be sensed, heard, and placed at a safe distance. Too close, and the patient is flooded. Too far, and the work becomes elegant dissociation.

The field creates relational distance: near enough to matter, far enough to observe.

Stutz's concept of Life Force can be reinterpreted sonically without turning it into doctrine. For Quantum Music Therapy, life force is not a metaphysical object that must be defined. It is an observable quality of state: vitality, impulse, readiness, breath, tone, movement, and the sense that action is possible. Many people are separated from their strength not because they lack ideas, but because the body has learned to extinguish impulse before it becomes action.

A brief sonic form can help reawaken agency. It may begin with recognition of collapse, introduce a pulse that the body can join, open a small field of choice, and close with a phrase: I stay. I move. I return. I choose. I breathe. The phrase should be the patient's own whenever possible. The sound prepares the act; the act gives the sound psychological consequence.

The value lies in repeatability. A tool that works only once as a dramatic experience is less useful than a modest form the patient can practice. Repetition trains access. Variation prevents dead ritual. MUMEx can preserve the identity of the tool while adjusting intensity, length, and color. This gives the patient continuity without mechanical sameness.

Daily practice deserves attention because many therapeutic insights weaken outside the session. Sonic inner tools may be designed for safe use in ordinary life: before a difficult conversation, after emotional collapse, during creative block, or when the body needs orientation. They should be short, simple, and bounded. They should not require deep altered states or complex interpretation.

Home use requires limits. Materials involving trauma, regression, intense shadow, violent imagery, dissociation, or unstable states should not be reactivated alone. A tool for daily use should focus on grounding, breath, agency, orientation, or gentle movement. The patient must know when to stop and when to seek professional support. The companion audio or MUMEx field must never imply that unsupervised practice replaces clinical care.

Documentation remains useful. The patient may record date, state before, tool used, state after, difficulty, and one sentence of reflection. Over time, the tool becomes not only an intervention but a map of state patterns. The logbook extends from therapist to patient in a simplified form.

The five operators translate naturally into inner tools. Resonance becomes the tool of returning to bodily support. Suspension becomes the tool of staying with the unknown without panic. Gentle Perturbation becomes the tool of moving a rigid state by one degree. Perceptual Collapse becomes the tool of allowing a hidden form to become visible without forcing revelation. Reintegration becomes the tool of returning to ordinary life after any opening.

Each operator can become a micropractice. A Resonance tool may last two minutes and ask only: where does the sound meet the body? A Suspension tool may train tolerance for ten seconds of silence. A Gentle Perturbation tool may introduce one unexpected sound and ask whether change can remain safe. A Perceptual Collapse tool may ask the patient to let one word, image, or gesture arise. A Reintegration tool may name room, feet, breath, and present time.

The strength of this approach is that it keeps the grand architecture of MUMEx close to daily life. The operators are not only theoretical categories. They become acts a person can learn. The model becomes embodied through practice.

There is nobility in simplicity. In work with image, will, and inner parts, excessive complexity often weakens the therapeutic act. The patient must remember the tool, feel it in the body, and be able to repeat it without theatricality. A single tone, one breath, one pulse, one word, one gesture, and one return may be enough. The field should have dignity, not spectacle.

Barry Simmons and Phil Stutz, placed within the path of Quantum Music Therapy, represent a shared question: how can an inner act modify a state? The sonic answer does not cancel visualization, cognitive work, or clinical relationship. It adds a temporal and bodily medium. Sound makes the act felt. MUMEx makes the act designable, repeatable, and revisable.

After Jungian symbol and Assagioli's synthesis, sonic inner tools bring transformation into ordinary life. The session does not remain an isolated event. It becomes the source of small rituals that help a person resist being devoured by automatic states. Modern life has replaced many rituals with instructions, diagnoses, and applications. Quantum Music Therapy restores a more ancient possibility in contemporary form: a sound, a breath, a gesture, and a return.

PART SEVEN

COSMOS, ALTERITY, AND FRONTIERS

CHAPTER 30

Quantum Vibrations of the Natural World and the Body-Mind Apparatus

EPISTEMOLOGICAL LEVEL: *Cosmological-metaphorical model. This chapter distinguishes physical vibration, biological oscillation, clinical resonance, and metaphor. It does not collapse quantum physics into therapy. It uses vibration as a disciplined bridge between scale, body, and perception.*

The word vibration has a double life. In one sense, it names a precise physical phenomenon: oscillation, periodic movement, energy moving through a structure, measurable change in a variable over time. In another sense, it has become a cultural and spiritual word, used to describe mood, atmosphere, resonance, attraction, intuition, and state. Quantum Music Therapy must hold these two lives together without confusing them.

A sound wave is not a metaphor. It is a physical event moving through a medium. A chest that trembles under a low tone is not only an image. It is a body receiving mechanical energy. At the same time, the experience of vibration is never merely mechanical. The patient hears with skin, memory, fear, expectation, and biography. The vibration that reaches tissue also reaches meaning.

This is why the phrase body-mind apparatus is useful. It names the human being as an active system in which body and consciousness are not separate territories. Breath, heart rhythm, muscular tone, attention, memory, internal imagery, and relational safety form a living apparatus. Sound enters that apparatus and is selected, resisted, amplified, interpreted, and transformed.

The quantum dimension must be handled with discipline. Quantum biology studies cases in which quantum effects may play roles in living systems, such as photosynthesis, enzyme processes, magnetoreception, and sensory mechanisms. This does not authorize vague claims that every therapeutic experience is quantum in a physical sense. The language of Quantum Music Therapy is stronger when it refuses inflation.

In this book, quantum refers primarily to a model of state: possibility, context, interference, transition, observation, and emergence. It does not claim that a MUMEx Sound Field manipulates subatomic processes in the patient. It proposes that a Generative Sound Field can work with human states in a way that resembles a quantum-like grammar: several possibilities coexist until a context, a sound, a question, or a silence helps one form become experience.

This distinction protects the project. A frontier discipline loses credibility when it uses scientific terms as ornaments. It becomes stronger when each term is sharpened until it can support method. The word quantum remains legitimate here because it organizes a theory of state change, not because it offers a miraculous credential.

The natural world vibrates across countless scales. Wind moves leaves with fluctuations that never repeat exactly. Water creates continuity and fracture. Insects produce dense fields of micro-pulses. Birds generate motifs, calls, alarm signals, and territorial forms. The body lives among these patterns and learns from them before it can name them.

The human organism is also polyrhythmic. Breath has frequency, depth, and variability. The heart accelerates and slows. Muscles contract and release. The vestibular system orients movement. Circadian rhythms organize sleep and wakefulness. The nervous system moves through activation, vigilance, rest, and repair. Music therapy works inside this polyrhythm.

A rhythm can support gait, a drone can expand the felt body, a voice can soften defensive attention, and a tactile vibration can make forgotten areas of the body perceptible. None of this implies a simple causal law. A low tone may ground one person and oppress another. A repetitive pulse may stabilize one state and trap another. Natural vibration becomes clinical only when it is mediated by assessment, consent, and observation.

Resonance must be protected as a technical and clinical word. In physics, resonance refers to a system responding with greater amplitude when driven near one of its natural frequencies. In clinical language, resonance often means compatibility, recognition, and the feeling that a sound meets the body without violating it. These meanings can dialogue, yet they cannot be collapsed into one another.

Mechanotransduction helps build a sober bridge between vibration and the body. Cells and tissues respond to physical forces: pressure, stretch, compression, movement, and tension. These processes remind us that the body is not acoustically passive. It converts force into biological signal. Vibroacoustic work occupies a related territory, especially when low frequencies or tactile transducers are used.

Clinical caution is essential. Vibratory stimulation may be valuable in some contexts and inappropriate in others. Pregnancy, implanted medical devices, acute inflammation, pain conditions, seizure vulnerability, cardiac instability, trauma history, sensory hypersensitivity, and anxiety states all require discernment. A Super Premium edition for North America must state this clearly: no vibrational method should be presented as universally safe or universally therapeutic.

MUMEx can learn from natural vibration without turning nature into decorative audio. A field inspired by water should not merely reproduce water. It should study continuity, microfracture, flow, surface, pressure, and return. A field inspired by birds should not merely imitate calls. It should study motif, response, spacing, interruption, and orientation. A field inspired by wind should study density, breath, fluctuation, and invisible movement.

Natural fields teach that living repetition is never mechanical. A forest repeats without looping. A stream continues without becoming identical to itself. Animal voices return while carrying context. This is precisely the differencc between a therapeutic Generative Sound Field and a passive ambience track. The field must remain alive, yet it must remain clinically inhabitable.

For MUMEx, natural vibration becomes a design matrix. The therapist can select density, register, texture, temporal variability, spatial motion, and silence according to the patient's state. The aim is not immersion for its own sake. The aim is to create conditions in which the body-mind apparatus can reorganize safely.

In trauma, the body may remain organized around alarm. A sudden sound can reopen threat grammar before the patient has time to think. For this reason, fields designed for traumatized states should privilege predictability, soft boundaries, low startle potential, patient control, and clear return. Gentle Perturbation must remain truly gentle. Intensity is not courage when it overwhelms the nervous system.

In depression, vibration may help restore world-contact. Depression often flattens time, dulls the environment, and makes the body heavy or remote. A subtle field can reintroduce texture, gravity, breath, and minute movement. The point is not to brighten the patient artificially. It is to restore the possibility that the world can be felt again.

In anxiety, vibration can function as boundary. The anxious organism often projects itself into anticipated danger. A bodily sound can return weight, edge, and rhythm. Yet a pulse that is too insistent can intensify control. A drone that is too dense can feel suffocating. The clinical question is always specific: what configuration of sound makes this person more able to stay present?

The word cosmos enters here because the body is never separate from the world. Every organism lives under gravity, light-dark cycles, weather, season, landscape, and acoustic environment. The body is not an isolated machine placed inside the universe. It is a rhythmic being inside a rhythmic order that exceeds it.

Quantum Music Therapy should not confuse cosmic scale with clinical proof. It should translate scale into method. Technical parameters—event density, dynamic range, dominant register, periodicity, spatial distribution, attack, decay, and duration—can be documented. State markers—breath, tension, presence, imagery, fear, calm, and return—can be observed. The bridge between cosmos and clinic is not enthusiasm. It is design, logbook, and accountability.

A MUMEx Sound Field can remind the body of its own oscillation, the mind of its plasticity, and perception of its capacity to widen without losing ground. That is the real promise. Not a universal frequency, not a cosmic cure, but a disciplined field in which scale, vibration, and human state can enter relation.

CHAPTER 31

Michael Wolf and Music Therapy Beyond the Boundaries of the System

EPISTEMOLOGICAL LEVEL: *Frontier territory. Michael Wolf, alienness, and controversial materials are treated as imagination, testimony, symbolic stimulus, and methodological provocation, not as scientific proof or established clinical evidence.*

The alien is one of the most powerful figures in contemporary imagination because it forces the human being to lose centrality. It is not only the being from elsewhere, the unknown creature, or the cosmic visitor entering terrestrial history. It is what exceeds our perceptual vocabulary. It is the face of radical alterity: a possible intelligence that might communicate without our language, perceive without our ear, remember without our memory, and inhabit time according to geometries we can barely imagine.

Music therapy has always worked with forms of alienness. The aphasic patient whose language no longer reaches the world, the traumatized person who experiences the body as foreign territory, the autistic child whose sensory maps do not obey social norms, the elder with dementia who seems to recede into another temporality, and the depressed person who feels reality as a dead planet all bring distance into the room. Therapy begins when that distance is heard without being colonized.

For this reason, alienness can be treated as a clinical metaphor of great force. The question is not whether a therapist believes in extraterrestrial life. The question is whether the therapist can meet what is radically other in the patient without reducing it too quickly to symptom, fantasy, resistance, or pathology.

Michael Wolf belongs to a controversial landscape of UFO narratives, alleged disclosure, insider testimony, and spiritual-extraterrestrial literature. His name is associated with The Catchers of Heaven and with claims that circulate in ufological environments. These materials must be handled with exceptional clarity in a North American scholarly edition.

The methodological position is firm: Wolf is not cited here as a clinical authority, a scientific source, or proof of extraterrestrial contact. He is treated as frontier material—an example of how contemporary culture imagines contact, secrecy, cosmic intelligence, and the expansion of human identity beyond ordinary systems. This distinction is not a retreat. It is what allows the topic to be discussed without collapsing into credulity or ridicule.

An unverified testimony can be scientifically weak and psychologically powerful. A contact narrative may fail as evidence and still reveal a deep hunger for cosmic communication, perceptual enlargement, and escape from anthropocentric imprisonment. Music therapy is not asked to certify aliens. It can study how images of absolute alterity modify body, listening, fear, hope, and the sense of human limit.

Extraterrestrial contact, even when it remains hypothesis or myth, challenges our idea of communication. Human culture tends to imagine language as the exchange of signs between similar minds. Radical alterity forces another possibility: communication based on pattern, rhythm, symmetry, repetition, variation, energy, distance, and response.

Before semantic meaning, there may be regularity. Before a sentence, there may be periodicity. Before argument, there may be shared temporal form. In this light, music appears less as entertainment and more as a primordial technology of recognition. It trains us to perceive relation before translation.

This has immediate relevance for the clinic. Many patients do not initially communicate in ordinary discursive forms. Their first language may be movement, sound avoidance, gaze, repetition, pressure, silence, rocking, vocal fragment, or refusal. The music therapist must know how to listen before language arrives.

MUMEx can become a poetic and experimental machine for exploring alienness without reproducing cinematic clichés. The alien sound field is not theremin, spaceship hum, metallic whistle, endless reverb, or filtered voice as effect. Those materials may have cultural charm, yet they do not constitute therapy.

A therapeutic field of radical alterity must remain inhabitable. It should allow the patient to sense strangeness without toxic disorientation. It should open imagination without dissolving orientation. It should create vastness without encouraging dissociative flight. Its power lies in function, not spectacle.

Such a field may be extremely simple: a remote pulse, an unstable harmonic, a barely moving granular texture, a transformed human voice that approaches nonhuman quality and then returns to recognizability. The trajectory matters: approach, perception, support, response, and return. The field becomes ethical when it brings the strange back into relation.

Patients may bring extraordinary narratives into therapeutic space: luminous beings, presences, nonhuman dreams, cosmic messages, memories beyond ordinary biography, or a sense of belonging to elsewhere. The therapist must neither automatically confirm nor automatically deride such material. The clinical question is state-based: what happens in the body while this is told? Does the narrative increase life or isolation? Does it bring orientation or disorganization? Does it soften fear or intensify grandiosity?

Sound can hold the quality of an experience before classification. Speech often rushes to categories: belief, fantasy, symptom, symbol, memory. A low-density MUMEx field, a distant bell, a quiet drone, a sparse granular texture, or a shared silence can give the image enough space to show its function. The aim is not to decide immediately what it is. The aim is to discover what it does to the human state.

This requires clinical maturity. Extraordinary imagery may carry trauma, loneliness, creativity, spiritual search, psychotic vulnerability, mythic imagination, or genuine symbolic transformation. The same image can be liberating in one subject and destabilizing in another. The sound field must follow the person, not the fascination of the theme.

Work with alienness, trance, regression, hypnosis, imagination, and generative fields must acknowledge suggestion. A vulnerable person can adopt cosmic narratives to defend against human pain. A facilitator's enthusiasm can amplify fragile beliefs. A sound field can dramatize material that should instead be grounded. These risks are not reasons to avoid the frontier. They are reasons to enter it with discipline.

Ethical containment means clear framing. The therapist can say that the session will work with images, sensations, and states, without validating extraordinary claims as literal facts. The patient remains free to describe experience, yet the therapist keeps attention on body, safety, breath, relationship, and return. This is respect, not skepticism disguised as coldness.

MUMEx design should avoid coercive atmospheres. Overwhelming spatialization, intense sub-bass, excessive darkness, suggestive verbal prompting, and theatrical build-ups can push the patient toward predesigned visions. A Super Premium clinical text must reject this. The field must invite, not impose.

The deepest value of the alien theme may be human hospitality. To imagine a nonhuman intelligence is to practice humility before another perceptual world. This humility returns to the clinic. The patient's way of hearing may differ from ours. Their silence may be full. Their repetition may be shelter. Their fear of voice may have logic. Their need for distance may be a precise form of contact.

MUMEx can help construct environments where the unfamiliar is not immediately normalized or expelled. The therapist becomes host to alterity. The room becomes a place where strange material can appear, be heard, be contained, and be returned to the body. In that sense, the alien is not an escape from music therapy. It is a severe test of its hospitality.

Music therapy beyond the boundaries of the system does not abandon the system's ethics. It expands the boundary of listening. It asks whether sound can meet what language has not yet domesticated. It answers with method: consent, field, observation, containment, and Reintegration.

CHAPTER 32

Cosmic Music Therapy

EPISTEMOLOGICAL LEVEL: *Frontier territory / experiential model. Cosmic Music Therapy addresses vastness, sonification, awe, symbolic scale, and bodily return. It distinguishes acoustic sound, data sonification, metaphor, and therapeutic experience.*

Cosmic Music Therapy begins when sound is taken to the outer limit of human scale: the relationship between the finite body and immensity. The cosmos does not offer only stars, planets, nebulae, pulsars, galaxies, dark matter, radiation, and gravitational fields. It offers a different measure of being. It reduces the tyranny of the small self, expands time, and places private suffering in relation to a depth no ordinary room can contain.

This vastness can be healing only if it returns. A session that opens the patient to cosmic scale but leaves the body behind is incomplete. The aim is not escape from Earth. The aim is a widened presence. The patient should return with more space inside, not with less orientation.

The formula is simple and demanding: sky and floor. The field may open to the stars, yet the body must feel the ground. The imagination may travel, yet the voice must bring it back. The therapeutic value of immensity is measured by the quality of return.

The first clarification concerns silence. Space does not sound like a terrestrial room because ordinary sound requires a material medium capable of transmitting pressure waves. Much rhetoric about "the sound of space" ignores this elementary fact. Cosmic phenomena may involve oscillations, radiation, impulses, field variations, electromagnetic signals, gravitational waves, and periodic patterns, yet to make them audible requires translation.

Sonification maps data into sound. It may compress time, assign pitch to a variable, translate brightness into register, convert intensity into loudness, or turn periodic signals into audible rhythm. The result is not a direct recording of celestial music. It is a sensory translation. This does not weaken the poetry. It makes it honest (Arcand et al., 2024; National Aeronautics and Space Administration, 2025).

Many astronomical images are also translations: data outside the visible spectrum are rendered through assigned color. Sonification performs a related act for the ear. It makes pattern, periodicity, density, distance, energy, and variation available in time. For music therapy, this is crucial because listening is always temporal. The patient experiences data as duration, not as a static image.

The pulsar is a powerful figure for this work. Its periodic signal can be imagined as a cosmic pulse: not human heartbeat, yet capable of entering dialogue with heartbeat. Used therapeutically, the point is not to create a science-fiction effect. The point is to study impulse, distance, regularity, density, and orientation. A pulsar-like field can give the patient a rhythm that is remote and stable enough to reframe inner time.

Nebulae suggest another quality: diffusion, birth, dissolution, matter before definitive form. A field inspired by a nebula may be useful when the patient cannot yet name what is emerging. It should not push the psyche toward premature definition. It should hold an atmosphere in which images can gather slowly.

Black holes carry an imagery of attraction, limit, event horizon, invisibility, density, and loss. Their use requires caution because they may activate fantasies of annihilation. Treated with precision, however, they can give form to states many patients know: being pulled inward, losing light, circling a dark center, feeling a force greater than will. A MUMEx field should not seek terror. It should work with edge: approach without falling, intensity without collapse, gravity followed by return.

Gravitational waves introduce a subtler model. Their audio translations can create the impression that the fabric of the universe has made a gesture. For therapeutic design, the principle is not spectacle. It is convergent transformation: tension, acceleration, contact, release. A field may use this logic to move a diffuse state toward a controlled point of change and then release it into quiet.

Cosmic experience often evokes awe: the encounter with something vast, complex, and difficult to assimilate. Awe can reorganize the self by reducing its claim to occupy the entire perceptual horizon. This matters clinically. A person trapped in failure, grief, injury, shame, or anxiety may benefit from a field in which the self becomes smaller without being humiliated.

This is not the same as telling a suffering person that their pain is insignificant. That would be cruel. The task is to let space appear around the pain. The body remains, the story remains, the wound remains; around it, a wider field emerges. This wider field may allow the patient to breathe differently.

Vastness must be dosed. For some people, immensity brings peace; for others, fear, derealization, or loss of boundary. Cosmic material is not automatically safe because it is beautiful. The beauty of a galaxy does not absolve the therapist from assessment. The field must be sized to the state.

A MUMEx cosmic field can be designed as a multi-layered matrix. A gravitational layer offers mass through slow low-register material. A pulsar layer introduces regular or near-regular impulses. A nebular layer creates diffuse matter. A stellar layer produces brief distant appearances. A human vocal layer guarantees return. A silence layer preserves distance between events.

The key is restraint. The cosmos is not full because everything is sounding at once. It is vast because distance exists between events. A cosmic field should therefore resist saturation. Too much material creates spectacle; too little structure creates emptiness without orientation. The therapeutic field needs vastness with architecture.

Generativity gives MUMEx a philosophical advantage. The universe itself appears as process: stars are born and die, elements form, planets gather, organic molecules emerge, life appears, consciousness listens. A Generative Sound Field does not imitate the universe. It echoes one of its formal laws: living stability contains variation.

The human voice remains indispensable. Even the most refined cosmic field often needs a voice that says presence. Not a voice that overexplains. Not a voice that interprets too quickly. A voice that marks return, names the body, offers orientation, and reminds the patient that the room exists, the breath is here, and the journey has an end.

Acoustic instruments can serve as anchors. A bell can mark emergence. A slow drum can offer gravity. A gong can expand if governed carefully. A small object close to the patient can restore proximity. Electronics should not devour acoustic matter. Cosmic Music Therapy is most powerful when remote and near coexist: a distant stellar pulse and a present breath, a galactic field and a human note, a huge silence and a hand on a drum.

Debriefing after a cosmic field should be simple. Asking too quickly, "What does it mean?" may compress a form that is still forming. Better questions begin with body, space, time, and image: where is the body now? Does the room feel closer or farther away? Was time slow or fast? Did an image arise? Is there something that should remain silent? Meaning can come later.

Cosmic sound also has an ethical dimension of accessibility. Sonification can make astronomical data available to blind and visually impaired people, reminding us that the cosmos does not belong only to the eye. The ear can become a way of entering the sky. In music therapy, this opens inclusive practices in which science, art, and perception meet without rigid sensory hierarchies (Arcand et al., 2024).

Research on sonification suggests that listening can increase access, engagement, and emotional relation to scientific data. For Quantum Music Therapy, this matters because it shows that translated data are not merely decorative. Sound is a mode of embodied knowledge. Where an image offers simultaneity, sound requires sequence. Sequence changes state.

Cosmic Music Therapy can therefore be summarized as the art of vastness and return. Human beings need sky and floor. They need to feel that their story is not the whole universe, yet their story still deserves care. MUMEx can generate the sonic sky. The music therapist must guarantee the floor.

CHAPTER 33

The Q-MUMEx SMP-001 Protocol

EPISTEMOLOGICAL LEVEL: *Experimental protocol / pilot research design. SMP-001 translates the model of Generative Sound Fields into a cautious, testable, ethically governed research procedure.*

The Q-MUMEx State Modulation Protocol (SMP-001) is the first operational bridge between the philosophy of the field and the science of the session. It asks a precise question: can a Generative Sound Field, designed through state operators and documented in its parameters, modify human experience differently from fixed music or a neutral condition?

This question matters because vision alone is not enough. Generativity is not enough. Beauty is not enough. The model becomes research only when it accepts interrogation: what happens, to whom, under which conditions, with which parameters, for how long, with what safety signals, and with what possibility of replication?

SMP-001 should begin modestly and strongly. Modestly, because the first study should involve healthy adults and exploratory outcomes. Strongly, because its structure must be clean enough to generate usable knowledge. The protocol should not seek to prove a cure. It should determine feasibility, tolerability, and preliminary state modulation.

The recommended first design is a randomized, counterbalanced, within-subject pilot study. Each participant experiences three conditions on separate sessions or in carefully separated blocks: a MUMEx Generative Sound Field, a fixed music condition matched as closely as possible in duration and broad affective profile, and a neutral or low-stimulation control condition.

The MUMEx condition must be defined by version, duration, operator profile, density, register, dynamic range, spatial behavior, and transition architecture. The fixed music condition must not be chosen casually. It should be selected or composed to provide a credible comparison without generative adaptation. The control condition should be quiet, ethically acceptable, and not humiliatingly empty.

Counterbalancing is essential because order changes state. A participant who hears the MUMEx field after silence is not the same as a participant who hears it after fixed music. SMP-001 must treat sequence as a variable, not as an administrative detail.

The initial sample should involve healthy adults with sufficient hearing and the capacity to give informed consent. Exclusion criteria should be explicit: acute psychiatric instability, recent severe trauma activation, active suicidal ideation, uncontrolled seizure vulnerability, severe sound hypersensitivity, acute panic instability, and any medical condition that would make immersive or vibratory listening unsafe (World Medical Association, 2024).

Consent must explain that the study examines responses to sound environments. It should not promise relaxation, healing, insight, or transformation. It should clearly state that participants may stop at any moment. The stop procedure should be simple: a word, gesture, or button. The facilitator must reduce or interrupt the field immediately when needed.

Safety is not a secondary section of the protocol. It is its ethical spine. The room should have stable light, a clear exit, water, seating or reclining support, and enough time for recovery. The participant must be oriented before leaving. No data point is worth a disorganized human being.

Each session should follow a stable structure: arrival, orientation, baseline state measures, baseline physiological recording when available, listening condition, immediate post-condition measures, short non-directive debriefing, grounding, and follow-up check. The facilitator's language must remain neutral across conditions.

The listening period should be long enough to allow state change and short enough to preserve safety and feasibility. Early versions may use ten to twenty minutes, depending on the population, equipment, and ethics approval. The protocol should not confuse endurance with depth. A short field can produce clearer data than a long journey.

The debriefing must avoid leading questions. It should not ask whether the participant felt the power of MUMEx. It should ask what was noticed: body, breath, time, images, comfort, discomfort, orientation, emotion, and return. A serious protocol protects the participant from the researcher's desire.

SMP-001 should combine subjective, physiological, and technical data. Subjective measures may include tension, calm, body presence, absorption, mental noise, state anxiety, perceived time, safety, and quality of return. Physiological measures may include HRV, respiration, movement, and skin conductance when available and appropriate. These are windows, not verdicts.

The MUMEx logbook is the methodological core. Every session should record the field code, system version, duration, operator profile, initial parameters, density changes, dynamic profile, register, spatial motion, perturbation events, return pattern, manual interventions, and facilitator notes. If a participant reports an image at minute fourteen, the logbook should allow the researcher to see what the field was doing at that point.

Traceability is the difference between a private experience and a researchable event. The field must be archived with enough detail for future comparison. A beautiful session that cannot be described technically remains anecdote. MUMEx becomes science when the field leaves a memory outside the therapist's impression (Edwards et al., 2023; Robb et al., 2025).

The first outcomes are feasibility and tolerability: completion rate, interruptions, adverse events, quality of physiological data, clarity of instructions, and acceptability of the setting. Exploratory outcomes may compare changes across conditions in tension, calm, body presence, absorption, mental noise, state anxiety, HRV, respiration, and richness of imagery.

Analysis should remain proportionate to the pilot nature of the study. Within-subject comparisons, mixed models, and qualitative thematic analysis may be appropriate depending on sample size and data quality. The protocol must distinguish exploratory signals from confirmatory evidence. A promising pattern is not proof. A negative result is not failure. It is information.

Interpretation must avoid inflation. If HRV changes, the study has not proven deep transformation. If participants describe vastness, the study has not proven cosmic healing. If MUMEx differs from fixed music, the next step is refinement and replication. Scientific maturity consists in letting the data alter the theory.

Public communication around SMP-001 must be restrained. It should speak of feasibility, tolerability, preliminary signals, subjective reports, limitations, and next research steps. It should never state that MUMEx cures, that Quantum Music Therapy has been proven, or that a physiological marker validates a metaphysical claim.

If SMP-001 produces useful results, subsequent studies can move gradually toward specific populations: mild anxiety, occupational stress, subclinical insomnia, music therapists in training, high sensory sensitivity, supportive oncology settings, older adults with mild cognitive change, or meditation groups. Each population will require new criteria, supervision, ethics review, and clinical adaptation.

Transparency must become part of the identity of the project. Every field used in research should be archived with code, version, parameters, duration, audio rendering when possible, logbook, facilitator notes, and context of use. Every protocol change should be justified. Every unexpected event should be recorded. Frontier research must be more disciplined than ordinary research because it carries more possibility and more suspicion.

For the protocol to function as an independent research document, the following requirements should be stabilized before any study with human participants:

- Design and sample: randomized, counterbalanced, within-subject pilot study; approximately thirty to thirty-six healthy adults; three comparable conditions.
- Inclusion and exclusion: informed consent, sufficient hearing, and absence of acute instability; exclusion of uncontrolled seizure vulnerability, acute psychiatric crisis, active suicidal ideation, severe sound hypersensitivity, and unstable trauma activation.
- Safety: word, gesture, or button for stopping; immediate reduction or interruption of the field; body orientation, stable light, water, and recovery time.
- Measures: feasibility, tolerability, completion, adverse events, tension, calm, body presence, absorption, respiration, HRV when available, and post-session narrative.
- Analysis: pre-post changes and models appropriate to the sample; rigorous distinction between exploratory and confirmatory claims.
- Ethics and communication: independent review when required, confidential data, non-directive debriefing, and no public promise of healing.

SMP-001 does not domesticate the mystery of sound. It gives that mystery a structure strong enough to be discussed, criticized, repeated, and improved.

CHAPTER 34

Manifesto for MUMEx Quantum Music Therapy

EPISTEMOLOGICAL LEVEL: *Theoretical-operational manifesto. This final chapter synthesizes the poetic, ethical, clinical, technological, and methodological position of the entire book.*

MUMEx Quantum Music Therapy rests on a simple and severe conviction: sound can modify the human state when it is conceived as a field, governed by method, held within relationship, and returned to the body. Sound is not only language. It is environment, pressure, vibration, temporal architecture, memory, and possibility.

The human being is sonic before being discursive. Before the sentence, there is heartbeat. Before argument, breath. Before narrated biography, rhythm, tone, vibration, gesture, tension, silence, cry, and song. Music therapy matters because it works at this primary layer of human organization.

A state is not an emotion. It is a configuration of body, attention, breath, memory, posture, imagery, safety, relationship, and choice. The task of Quantum Music Therapy is to design fields in which the state can move without being forced.

MUMEx does not replace music therapy. It extends its frontier. The patient is not a receiver of sound effects. The patient is part of the field. The therapist is not an operator of a machine. The therapist is custodian of the field. The technology is not the center. The human relationship is the center.

The most advanced therapeutic technology is not the one that does the most. It is the one that knows how to withdraw. A MUMEx field must be able to become quieter, simpler, less beautiful, less dense, more spacious, and finally silent when the state requires it. Clinical intelligence is often the art of doing less at the decisive moment.

No algorithm responds morally for the state it helps to change. The music therapist remains responsible for timing, intensity, consent, containment, meaning, and return. MUMEx generates the field; human presence decides whether the field can become transformative experience.

The five sonic operators form the grammar of the model. Resonance establishes compatibility between body and field. Suspension opens a duration in which the patient can remain among possibilities without premature definition. Gentle Perturbation introduces difference without violence. Perceptual Collapse marks the moment when a diffuse plurality becomes image, breath, word, gesture, or orientation. Reintegration returns experience to body, room, speech, and shared time.

These operators are not recipes. They are functions. They may combine, return, interrupt one another, reverse intensity, or remain latent. Every patient requires a trajectory. An anxious person may need long Resonance before any perturbation. A depressed person may need Gentle Perturbation before Suspension becomes possible. A traumatized person may need Reintegration from the first minute.

The operators protect the model from vagueness. They allow practitioners to ask concrete questions: what is this field doing? Which state is it addressing? What is being opened? What is being protected? What marks the return?

The body is the first laboratory. Ear, skin, bone, chest, diaphragm, abdomen, throat, skull, vestibular system, hands, feet, posture, and breath all participate in listening. A therapy of sound that forgets the body becomes abstraction. MUMEx must remain bodily or it loses its truth.

The voice has absolute precedence. No generative system, however refined, can equal the incarnate quality of the human voice. The voice carries breath, age, wound, authority, tenderness, fear, courage, and presence. In many sessions, the voice is the bridge between field and person.

Improvisation is the living proof of the field. To improvise in music therapy is not to display freedom. It is to recognize another's sonic gesture, answer it, transform it, hold it, and return it. MUMEx must serve this relational intelligence, not replace it.

Nature is matrix, not ornament. Garden, forest, wind, water, stone, insects, birds, animals, rain, sea, cave, and storm should not be reduced to a catalog of relaxing sounds. Each natural world contains structures of time, density, repetition, alarm, shelter, and return. MUMEx can learn from them without flattening them into background ambience.

Frontier territories require courage and distinction. Radionics, dowsing, past lives, alienness, vibrational medicine, nonordinary states, cosmic intuition, and extraordinary narratives should not be discarded because they disturb institutional comfort. They should also not be smuggled into the book as established evidence. They need language, frame, and method.

The epistemological spectrum is therefore not a decorative device. It is a moral instrument. Established evidence, theoretical model, wisdom tradition, clinical practice, symbolic imagination, and frontier testimony must remain distinguishable. The reader should always know what kind of claim is being made.

This is how a visionary work survives the North American market. It does not lower its ambition. It makes its distinctions sharper. It dares to speak about the edge without pretending the edge is already the center.

Research is constitutive of MUMEx Quantum Music Therapy. Without logbooks, protocols, observable markers, comparison, and revision, the vision would remain narrative. Every Generative Sound Field used in serious practice should be documented: parameters, duration, operator profile, state goal, patient response, safety events, debriefing, and return.

SMP-001 is the first sign of this responsibility. Healthy adult participants, comparison among Generative Sound Field, fixed music, and neutral control, subjective measures, HRV when available, breath, imagery, tolerability, and logbook traceability create a first bridge between philosophy and study (Edwards et al., 2023; Robb et al., 2025; World Medical Association, 2024).

Ethics precedes effect. Every field that modifies state requires consent, graduality, possibility of interruption, return, attention to limits, and respect for vulnerability. A session is not successful because it is intense. It is successful when the person returns more present, more inhabitable, and more able to choose.

The freedom of the researcher remains decisive. Dominant paradigms often protect their boundaries, funding languages, accepted methods, and hierarchies. A new field is born when someone refuses to confuse method with obedience. MUMEx belongs to this line not as a brand to celebrate but as an architecture to test.

If the system does not withstand verification, it must change. If some fields saturate, they must be reduced. If certain hypotheses fail, they must be rewritten. If some intuitions prove fertile, they must become protocols. The nobility of a frontier discipline lies in its willingness to be corrected without losing courage.

The core is this: sound becomes a state operator when it is generated as a field, read by competent presence, attuned to the body, placed within an ethical context, documented by method, and returned to the person. From here, a larger music therapy can emerge: one in which the piece remains, the voice remains, the instrument remains, improvisation remains, and beside them appears the Generative Sound Field as a new clinical, artistic, and research form.

The manifesto closes not with a slogan but with an operational sequence: listen to the state, generate the field, protect the body, allow the form to emerge, accompany the return, record the trace, and refine the method. Quantum Music Therapy begins here: where sound stops being a thing and becomes a living architecture of transformation.

APPENDICES

APPENDIX A

Glossary of Quantum Music Therapy

EPISTEMOLOGICAL NOTE: The glossary defines operative terms used throughout the book. Each definition distinguishes established evidence, theoretical model, clinical practice, and frontier language so that conceptual ambition never substitutes for precision.

MUMEx—MUSIC MULTIVERSE EXPLORATION

The glossary gathers the operative language developed across the theoretical, clinical, sonic, and experimental arc of MUMEx Quantum Music Therapy. Each entry should be read as a tool of precision, not as decorative terminology.

Quantum Music Therapy—A research and practice perspective that treats sound as an operator capable of modifying configurations of the human state. The term quantum does not claim that the brain is physically quantum; it indicates a model of possibility, context, transition, and emergence.

MUMEx (MUSIC MULTIVERSE EXPLORATION)—A generative architecture conceived to produce living, variable, traceable, and orientable sound fields. MUMEx is neither a playlist nor a fixed ambient track. It is a field engine.

Generative Sound Field—An evolving acoustic environment with continuity, variation, density, formal memory, and the possibility of modulation. Unlike a fixed musical piece, the field can change while preserving identity.

Human State—A temporary and complex configuration of body, attention, breath, memory, emotional tone, posture, internal imagery, orientation, safety, relationship, and possibility of choice.

State Operator—A transformative function applied to a psychophysical configuration. A sonic operator is not a generic musical effect; it is a way of acting on the field and altering the probability of certain internal configurations.

Resonance—The operator that seeks compatibility between body and sound field. Resonance does not impose movement; it creates conditions of recognition.

Suspension—The operator that reduces the pressure of immediate response and opens an inhabitable duration. In Suspension the subject may remain among possibilities without being forced to choose too soon.

Gentle Perturbation—The operator that introduces difference without violence. A successful perturbation does not break the field; it moves it.

Perceptual Collapse—The moment when an internal plurality assumes lived form: image, word, gesture, breath, tears, memory, decision, or bodily orientation. The term is psychological and phenomenological, not a claim about physical collapse in the brain.

Reintegration—The operator that returns experience to body, room, language, and shared time. Every opening of state must include a way back.

Quantum Cognition—A scientific program that uses the formalism of quantum probability to model cognitive phenomena such as judgment, decision, memory, order effects, ambiguity, and context dependence. In this book it functions as a formal reference for state-based thinking.

Possibility—A latent form of the human state. Possibility is not vague fantasy; it is a configuration that can become accessible when the relational and sonic field supports it.

Psychological Superposition—The coexistence of internal states that may be different or incompatible: desire to change and fear of change, need for contact and defense against contact, silence and voice.

Interference—A dynamic relation among internal possibilities that modify one another. Fear can reduce the weight of trust; memory can transform the meaning of present sound.

Context—The conditions that make an experience possible: room, posture, light, distance, therapist presence, patient history, proposed sound, sequence of events, and frame of the session.

Observable—An aspect of the human state that can be noticed, described, or measured: breath, heart rate variability, posture, vocal tone, movement, instrumental choice, reported image, time perception, or return quality.

Measurement—An act that makes an aspect of experience legible and also modifies it. A question, scale, physiological recording, invitation to vocalize, or debriefing is never neutral.

Logbook—The technical and clinical record of a MUMEx session or experiment. It includes sound parameters, duration, variations, operators activated, contextual notes, clinical observations, and debriefing material.

Traceability—The capacity to reconstruct what was generated, heard, modified, and observed during a session. Without traceability, a powerful experience remains anecdote.

Vibroacoustics—A field of practices and studies using sound vibrations perceived by the body, often through beds, transducers, chairs, or vibrating surfaces. In Quantum Music Therapy, vibroacoustic work requires caution, consent, and clear boundaries.

Interoception—The capacity to perceive internal bodily signals: breath, heartbeat, tension, hunger, pressure, heat, vibration, or visceral movement.

Heart Rate Variability (HRV)—Variation in the intervals between consecutive heartbeats. HRV can serve as a cautious observable of autonomic regulation, never as a total measure of transformation.

Window of Tolerance—The zone of activation within which a subject can remain present, oriented, and capable of integrating experience. A Generative Sound Field must respect this window.

State Modulation—The process by which a sound field, voice, gesture, instruction, or context modifies the configuration of the human state.

Co-Modulation—Reciprocal regulation among patient, therapist, and sound field. The field modulates the state; the patient's state informs the therapist's choices; the therapist remodulates the field.

Biofeedback—The return to the subject of physiological signals detected in real time or near-real time, such as breathing, heart rate, muscular tension, or skin conductance.

Neurofeedback—A specific form of feedback based on brain activity signals, often electroencephalography (EEG). In the MUMEx perspective it can inspire responsive sonic systems but requires specialized competence.

Light EEG—Noninvasive and simplified use of electroencephalographic signals to observe attention, relaxation, absorption, or activation in exploratory contexts.

Sound Spatialization—The organization of sound in perceived space: distance, depth, movement, height, lateralization, proximity, and envelopment.

Binaural—A reproduction technique using differences between the two ears to create spatial perception through headphones. It must be distinguished from simplistic claims about binaural beats.

Ambisonics—A technique for recording, encoding, and reproducing three-dimensional sound fields. It can widen spatial perception in music-therapy contexts when used carefully.

Soundscape—A sonic environment as lived perception, not a mere sum of sounds. Water, wind, distant traffic, voice, insects, room resonance, silence, and memory may all compose it.

Field Recording—The recording of environmental sounds in real places: forests, gardens, sea, city, interiors, sacred spaces, caves, wind, insects, and footsteps. In MUMEx it can become a matrix for transformation rather than a decorative layer.

Natural Soundscape—A sound field produced by living or geophysical environments: water, leaves, birds, insects, wind, sea, rain, fire, stone, or storm.

Nada Yoga—A contemplative path of sound in the Indian tradition, centered on external and internal listening, vibration, mantra, and sound as a path of knowledge.

Mantra—A repeated sonic formula with attentional, respiratory, symbolic, and transformative function. Its force lies not only in semantic meaning but in rhythm, articulation, breath, and continuity.

Voice—The first instrument of state modulation. Voice carries breath, identity, vulnerability, body, and relationship. Before communicating content, it communicates presence.

Improvisation—Real-time sonic creation grounded in listening and response. In music therapy it is not display; it is embodied relationship.

Animal Body—The instinctive, vocal, motor, and preverbal dimension of the human being. Work with animal sounds, postures, growls, breath, calls, steps, or guttural vocality can return the patient to a less domesticated layer of embodiment.

Sonic Archetype—A sonic configuration capable of evoking deep psychic forms: forest, mother, animal, wind, abyss, bell, choir, sea, drum, lament, or distant voice.

Sonic Imagination—The capacity to generate images, scenes, memories, figures, and sensations from sound. It can become clinical, symbolic, and creative material.

Regressive Hypnosis—The use of hypnosis to facilitate the emergence of memories, images, scenes, or lived impressions perceived as belonging to earlier psychic time. It must be distinguished from factual memory retrieval.

Past Lives—Subjective experiences in which a person reports images, scenes, identities, or bodies perceived as belonging to other existences. The safest methodological position is phenomenological: such material is treated as experience, image, and narrative, not as verified history.

Radionics—A historical and controversial system of diagnosis or intervention based on ideas of frequencies, subtle correspondences, and devices not recognized by mainstream scientific medicine.

Dowsing—A practice using pendulums, rods, or subtle bodily responses to detect correspondences, places, objects, or states. It can be reread phenomenologically as a practice of attention, ideomotor response, and symbolic choice.

Vibrational Medicine—A broad and ambiguous expression that includes diverse practices, some grounded in measurable physical vibration and others in hypotheses about subtle energy fields. The term requires epistemological labeling.

Biofield—A term used in some complementary-medicine contexts to indicate an energetic or informational field associated with living organisms. Mainstream science has not established it as a clinical mechanism.

Sonification—The translation of data into sound. In astronomy, for example, telescope data can be made audible, creating multisensory access to otherwise non-audible phenomena.

Cosmic Music Therapy—An expansion of sound practice toward the imagination of the cosmos, deep space, stars, pulsars, silence, and immensity. Its value is symbolic, perceptual, educational, and experiential, not proof of cosmic causality.

Radical Alterity—An encounter with what exceeds ordinary categories of self: animal, forest, cosmos, alien, ancestor, dead, archetypal image, or unknown voice.

Q-MUMEx State Modulation Protocol (SMP-001)—The first exploratory experimental design for observing the effects of a MUMEx Generative Sound Field on healthy adult participants, compared with fixed music and a neutral condition.

Epistemological Spectrum—The editorial and methodological map that distinguishes established evidence, theoretical model, wisdom tradition, clinical practice, symbolic imagination, and frontier testimony.

APPENDIX B

MUMEx Sound Field Design Sheet

PROFESSIONAL USE NOTE: This design sheet is intended for trained professionals and supervised research settings. It does not authorize unsupervised clinical use, diagnosis, treatment, or medical decision-making.

A design sheet does not exist to rigidify the session. It exists to prevent intuition from remaining vague. A Generative Sound Field, if it is to become a professional instrument, must be thinkable before the session, observable during it, and discussable afterward. Every parameter has weight: density, register, timbre, duration, silence, spatiality, microvariation, response to voice, predictability, and return strategy.

Session Identification

Patient or group code:

____

Date:

____

Place and setting:

____

Responsible music therapist:

____

People present in the room:

____

Planned session duration:

____

Planned MUMEx field duration:

____

Acoustic instruments present:

____

Active technological devices:

Individual or group condition:

Observed Initial State

Design begins with the real state, not with an abstract idea of technique. Record what appears in the body, voice, breath, orientation, energy, and relational availability.

Patient's initial words:

Breath quality:

Posture and bodily tone:

Voice, volume, rhythm, presence:

Spatial orientation:

Perceived activation level:

Signs of closure, defense, hypervigilance, or dispersion:

Signs of opening, trust, curiosity, or contact:

Transformation Question

The question of transformation often concerns a minimal transition: breathing with less effort, tolerating silence, sensing the chest, remaining in the room, emitting one note, accepting a vibration, or allowing an image to emerge without being invaded by it.

Starting state to be held:

Desired transition:

Minimal observable sign of change:

Condition indicating excess or intrusion:

Condition requiring interruption or reduction of the field:

Perceptual-Sonic Profile

Sounds experienced as pleasant, sought, or reassuring:

Sounds experienced as unpleasant, intrusive, or risky:

Relationship to the human voice:

Relationship to rhythm and pulse:

Relationship to drones, pedal tones, and sustained sounds:

Relationship to natural sounds:

Relationship to electronic and spatialized sound:

Relevant sonic memories:

Sensitivity to volume, register, or unpredictability:

Bodily and Vibrational Profile

Body areas easily perceived:

Body areas experienced as muted, absent, or foreign:

Hypersensitive body areas:

Relationship to chest vibration:

Relationship to abdominal vibration:

Relationship to bone or cranial sound:

Known physical limitations:

Medical conditions to respect:

Risks and Protections

Every powerful sound field must be designed also from the perspective of what may go wrong. The possibility of stopping, reducing, simplifying, or returning to the therapist's voice must be defined before the field begins.

Possible factors of excessive activation:

Possible factors of closure or withdrawal:

Agreed signal to stop or reduce the field:

Immediate stabilization strategy:

Bodily return strategy:

Traumatic or regressive material requiring caution:

Notes on informed consent and patient control:

Operator Profile

Primary operator:

Secondary operators:

Reason for the choice:

Operator to avoid or use with extreme caution:

Planned form of return:

Sonic Parameter Design

Overall field density:

Predominant register:

Distribution among low, middle, and high registers:

Primary timbres:

Degree of stability:

Degree of microvariation:

Allowed degree of unpredictability:

Pulse, rhythm, or absence of pulse:

Use of silence:

Use of space and distance:

Possible movement of sound:

Presence or absence of melodic elements:

Presence or absence of natural elements:

Presence or absence of generative vocal elements:

Starting volume and variation range:

Duration of phases:

Criteria for field reduction:

Session Trajectory

Entry phase:

Stabilization phase:

Variation or perturbation phase:

Possible emergence phase:

Return phase:

Final silence:

Planned debriefing:

Voice, Improvisation, and MUMEx

Planned therapist voice:

Possible patient voice:

Planned instrumental improvisation:

Moments when MUMEx must withdraw:

Moments when MUMEx must support:

Room, Space, and Technical Setting

Patient position:

Therapist position:

Loudspeaker placement:

Transducers or vibrational surfaces:

Natural or artificial reverberation:

Available sonic objects:

Light, temperature, and physical comfort:

Possibility of movement:

____

Possibility of immediate interruption:

____

Observation During the Field

Changes in breath:

____

Changes in posture:

____

Changes in voice:

____

Changes in orientation:

____

Spontaneous movements:

____

Images or words that emerged:

____

Signs of absorption:

____

Signs of excess:

____

Points at which the therapist modified the field:

____

Points at which the patient modified or oriented the field:

____

Technical Logbook

Initial preset or configuration:

Seed or generative identifier:

Main parameters recorded:

Manual variations during the session:

Relevant sonic events:

Reductions or interruptions:

Actual field duration:

Technical notes:

Debriefing and Integration

Patient's first sentence after the field:

Reported bodily sensations:

Reported images:

Perception of time:

Predominant emotional quality:

Memories that emerged:

Need for silence:

Therapist's words for return:

Minimal Outcome Notes

Perceived state before the session:

Perceived state after the session:

Perceived calm:

Perceived tension:

Perceived bodily presence:

Absorption:

Sense of safety:

Quality of return:

Available physiological measures:

Final clinical note:

MUMEx Session Sheet

COMPLETION NOTE: Fields marked as essential should be completed in every session whenever possible. Other fields may be adapted to the setting, patient, and purpose of data collection.

The MUMEx session sheet exists to preserve what happens during a sound practice without turning the experience into bureaucracy. Its task is to record the relation among person, sound field, therapeutic presence, initial state, observable variations, emergent images, bodily signs, return, and quality of integration.

Administrative and Safety Frame

Session code:

Date:

Start time and closing time:

Place and type of setting:

Responsible professional:

Co-therapist, observer, or sound technician:

Patient or participant code:

Age or age range:

Session context:

Informed consent collected:

Safety conditions verified:

Known contraindications, cautions, or vulnerabilities:

Aim and Initial State

Primary aim of the session:

Initial state observed by the therapist:

Initial state reported by patient or participant:

Initial bodily perception:

Dominant emotional quality:

Initial attentional quality:

Initial sense of safety:

Field Used and Technical Configuration

MUMEx field used:

Technical configuration:

Initial sound parameters:

Sonic operators activated:

Role of the voice:

Acoustic or bodily instruments integrated:

Course of the Session

Opening instructions:

Patient choices before the field:

Observable changes during the field:

Unexpected events:

Therapist decisions during the session:

Essential MUMEx logbook:

Physiological measures available:

Bodily observations during the session:

Vocal observations:

Imagery, Space, Time, and Debriefing

Images, memories, or symbols that emerged:

Perception of time:

Perception of space:

Immediate debriefing:

Final state reported:

Final state observed:

Perceived difference between beginning and end:

Residual risks or elements to monitor:

Post-session return instructions:

Therapist note on field quality:

Methodological note for the next session:

Professional signature or initials:

The MUMEx session sheet does not measure the entire human being. It records a relationship among state, sound, body, and context. Its strength lies in continuity: a single note may remain fragile; a sequence of sessions may reveal trajectories.

APPENDIX D

Experiential Practices and Composite Clinical Cases

SAFETY NOTE: The following practices are educational and exploratory. They do not replace medical, psychological, or clinical treatment. Any use with patients requires appropriate professional competence, consent, contraindication screening, and a clear return procedure.

Synthetic Matrix of Indications, Contraindications, and Duration

Sounded Breath

- Suggested duration: one to five minutes
- Possible use: orientation, mild anxiety, entry into the field
- Cautions: panic escalation, acute respiratory distress, strong performance anxiety around breathing

Vocalization

- Suggested duration: one to seven minutes
- Possible use: voice access, embodiment, agency
- Cautions: severe shame activation, acute dissociation, refusal of vocal exposure

Chest Vibration

- Suggested duration: one to four minutes
- Possible use: body presence, containment, resonance
- Cautions: chest pain, cardiac instability, trauma linked to bodily invasion

Bone Listening

- Suggested duration: one to three minutes
- Possible use: internal orientation and quiet attention
- Cautions: migraine, cranial sensitivity, vertigo, sensory overload

Dialogue with a Drone

- Suggested duration: five to fifteen minutes
- Possible use: stability, Suspension, slow imagery

- Cautions: claustrophobic response, dissociation, excessive absorption

Animal Imitation

- Suggested duration: three to ten minutes
- Possible use: instinctive voice, movement, play
- Cautions: humiliation risk, group pressure, traumatic animal associations

Garden Session

- Suggested duration: ten to thirty minutes
- Possible use: orientation, nature contact, gentle perturbation
- Cautions: allergies, weather instability, loss of privacy, environmental distraction

Forest Listening

- Suggested duration: ten to forty minutes
- Possible use: attention restoration, deep listening, ecological presence
- Cautions: hypervigilance in open environments, mobility limitations, safety concerns

Birdsong Listening

- Suggested duration: five to twenty minutes
- Possible use: motif recognition, attention, nonhuman voice
- Cautions: sensory overload, irritability, triggering memories

Sound Regression

- Suggested duration: five to fifteen minutes
- Possible use: imagery and autobiographical material
- Cautions: psychosis risk, acute trauma instability, suggestibility without containment

MUMEx Cosmic Field

- Suggested duration: eight to twenty minutes
- Possible use: vastness, awe, symbolic expansion
- Cautions: derealization, panic, spiritual bypassing, lack of grounding

Return and Reintegration

- Suggested duration: two to ten minutes
- Possible use: closing, grounding, orientation

- Cautions: none as a category; must always be adapted and included

Sounded Breath

The participant is invited to listen to the breath without changing it, then to allow a barely audible tone to ride on the exhalation. The goal is not vocal beauty. The goal is to notice the bridge between breath, sound, and state.

Vocalization

A single vowel is chosen and held briefly, with the therapist supporting through humming, drone, or silence. The voice is treated as an inhabited body, not as performance.

Chest Vibration

A low and gentle tone, humming, or safe resonant instrument is used to explore chest perception. The therapist asks for consent and monitors discomfort, constriction, or fear.

Bone Listening

The participant attends to subtle vibrations through jaw, skull, sternum, hands, or feet, using very low intensity. The purpose is internal orientation, not stimulation for its own sake.

Dialogue with a Drone

A stable drone is introduced as a sonic floor. The participant may listen, breathe, vocalize, or remain still. The field must remain simple enough to be inhabited.

Animal Imitation

Animal vocality is used as a protected entrance into instinctive body. Growl, breath, pawing movement, bird call, or low mammalian tone may appear. The therapist protects dignity and play.

Garden Session

The garden is treated as a living sound field. The patient listens to near and distant layers, then a MUMEx field may echo density, air, leaves, insects, or water without becoming imitation.

Forest Listening

The forest is approached as architecture: verticality, distance, canopy, ground, alarm, shelter, and silence. The work requires orientation, clear boundaries, and return.

Birdsong Listening

Birdsong is used as a model of motif, variation, territory, and call-response. The goal is not romantic relaxation but attention to living pattern.

Sound Regression

Sound may open images or earlier subjective material. The therapist must avoid leading questions, factual claims, and interpretive pressure. All material is treated phenomenologically unless otherwise clinically established.

MUMEx Cosmic Field

A field of vastness may use low density, long silences, distant events, and spatial depth. It must include a return path: voice, floor, hands, room, date, and present orientation.

Return and Reintegration

The session closes by reducing complexity, naming the room, sensing the body, restoring ordinary time, and allowing speech or silence. Reintegration is not an optional ending; it is the ethical seal of the work.

Composite Clinical Cases

The following cases are composite, anonymized, and not linked to identifiable patients. They function as operational models showing how the five operators can be translated into setting, MUMEx field, observation, and Reintegration. They have no statistical value and must not be read as clinical proof.

Composite Clinical Case 1—Generalized Anxiety: Resonance and Suspension

Context: Individual session, stable room, soft light, eighteen-minute field. Initial state: high breathing, lifted shoulders, cold hands, rapid speech, implicit demand for control.

Aim: Transition from hypervigilance to bodily orientation. Preferred operators: Resonance and Suspension.

MUMEx Field: Mid-low drone, low density, slow microvariations, no abrupt events, contained dynamic range, gradual return in the final four minutes.

Observation: After six minutes the shoulders lower; after nine minutes the breath loses its initial fragmentation. The patient reports, "I feel that the sound is not asking anything from me."

Reintegration: Brief silence, feet on the floor, naming three objects in the room, final chosen word: "boundary."

Clinical Reflection: Resonance functioned when the field stopped being perceived as stimulus and became floor. Suspension should remain brief in early sessions to avoid dependence on sonic containment.

Composite Clinical Case 2—Depression: Gentle Perturbation

Context: Individual session with slowing, low voice, limited gaze, and difficulty naming desire or imagery. Twenty-minute field.

Aim: Transition from stasis to micro-movement. Preferred operator: Gentle Perturbation, supported by minimal resonance.

MUMEx Field: Mid-low register, warm timbral grain, sparse non-metric impulses, small luminous openings every ninety to 120 seconds, no emotional crescendo.

Observation: The patient slowly moves one foot at the twelfth minute and later says, "There was a small point that returned, as if something was not switched off."

Reintegration: One short vocal tone, then a neutral spoken sentence. Image noted: "light under a door."

Clinical Reflection: Gentle Perturbation does not seek cheerfulness. It introduces difference without demanding energy the patient does not have. The risk is acceleration too soon.

Composite Clinical Case 3—Complex Trauma: Reintegration

Context: Individual session with hyperarousal history. The field is set at very low volume and the possibility of stopping is verbally recalled.

Aim: Maintain presence, boundary, and control. Preferred operator: Reintegration, prepared from the first minute.

MUMEx Field: Stable texture, few variations, no invasive low frequency, early return if overload signs appear.

Observation: At minute five the patient opens the eyes and looks at the door. The therapist reduces the field, names the room, and invites the patient to sense the weight of the feet. The patient chooses to continue with a nearer sound.

Reintegration: Spatial orientation, water, finger movement, date, place, and a very short closing sound chosen by the patient.

Clinical Reflection: In trauma, success is not depth or intensity. It is control, presence, and return. Reintegration is not the end: it governs the whole trajectory.

Composite Clinical Case 4—Vocal Block: Voice and Improvisation

Context: Brief individual laboratory with fear of "singing out of tune" and strong judgment around the voice. MUMEx field almost imperceptible.

Aim: Move from judged voice to inhabitable voice. Operators: Resonance, Gentle Perturbation, and Reintegration.

MUMEx Field: Poor harmonic floor, middle register, no explicit melody, space left for the voice. The therapist uses minimal humming as mirroring.

Observation: The first sound is almost silent. After several attempts the patient emits a short vowel and laughs: "It was not beautiful, but it was mine."

Reintegration: From sound to speech: first name, then a simple sentence. The field fades before the voice is discussed.

Clinical Reflection: The voice emerges when the field stops competing with it. The aim is not performance but sonic agency.

Composite Clinical Case 5—Archetypal Imagery: Perceptual Collapse

Context: Individual session with strong imaginative capacity. Sixteen-minute Suspension field and non-directive debriefing.

Aim: Allow a diffuse image to assume sustainable form. Operators: Suspension and Perceptual Collapse, with final Reintegration.

MUMEx Field: Rare bells, spatial depth, barely mobile drone, long pauses, distant non-descriptive events.

Observation: At the eleventh minute light tears appear. After return the patient reports, "I saw a staircase inside an empty house." The therapist avoids immediate symbolic interpretation.

Reintegration: Quick drawing of the staircase, three body words, return to the room, and choice of one closing gesture.

Clinical Reflection: Perceptual Collapse has value when an internal form becomes inhabitable, not when it produces spectacular narrative. Interpretive prudence protects the image.

References

The references below are limited to works cited directly in the text. Clinical evidence, professional standards, research methods, theoretical models, and data-sonification sources are kept within one alphabetized reference list. Authorial MUMEx materials, foundational reading, and frontier sources are separated afterward so that different levels of evidentiary weight are not conflated.

Aalbers, S., Fusar-Poli, L., Freeman, R. E., Spreen, M., Ket, J. C. F., Vink, A. C., Maratos, A., Crawford, M., Chen, X.-J., & Gold, C. (2017). Music therapy for depression. *Cochrane Database of Systematic Reviews, 2017*(11), Article CD004517. https://doi.org/10.1002/14651858.CD004517.pub3

American Music Therapy Association. (n.d.). *Standards of clinical practice*. https://www.musictherapy.org/about/standards/

American Music Therapy Association. (2019). *Code of ethics*. https://www.musictherapy.org/about/ethics/

American Music Therapy Association, & Certification Board for Music Therapists. (2015). *Scope of music therapy practice*. https://www.musictherapy.org/about/scope_of_music_therapy_practice/

Arcand, K. K., Schonhut-Stasik, J. S., Kane, S. G., Sturdevant, G., Russo, M., Watzke, M., Hsu, B., & Smith, L. F. (2024). A universe of sound: Processing NASA data into sonifications to explore participant response. *Frontiers in Communication, 9*, Article 1288896. https://doi.org/10.3389/fcomm.2024.1288896

Bolhuis, J. J., Okanoya, K., & Scharff, C. (2010). Twitter evolution: Converging mechanisms in birdsong and human speech. *Nature Reviews Neuroscience, 11*(11), 747–759. https://doi.org/10.1038/nrn2931

Bradt, J., Dileo, C., Myers-Coffman, K., & Biondo, J. (2021). Music interventions for improving psychological and physical outcomes in people with cancer. *Cochrane Database of Systematic Reviews, 2021*(10), Article CD006911. https://doi.org/10.1002/14651858.CD006911.pub4

Buxton, R. T., Pearson, A. L., Allou, C., Fristrup, K., & Wittemyer, G. (2021). A synthesis of health benefits of natural sounds and their distribution in national parks. *Proceedings of the National Academy of Sciences, 118*(14), Article e2013097118. https://doi.org/10.1073/pnas.2013097118

Busemeyer, J. R., & Bruza, P. D. (2012). *Quantum models of cognition and decision*. Cambridge University Press.

Certification Board for Music Therapists. (2025). *Board certification domains—2025: From the 2024 music therapy practice analysis study* [PDF]. https://www.cbmt.org/wp-content/uploads/2025/07/CBMT-BOARD-CERTIFICATION-DOMAINS-DOCUMENT-0725-50463-V2-F.pdf

Chanda, M. L., & Levitin, D. J. (2013). The neurochemistry of music. *Trends in Cognitive Sciences, 17*(4), 179–193. https://doi.org/10.1016/j.tics.2013.02.007

Craig, A. D. (2002). How do you feel? Interoception: The sense of the physiological condition of the body. *Nature Reviews Neuroscience, 3*(8), 655–666. https://doi.org/10.1038/nrn894

Craig, A. D. (2009). How do you feel—now? The anterior insula and human awareness. *Nature Reviews Neuroscience, 10*(1), 59–70. https://doi.org/10.1038/nrn2555

de Witte, M., da Silva Pinho, A., Stams, G.-J., Moonen, X., Bos, A. E. R., & van Hooren, S. (2022). Music therapy for stress reduction: A systematic review and meta-analysis. *Health Psychology Review, 16*(1), 134–159. https://doi.org/10.1080/17437199.2020.1846580

de Witte, M., Aalbers, S., Vink, A., Friederichs, S., Knapen, A., Pelgrim, T., Lampit, A., Baker, F. A., & van Hooren, S. (2025). Music therapy for the treatment of anxiety: A systematic review with multilevel meta-analyses. *EClinicalMedicine, 84*, Article 103293. https://doi.org/10.1016/j.eclinm.2025.103293

Edwards, E., St. Hillaire-Clarke, C., Frankowski, D. W., Finkelstein, R., Cheever, T., Chen, W. G., Onken, L., Poremba, A., Riddle, R., Schloesser, D., Burgdorf, C. E., Wells, N., Fleming, R., & Collins, F. S. (2023). NIH Music-Based Intervention Toolkit: Music-based interventions for brain disorders of aging. *Neurology, 100*(18), 868–878. https://doi.org/10.1212/WNL.0000000000206797

Elkins, G. R., Barabasz, A. F., Council, J. R., & Spiegel, D. (2015). Advancing research and practice: The revised APA Division 30 definition of hypnosis. *International Journal of Clinical and Experimental Hypnosis, 63*(1), 1–9. https://doi.org/10.1080/00207144.2014.961870

Fancourt, D., & Finn, S. (2019). *What is the evidence on the role of the arts in improving health and well-being? A scoping review*. World Health Organization Regional Office for Europe. https://iris.who.int/handle/10665/329834

Hanson-Abromeit, D. (2025). The therapeutic function of music plan: A tool to specify the theory of music in music-based interventions. *Frontiers in Psychology, 16*, Article 1577176. https://doi.org/10.3389/fpsyg.2025.1577176

Huang, J., Epping, G., Trueblood, J. S., Yearsley, J. M., Busemeyer, J. R., & Pothos, E. M. (2025). An overview of the quantum cognition research program. *Psychonomic Bulletin & Review, 32*, 2507–2556. https://doi.org/10.3758/s13423-025-02675-9

Jarvis, E. D. (2004). Learned birdsong and the neurobiology of human language. *Annals of the New York Academy of Sciences, 1016*(1), 749–777. https://doi.org/10.1196/annals.1298.038

Khalsa, S. S., Adolphs, R., Cameron, O. G., Critchley, H. D., Davenport, P. W., Feinstein, J. S., Feusner, J. D., Garfinkel, S. N., Lane, R. D., Mehling, W. E., Meuret, A. E., Nemeroff, C. B., Oppenheimer, S., Petzschner, F. H., Pollatos, O., Rhudy, J. L., Schramm, L. P., Simmons, W. K., Stein, M. B., ... Zucker, N. (2018). Interoception and mental health: A roadmap. *Biological Psychiatry: Cognitive Neuroscience and Neuroimaging, 3*(6), 501–513. https://doi.org/10.1016/j.bpsc.2017.12.004

Koelsch, S. (2014). Brain correlates of music-evoked emotions. *Nature Reviews Neuroscience, 15*(3), 170–180. https://doi.org/10.1038/nrn3666

National Aeronautics and Space Administration. (2025, June 10). *Data sonifications*. https://www.nasa.gov/data-sonifications/

Pothos, E. M., & Busemeyer, J. R. (2013). Can quantum probability provide a new direction for cognitive modeling? *Behavioral and Brain Sciences, 36*(3), 255–274. https://doi.org/10.1017/S0140525X12001525

Robb, S. L., Springs, S., Edwards, E., Golden, T. L., Johnson, J. K., Burns, D. S., Belgrave, M., Bradt, J., Gold, C., Habibi, A., Iversen, J. R., Lense, M., MacLean, J. A., & Perkins, S. M. (2025). Reporting guidelines for music-based interventions: An update and validation study. *Frontiers in Psychology, 16*, Article 1551920. https://doi.org/10.3389/fpsyg.2025.1551920

Seo, J. S. (2026). A focused survey of generative AI-based music therapy systems: Recent progress and open challenges. *Applied Sciences, 16*(9), Article 4120. https://doi.org/10.3390/app16094120

Trueblood, J. S., & Busemeyer, J. R. (2011). A quantum probability account of order effects in inference. *Cognitive Science, 35*(8), 1518–1552. https://doi.org/10.1111/j.1551-6709.2011.01197.x

Wei, Q., & He, W. (2026). The application of AI-assisted music therapy tools in mental health interventions. *Frontiers in Psychology, 17*, Article 1741463. https://doi.org/10.3389/fpsyg.2026.1741463

World Medical Association. (2024). *Declaration of Helsinki: Ethical principles for medical research involving human participants*. https://www.wma.net/what-we-do/medical-ethics/declaration-of-helsinki/

Published Books by Louis Siciliano

Siciliano, L. (2026). MUMEx A New Sound Cosmology. MAGIC&UNIQUE BOOKS.

Siciliano, L. (2026). The Frequency of the Earth. MAGIC&UNIQUE BOOKS.

Siciliano, L. (2026). The Ecosystem of the Music. MAGIC&UNIQUE BOOKS.

Siciliano, L. (2026). *The engineering of conscious melodies: How sound and vibration shape our everyday reality.* MAGIC&UNIQUE BOOKS.

Siciliano, L. (2026). *Toward the Ganga: Poems.* MAGIC&UNIQUE BOOKS.

Foundational and Further Reading

The works in this section inform the book's intellectual genealogy, clinical imagination, or historical context. They are not used as substitutes for contemporary empirical evidence.

Assagioli, R. (1965). *Psychosynthesis: A manual of principles and techniques*. Hobbs, Dorman & Company.

Grocke, D., & Wigram, T. (2007). *Receptive methods in music therapy: Techniques and clinical applications for music therapy clinicians, educators and students*. Jessica Kingsley Publishers.

Jung, C. G. (1964). *Man and his symbols*. Doubleday.

Jung, C. G. (1969). *The archetypes and the collective unconscious* (R. F. C. Hull, Trans.; 2nd ed.). Princeton University Press.

Kaplan, R., & Kaplan, S. (1989). *The experience of nature: A psychological perspective*. Cambridge University Press.

Krause, B. (2012). *The great animal orchestra: Finding the origins of music in the world's wild places*. Little, Brown and Company.

Levitin, D. J. (2006). *This is your brain on music: The science of a human obsession*. Dutton.

Porges, S. W. (2011). *The polyvagal theory: Neurophysiological foundations of emotions, attachment, communication, and self-regulation*. W. W. Norton.

Rouget, G. (1985). *Music and trance: A theory of the relations between music and possession* (B. Biebuyck, Trans.). University of Chicago Press.

Sacks, O. (2007). *Musicophilia: Tales of music and the brain*. Knopf.

Schafer, R. M. (1994). *The soundscape: Our sonic environment and the tuning of the world*. Destiny Books. (Original work published 1977)

Stutz, P., & Michels, B. (2012). *The tools: Transform your problems into courage, confidence, and creativity*. Spiegel & Grau.

Truax, B. (2001). *Acoustic communication* (2nd ed.). Ablex Publishing.

Wigram, T., Pedersen, I. N., & Bonde, L. O. (2002). *A comprehensive guide to music therapy: Theory, clinical practice, research, and training*. Jessica Kingsley Publishers.

Yapko, M. D. (2019). *Trancework: An introduction to the practice of clinical hypnosis* (5th ed.). Routledge.

Frontier / Exploratory Sources—Not Clinical Evidence

These works are retained only because the book discusses frontier narratives, nonverbal-hypnosis traditions, or extraterrestrial testimony as cultural, phenomenological, or authorial material. Their presence does not validate clinical efficacy, paranormal claims, medical diagnosis, or extraterrestrial contact.

Paret, M. (2011). *The magnetic gaze*. International Academic Productions.

Paret, M., & Atkinson, W. W. (2011). *Hypnotic fascination*. International Academic Productions.

Wolf, M. (1996). *The catchers of heaven: A trilogy*. Dorrance Publishing Co.

INDEX

A

acoustic instruments, 6, 49, 141–145, 147–148
adaptivity, 9, 121, 124–126
agency, 21, 53, 61, 66, 135, 139, 144–148, 154, 167–168, 172, 227, 232
altered states, 32–38, 73–83, 172
alterity, 110–113, 181–188, 203
animals and animal sound, 110–113, 117, 123, 153, 162, 165, 179, 202–204, 228–229
anxiety, 25–28, 39–42, 50–53, 68, 87, 99–100, 104, 108, 112, 123, 129, 146–147, 151, 158–160, 171, 179–180, 186, 191–192, 227, 231
clinical orientation, 39–42, 50–53, 158–160
sound-field design, 40–42, 68, 129, 146–147
archetype, sonic, 162–165, 202
Assagioli, Roberto, 166–169, 173
attention, 13–23, 32–38, 73–78, 157–162, 172, 177–178, 183, 193–195, 199, 202–203, 227–230
autonomic nervous system, 50, 55–58, 64, 68, 158–160, 201
awe, 185–186, 228

B

Barry Simmons, 170–173
biofeedback, 64–69, 201
biofield, 203
birdsong, 106–109, 115, 228, 230
body as instrument, 49–54
body–mind apparatus, 177–180
bone conduction, 51, 53
breath, 6–8, 10–11, 15–16, 19–20, 22–26, 28, 31–34, 37–38, 42–44, 49–52, 56–58, 62, 66–70, 73–74, 77, 80, 84–93, 97, 99–101, 103–105, 107, 110–117, 121–127, 129, 131–135, 137, 139–143, 145–148, 150–153, 157–161, 164–165, 170–173, 177–180, 183, 187, 190, 193–195, 199–202, 206, 213, 227, 229, 231

C

clinical evidence, 4–5, 33, 60, 63, 79, 89, 157–161, 181, 189–192
clinical relationship, 4–12, 173
cognitive decline, 18
consent, 34, 42, 45, 52–53, 57, 63, 65, 67–68, 73, 77, 81, 84, 87, 89, 92, 112, 122, 127, 130–131, 143, 147, 150, 161, 163, 178, 184, 190–195, 201, 209, 218, 227, 229
cosmic music therapy, 185–188, 203
cosmos, 177–188

D

data privacy, 67–68
debriefing, 16, 29, 35, 38, 77–78, 81–82, 101, 130, 135, 151, 153, 159–160, 187, 190–192, 195, 200–201, 212, 214, 223–224, 233

density, 20, 27, 38, 40–42, 52–53, 66, 68, 76–77, 100–101, 114–117, 121–126, 130–139, 141–148, 150–154, 159, 161–162, 164, 167, 171, 179–180, 183, 185–186, 189, 191, 194, 199, 205, 210, 230–231
depression, 25–28, 39–41, 50, 53, 68, 87, 99–100, 104, 108, 112, 123, 133, 151, 158–160, 179, 231
dissociation, 26, 35, 50, 73, 82, 99, 123, 133, 135, 139, 160, 169–172, 227–228
dowsing, 60–63, 194, 203
drone, 8, 11, 14–15, 20, 22, 27–29, 32, 34–35, 39, 41, 52–53, 70, 74–76, 80, 84–88, 100, 122, 129, 132, 137, 151, 154, 178, 180, 183, 227, 229, 231, 233

E

EEG (electroencephalography), 64, 66–67, 160, 201–202
electromedical devices, 64–70
empty infinity, 73–78
entrainment, 133, 158, 161
epistemological spectrum, 195, 204
ethics, 4, 30, 34–38, 42, 45, 51–70, 79–83, 89–93, 127–131, 150–154, 189–196

F

fascination, 32–38, 65, 79, 124–125, 129, 136, 154, 160, 183
field; see sound field
field design, 11, 56, 103, 117, 137–140, 205–216
forest and woods, 102–105, 115, 117, 179, 194, 203–204, 228, 230

G

garden, 97–101, 194, 228, 230
gaze, hypnotic, 32–38
generative sound field, 8–12, 27, 43, 51, 63, 99, 121–126, 141, 157, 160, 178–179, 187, 189, 195–196, 199, 201, 204–205
adaptivity and memory, 121–126
design parameters, 137–140, 205–216
experiential protocols, 150–154, 227–233
state modulation, 189–192
voice and improvisation, 141–144
grounding, 18, 36–37, 40, 49, 52, 57–58, 65, 67, 104, 135, 143, 163, 167, 172, 190, 228–229

H

heart rate variability (HRV), 64, 124, 126, 158–161, 191–192, 195, 200–201
hypnosis, 32–38, 74, 79–83, 85, 158, 183, 203
nonverbal, 32–38
regressive, 79–83, 203

I

imaginal experience, 62–63, 67, 78–83
immersion, 21, 34, 42, 64–70, 127–131, 184
improvisation, 4, 6, 8–9, 12, 57, 66, 68–69, 125, 141–144, 160, 194, 196, 202, 212, 232
informed consent, 65–66, 190–192, 209, 218
inner orchestra, 166–169
instrumentation, 49–54, 64–70, 145–148

interference, 13, 17, 21, 24, 30–31, 177, 200
interoception, 50, 55, 154, 201

J

Jung, Carl Gustav, 162–165

L

logbook, 9–10, 38, 45, 50, 53, 63, 77, 81, 92, 101, 124, 139–140, 148, 151, 161, 164, 168, 172, 180, 191–192, 195, 201, 214, 222

M

mantra, 84–88, 202
measurement, 13, 15–16, 21–22, 24, 27, 29–30, 38, 49, 61, 64, 129, 153, 157–161, 173, 200
meditation, 63, 73–78, 84–93, 124, 192
memory, 4, 6–31, 36–37, 39–46, 49, 54–55, 62, 64, 69–70, 73, 76, 78–80, 85–86, 89, 104, 106, 108–109, 115–116, 121–128, 133–135, 137, 141, 143–144, 147–148, 157, 159–166, 177, 181, 183, 191, 193, 199–203
Michael Wolf, 181–184
microvariation, 16, 20, 27, 40–41, 51, 63, 68, 76, 80, 85, 87, 97, 106, 114–115, 122, 130, 134, 158, 205, 210
mind as a field of possibility, 13–23
music therapy, 4–12, 24–46, 49–70, 73–93, 97–117, 121–148, 150–154, 157–173, 177–196
MUMEx, 4–31, 33–38, 40–46, 49–70, 76–93, 97–117, 121–148, 150–154, 157–173, 177–196, 199–233
architecture and philosophy, 121–126
experiential laboratory, 145–148
five operators, 132–136
glossary, 199–204
manifesto, 193–196
session design, 137–140, 205–226
SMP-001 protocol, 189–192

N

Nada Yoga, 84–88, 202
natural soundscapes, 114–117, 202
nature, 97–117, 126, 134, 179, 191, 194, 228
neuroaesthetics, 157
neuroscience, 50, 73, 154, 157–161, 165, 173
neurofeedback, 64, 201
nonverbal hypnosis, 32–38

O

operators, five sonic, 132–136, 199–200
Gentle Perturbation, 134–136, 138, 140, 151–153, 168, 173, 194, 200, 231–233
Perceptual Collapse, 132, 134–136, 138, 140, 152–153, 168, 173, 194, 200, 233
Reintegration, 132, 134–140, 142, 144, 148, 151–154, 159, 164–165, 168–169, 171, 173, 184, 194, 200, 229–233
Resonance, 132–138, 140, 142–146, 150–154, 158, 164–165, 167, 173, 177–178, 194, 199, 202, 227, 231–232

Suspension, 132–138, 140, 151–154, 158, 167, 173, 194, 200, 228, 231, 233

P

Paret, Marco, 33
past lives, 79–83, 194, 203
perceptual collapse; see operators, five sonic
perceptual field, 25–26, 32–38, 46, 75, 102, 125
perceptual-sensory world, 38–46
Phil Stutz, 170–173
plasticity, 157, 160–161, 180
posture, 8–9, 15, 27, 32, 34, 42, 49–54, 56, 65, 78, 81, 86, 99, 101–102, 109–113, 117, 125, 129, 132–139, 145, 148, 152, 159–160, 166, 171, 193–194, 199–200, 206, 213
prediction, 36, 86, 157–161, 173
psychosynthesis, 166–169

Q

quantum cognition, 13–17, 21, 24, 200
quantum psychology, 24–31
Q-MUMEx State Modulation Protocol (SMP-001), 148, 153, 189–192, 195, 203

R

radionics, 60–63, 194, 203
raga, 84–86
regressive hypnosis, 79–83, 203
reintegration; see operators, five sonic
resonance; see operators, five sonic
rhythm, 6–7, 9–10, 14, 16, 20–21, 25, 27–30, 32–39, 41, 49, 52–53, 56–57, 64, 67, 74, 80, 86–87, 99–100, 103, 106, 111, 122–123, 137–138, 142–144, 146, 152, 157–160, 163, 166–167, 170, 173, 177–178, 180, 182, 185–186, 193, 202, 206–207, 210
ritual, 6, 10, 34, 60–63, 80–81, 89, 91–92, 164, 171–172

S

sacred song, 89–93
safety, 14–15, 19–21, 30, 34–38, 42, 44–45, 49, 51–54, 56–58, 64–68, 82, 85, 97–100, 112, 115–116, 122, 132–134, 137, 140, 150, 158–160, 177, 183, 189–195, 199, 216–219, 227–228
silence, 6, 9–11, 14–20, 22–23, 25–26, 29–30, 32–38, 40–44, 54, 63, 73–78, 80, 86–89, 91–93, 97–98, 100, 103–104, 107, 109, 111, 114–117, 122–124, 130, 132–145, 147–148, 150–153, 157–158, 160–161, 165–168, 171, 173, 178–179, 182–185, 187, 189, 193, 200, 202–203, 205–206, 210–211, 215, 229–231
SMP-001; see Q-MUMEx State Modulation Protocol
sonification, 185, 188, 203
sonic anamnesis, 43
sonic archetype, 162–165, 202
sonic diagnosis, 29
sonic imagination, 162–165, 202
sonic memory, 43–44

sound field, 4, 8–12, 16, 19–20, 25–27, 29–30, 34, 39–43, 45, 49–52, 55, 58, 63, 66, 73, 75–76, 81, 85–87, 90, 99–100, 103, 121–131, 137–141, 147, 153, 157, 160, 166, 168, 177–183, 187, 189, 195–196, 199, 201–205, 208, 217, 230
sound healing, 89–90, 93
soundscape, 97, 107, 114–117, 202
spatialization, 10–11, 20, 22, 36, 42, 44, 76, 81, 116, 127–131, 183, 201
state, human, 4–46, 49, 56, 66, 68–69, 73, 76–87, 91, 97–103, 107–108, 116, 121–126, 128, 130, 132–140, 143–148, 150–154, 158, 161–162, 165–173, 177–180, 183, 186–191, 193–196, 199–207, 215, 217–219, 224, 226, 229, 231
Stutz, Phil, 170–173
sub-bass, 36, 42, 53, 129–130, 139, 159, 183
suggestion, 32, 36–38, 55–56, 62–63, 79, 81, 86, 136, 144, 151, 183
suspension; see operators, five sonic
symbol, 111, 162–165, 173, 183

T

tala, 84, 86
therapist, 4–12, 14–23, 26–31, 34–38, 40–44, 49–58, 61–69, 73–83, 85–93, 99–117, 122–145, 150, 153–154, 159–173, 179, 181–184, 187–188, 191, 193, 200–201, 205–233
threshold, 35, 37–38, 53, 80, 92, 127, 135, 138, 143, 150, 162, 164, 171
timbre, 9–10, 16–17, 20, 25–27, 30, 37, 39, 50, 80–81, 85, 106, 122–123, 133–134, 138, 140, 148, 150, 157, 159, 163, 171, 205
trance, 11, 35–36, 73, 123, 183
trauma, 13, 25–26, 28, 39, 42, 50–53, 56–57, 62, 66, 78–79, 82, 88–89, 100, 104, 107, 112, 123, 128, 133, 137, 139, 160, 163–164, 169, 172, 179, 183, 190, 192, 227–228, 232

V

vibration, 8, 11, 16, 25–26, 30, 43, 45, 49–58, 61–62, 64–70, 75–76, 84–87, 90, 110–111, 127, 130, 137, 141, 146, 151, 160, 177–180, 193, 201–203, 207–208, 227, 229
vibroacoustics, 65–69, 91, 152, 179, 201
voice, 6, 8, 11–23, 26, 29, 31–45, 49–58, 66–67, 69, 74–80, 85, 87–93, 99–100, 107, 109–117, 122–123, 125, 131–139, 141–148, 150–154, 160–162, 166–171, 178, 182–187, 194, 196, 200–208, 212–213, 220, 227–232

W

well-being, 7, 40, 102, 159
woods; see forest and woods

CONTENTS

Foreword 5
Introduction — From the Musical Piece to the Sound Field 10
Reader's Guide 15
List of Plates 17
Iconographic Orientation Plates 18

PART ONE — FOUNDING THE FIELD 2

Chapter 1 — Music Therapy Before Its New Frontier 4
Chapter 2 — The Mind as a Field of Possibility 13
Chapter 3 — Quantum Psychology and the Transformation of the Human State 24
Chapter 4 — Nonverbal Hypnosis, Fascination, and the Perceptual Field 32
Chapter 5 — Reconstructing the Patient's Perceptual-Sensory World Through Sound 39

PART TWO — THE VIBRANT BODY 48

Chapter 6 — The Body as Instrument 49
Chapter 7 — Stimulating the Internal Organs Through Vibration 55
Chapter 8 — Radionics, Dowsing, and Vibrational Medicine 60
Chapter 9 — Electromedical Devices and Advanced Vibrational Instrumentation 64

PART THREE — EMPTY INFINITY, TRANCE, AND MEDITATION 72
Chapter 10 — Bringing the Mind into Empty Infinity Through Sound 73
Chapter 11 — Music Therapy, Regressive Hypnosis, and Past Lives 79
Chapter 12 — Nada Yoga and the Eastern Paths of Sound 84
Chapter 13 — Sacred Song, Western Meditation, and Sound Healing 89

PART FOUR — VIBRANT NATURE 96
Chapter 14 — The Garden as a Living Vibrant Organism 97
Chapter 15 — Trees, Forests, Woods, and Music Therapy 102
Chapter 16 — Birdsong as a Replicable Sonic Model 106
Chapter 17 — The Sonic World of Animals 110
Chapter 18 — Natural Soundscapes and Perceptual Healing 114

PART FIVE — MUMEx AND GENERATIVE SOUND FIELDS 120
Chapter 19 — MUMEx: Generative Architecture and Philosophy 121
Chapter 20 — Immersive and Spatialized Electronic Sound in Music-Therapy Practice 127
Chapter 21 — The Five Sonic Operators 132

Chapter 22 — Designing a MUMEx Sound Field for the Session 137
Chapter 23 — MUMEx, Voice, and Improvisation 141
Chapter 24 — The Experiential Laboratory and Musical Instruments 145
Chapter 25 — Practices, Exercises, and Experiential Protocols 150

PART SIX — NEUROSCIENCE AND DEPTH PSYCHOLOGY 156
Chapter 26 — Neuroscience and Music Therapy 157
Chapter 27 — Jung, Symbol, and Sonic Imagination 162
Chapter 28 — Roberto Assagioli, Psychosynthesis, and the Inner Orchestra 166
Chapter 29 — Barry Simmons, Phil Stutz, and Sonic Inner Tools 170

PART SEVEN — COSMOS, ALTERITY, AND FRONTIERS 176
Chapter 30 — Quantum Vibrations of the Natural World and the Body-Mind Apparatus 177
Chapter 31 — Michael Wolf and Music Therapy Beyond the Boundaries of the System 181
Chapter 32 — Cosmic Music Therapy 185
Chapter 33 — The Q-MUMEx SMP-001 Protocol 189
Chapter 34 — Manifesto for MUMEx Quantum Music Therapy 193

APPENDICES 198
Appendix A — Glossary of Quantum Music Therapy 199
Appendix B — MUMEx Sound Field Design Sheet 205
Appendix C — MUMEx Session Sheet 217
Appendix D — Composite Clinical Cases 227

REFERENCES 235
INDEX 241
CONTENTS 247

MAGIC & UNIQUE
BOOKS

www.ingramcontent.com/pod-product-compliance
Lightning Source LLC
LaVergne TN
LVHW041207061126
851857LV00018B/1968
* 9 7 8 9 6 9 7 6 6 0 0 0 1 *